Smart Service Management

Maria Maleshkova • Niklas Kühl • Philipp Jussen
Editors

Smart Service Management

Design Guidelines and Best Practices

 Springer

Editors
Maria Maleshkova (iD)
University of Bonn
Bonn, Germany

Niklas Kühl (iD)
Karlsruhe Institute of Technology
Karlsruhe, Germany

Philipp Jussen
Schaeffler Monitoring Services GmbH
Herzogenrath, Germany

ISBN 978-3-030-58184-8   ISBN 978-3-030-58182-4   (eBook)
https://doi.org/10.1007/978-3-030-58182-4

This Springer imprint is published by the registered company Springer Nature Switzerland AG.
The registered company address is: Gewerbestrasse 11, 6330 Cham, Switzerland

Foreword

What are the characteristics of smart service systems and offerings? How are they engineered? How should they be priced? How can a traditional manufacturing company transform its current offerings into high-value smart service systems? What role does artificial intelligence (AI) play in smart service management and engineering? Today's companies are faced with more questions than answers as they digitally transform. While there is a large amount of high-quality service research on a range of topics related to digital transformation of business, the adoption into practice, especially in traditional manufacturing companies, is still lacking. SMEs (small and medium-sized enterprises) are struggling to adopt a "smart service mindset" to keep up with the pace of change and continue their journey to become T-shaped adaptive service innovation professionals, with technical depth and business communications breadth. This task is especially difficult as businesses and governments dynamically reconfigure business models and social contracts (value propositions) interconnecting people, technology, organizations, and shared information in order to build smarter service systems that strive to meet ever-changing business and societal needs.

To become oriented quickly, practitioners and also junior researchers will need good guidance. In *Smart Service Management*, Maria Maleshkova, Niklas Kühl, and Philipp Jussen provide a map with multiple entry points for industry professionals and researchers. In a unique way, they cover the entire life cycle of smart service offerings—from business models to technology to market launch.

As the area of smart service offerings is vast, and growing rapidly, the editors first emphasize basic concepts (like service systems) to allow for a shared understanding of terms, which commonly lead to confusion if the reader is not deeply rooted in the academic community. With the nomenclature established, industrial maintenance and how an organization can enhance and adjust its management of business processes and relationships are explored with motivating examples (Part I).

With the fundamental and motivating aspects set, the editors elaborate on the design of smart service offerings and systems. They describe what constitutes a successful smart service and emphasize how to develop the right strategy for a smart service portfolio. This is especially commendable, as SMEs need early orientation to position themselves strategically. While the next step in a product-oriented business would be one or more long research and development phases, the editors stress the importance of early prototyping activities inspired by agile methods like design thinking or extreme programming. Finally, they give insights on the challenging topic of pricing smart service offerings as well as preparing smart service systems for market launch. Each step is demonstrated with real-world examples from the experience of industry projects (Part II).

While the business aspects of smart service offerings are of high importance, the authors take an interdisciplinary perspective and also focus on the technical architectures of smart service systems. Only with proven architectural concepts can smart service systems simultaneously achieve scalable and efficient performance as well as high customer satisfaction and regulatory compliance. This includes topics on the design of digital twins in cyber-physical systems, the communication between entities and sensors in the age of Industry 4.0, as well as data management and integration (Part III).

Artificial intelligence provides a wide range of possibilities for data analysis, which is a key component of data-driven service systems. AI puts the technological "smart" into smart service by providing the capability of intelligently analyzing data and learning patterns within typical service transactions, e.g., interactions between customers and providers. The authors refer to these activities as service analytics. They describe how the concept of service analytics is implemented and show examples from industry and research (Part IV).

To give the reader even more actionable content, they demonstrate the applicability of the introduced method for smart service management by presenting more real-world use cases from the related areas of IT service management, IoT (Internet of Things), and condition monitoring (Part V).

The result is a comprehensive "end-to-end" textbook that clearly and concisely introduces service-oriented ways for industry. For practitioners, this book will be a valuable reference to learn the fundamentals and repeatedly consult on their digital transformation journey to smarter service offerings and systems. Both practitioners and researchers will find that it augments their own core areas expertise, and they will appreciate the carefully selected use cases, additional readings, and extensive references that accompany each of the chapters. In sum, this book provides the most complete overview of the world of smart service that I have seen to date. I am truly delighted by the tremendous contribution of this book, as well as the great progress the community continues to make in advancing the emerging trans-discipline of service science, management, engineering, design, arts, and policy. There is more work to be done for sure, but with the help of this comprehensive book, the next generation will be better prepared to tackle the challenges of smarter service.

Cognitive Opentech Group (COG), IBM Research,   Jim Spohrer
San Jose, CA, USA

Preface

Concept of the Book

This book aims to communicate the main theoretical foundations behind smart services and to give specific guidelines and practically proven methods on how to design these. Furthermore, it gives an overview of the possible implementation architectures and shows how the designed smart services can be realized with specific technologies. Finally, it provides four specific use cases that show how smart services have been realized in practice and what impact they have within the businesses.

The first part of the book defines the basic concepts and also aims to establish a shared understanding of terms, which are commonly misused or lead to confusion, such as *smart services*, *service systems*, *smart service systems*, and *cyber-physical systems*. On this basis, it also provides an analysis of existing work, especially in the field of management science, with the goal to lay the foundation for aligning state-of-the-art research, technology, and business. Furthermore, this includes insights on how organizations incorporating smart services could enhance and adjust their management and business processes with the help of smart services.

With the organizational and fundamental aspects set, the focus is shifted to the design of smart services. Here, the aim is to elaborate on what constitutes a successful smart service and to describe experiences in the area of interdisciplinary teams, strategic partnerships, the overall service systems, as well as the common, broad data basis. The necessity of rapid prototyping is emphasized, which goes hand in hand with recent procedure models such as design thinking or Scrum. After the design phase, a methodology is presented on how to realize smart services within an organization and how to successfully introduce a smart service to market. This step covers multiple aspects, including the customer targeting and acquisition, the different phases with its individual challenges, as well as communication and service pricing.

While the business and service development sides of smart service are of high importance, the technical architectures need to be handled with the same level of detail, as they ensure a scalable and efficient realization. This includes topics on the design of digital twins in cyber-physical systems, the communication between entities and sensors in the age of Industry 4.0, as well as data management and integration. On this basis, there are a number of analytical possibilities that can be realized and that can constitute—or be included into other—smart services. This includes machine learning and artificial intelligence methods, which can lead to value added for customers and providers.

Finally, the applicability of the introduced design and development method for smart services is demonstrated by considering specific real-world use cases. These include services in the industrial and mobility sector, which were developed in direct cooperation with industry partners.

In the following paragraphs, each of the parts of the book is described in further detail.

Target Audience and Prerequisites

The main target audience of this book is industry-focused readers, especially practitioners from the industry, who are involved in supporting and managing digital business. These include professionals working in business development, product management, strategy, and development or as chief digital officers. The content of this book is relevant and beneficial for top level to middle management. To this end, it conveys the basics needed for developing smart services, given a consistent digital transformation strategy, and successfully placing them on the market. Furthermore, the necessary understanding of the technical aspects as well as practical use cases is taught.

There are no specific prerequisites necessary for appreciating the content presented here. However, some previous knowledge related to the background of smart services, such as a basic understanding of the effects of digitization, can be helpful. Similarly, a general understanding of components and architectures, as well as of business processes, could be beneficial too. The contents of the book are understandable regardless of the reader's academic background.

Overview of the Chapters

This book consists of five main parts, which build up from fundamental to more advanced topics.

Part I: Introduction

This part describes the central challenges in the management of smart services. This includes aligning business and technology, integrating smart services with the core business, and creating scalability. Solutions are shown for the challenges, and typical tasks of a smart service organization are presented.

Part II: Smart Service Design

Here, Smart Service Engineering—a development approach for smart services—is introduced. Based on fundamental principles of success in the development of smart services (interdisciplinary teams, strategic partnerships, etc.), Smart Service Engineering shows how smart services can be developed agilely from strategy development to market launch. It should be emphasized that the approach considers the entire development process. In particular, the step of market introduction with questions of pricing, communication of customer benefits, or the establishment of a sales organization represents a central challenge for the success of smart services.

Part III: Smart Service Architecture

This part describes how the smart services, which are designed by following the methods described in the previous part, can be turned into actual implementations. The foundation for realizing smart services is based on introducing reference architectures for guiding the installment of smart services. The currently very prominent approach of the digital twin is also described, as an example of a model-based representation of hardware. Finally, the communication between the components of a smart service is discussed, followed by a description of how data integration and management can be realized.

Part IV: Smart Service Analytics

This part describes the necessary foundations for quantitative analytics, especially the AI-based process of capturing, processing, and analyzing data generated from the execution of (smart) services, which then enables to improve, extend, and personalize services internally or externally, e.g., creating value for providers and/or customers.

Part V: Smart Service Use Cases

The applicability of the introduced design and development methods for smart services is demonstrated by considering specific real-world use cases. In particular, four different use cases are presented in detail. These include services in the industrial and mobility sector, which were developed in direct cooperation with industry partners.

Bonn, Germany   Maria Maleshkova
Karlsruhe, Germany   Niklas Kühl
Herzogenrath, Germany   Philipp Jussen
July 2020

Contents

Contributors

Muhammad Intizar Ali Data Science Institute, NUI Galway, Galway, Ireland
Dublin City University, Dublin, Ireland

Can Azkan Fraunhofer ISST, Dortmund, Germany

Sebastian R. Bader Fraunhofer IAIS, Schloss Birlinghoven, Sankt Augustin, Germany

Lena Eckstein IBM Deutschland GmbH, Ehningen, Germany

Tobias Enders Karlsruhe Institute of Technology (KIT), Karlsruhe, Germany

Marcel Faulhaber Institute for Industrial Management (FIR) at RWTH Aachen University, Aachen, Germany

Jana Frank Institute for Industrial Management (FIR) at RWTH Aachen University, Aachen, Germany

Hansjörg Fromm Karlsruhe Institute of Technology (KIT), Karlsruhe, Germany

Katarina Heeg Institute for Industrial Management (FIR) at RWTH Aachen University, Aachen, Germany

Jan Hicking Institute for Industrial Management (FIR) at RWTH Aachen University, Aachen, Germany

Philipp Jussen Schaeffler Monitoring Services GmbH, Herzogenrath, Germany

Niklas Kühl Karlsruhe Institute of Technology (KIT), Karlsruhe, Germany

Tobias Leiting Institute for Industrial Management (FIR) at RWTH Aachen University, Aachen, Germany

Maria Maleshkova University of Bonn, Bonn, Germany

Dominik Martin Karlsruhe Institute of Technology (KIT), Karlsruhe, Germany

Benedikt Moser Institute for Industrial Management (FIR) at RWTH Aachen University, Aachen, Germany

Pankesh Patel Data Science Institute, NUI Galway, Galway, Ireland

Gerhard Satzger Karlsruhe Institute of Technology (KIT), Karlsruhe, Germany IBM Deutschland GmbH, Ehningen, Germany

Maximilian Schacht Institute for Industrial Management (FIR) at RWTH Aachen University, Aachen, Germany

Jakob Schöffer Karlsruhe Institute of Technology (KIT), Karlsruhe, Germany

Ronny Schüritz Karlsruhe Institute of Technology (KIT), Karlsruhe, Germany

Ljiljana Stojanovic Fraunhofer IOSB, Karlsruhe, Germany

Jarno Suomela Schaeffler Finland Oy, Jyväskylä, Finland

Johannes Kunze von Bischhoffshausen Trelleborg Sealing Solutions Germany GmbH, Stuttgart, Germany

Michael Vössing Karlsruhe Institute of Technology (KIT), Karlsruhe, Germany

Part I
Introduction to Smart Services

Introduction to Smart Service Management

Maria Maleshkova, Niklas Kühl, and Philipp Jussen

Abstract Technology and customer focus lead to a new vision of integrated and digitized industries, fostering the development of a new kind of services—the smart services. In this introduction, we give a short overview and motivate our book on the topic of smart service management.

1 Introduction

The design and evolution of services and products are continuously influenced by multiple factors. On the one hand, market needs and demands determine the shape of new solutions. On the other hand, technology developments dictate what the new actual realization frontiers are and what practical implementation limits exist. The market influence and the technology state can be seen as two main creative forces behind services and products, which represent counterparts that need to be balanced out in order to be able to provide feasible solutions of superior quality.

Product and service evolution can be witnessed in multiple domains. These are shaped by a variety of forces driving the market. Especially in the context of services, shorter and shorter innovation cycles have been becoming more and more characteristic for the development process. The users are no longer only involved by consuming the finalized service but they take up the role of service co-creators and designers. User preferences, priorities, and needs become an integral part of the

M. Maleshkova (✉)
University of Bonn, Bonn, Germany
e-mail: maleshkova@cs.uni-bonn.de

N. Kühl
Karlsruhe Institute of Technology (KIT), Karlsruhe, Germany
e-mail: kuehl@kit.edu

P. Jussen
Schaeffler Monitoring Services GmbH, Herzogenrath, Germany
e-mail: philipp.jussen@schaeffler.com

© Springer Nature Switzerland AG 2020
M. Maleshkova et al. (eds.), *Smart Service Management*,
https://doi.org/10.1007/978-3-030-58182-4_1

service requirements and thus the service design. As a result, continuous adaptation and customized solutions are not a commodity but rather a prerequisite in terms of expectations.

At the same time, technology developments determine the implementation limits of services and products but also inspire innovative solutions. Current trends, such as ubiquitous access, remote and distributed cloud storage, and distributed component-based applications, predefine user expectations and directly shape the realization of the service. In the context of smart services, data availability and abundancy, data analytics, and artificial intelligence (AI) methods have been particularly impactful in terms of enabling their development and shaping the specific functionalities.

Naturally, market push and technology developments are not the only factors that aid to promote the emergence of innovative services. A suitable environment that supports the adoption of new solutions is just as crucial. In the context of smart services, this environment was provided by the Industry 4.0 initiative, which was initially coined in 2011 by the high-tech strategy of the German government with the aim to promote the digital transformation of manufacturing. Industry 4.0, as originally conceptualized, focuses on providing custom and individualized solutions, which are enabled by adaptable and highly flexible production processes. These are realized by introducing new methods for self-optimization, self-configuration, and self-diagnosis leading to the development of cognitive and intelligent decision processes. Real-time monitoring and optimization of the complete value chain are the basis for ensuring the smooth running of the production processes.

This new vision of integrated and digitized industry fostered the development of a new kind of services—the smart services. There are multiple, partially inconsistent, definitions in terms of what smart services are. However, there is a general agreement on the key shared characteristics. Smart services are user-centered and cover a scope that goes beyond a single company. Furthermore, they are usually industry specific and rely on the integration of data, processes, value chains, and even business models. In terms of technology, smart services are highly dependent on the availability of data and integrated system and sensors. In some cases, smart services are used to refer to cognitive services or services that automatically adapt to user preferences, and recognize and support user needs. However, these are not the main focus of this book. In the following chapters, smart service characteristics and further relevant definitions are discussed in more detail.

Digital transformation, integration, and artificial intelligence are current main driving forces in both research and industry. Smart services unite these three concepts in order to enable the development of innovative services, which target a high-level of customization and automation. Thus, smart services are on the rise. However, while academia describes the theoretical background, the industry-wide take-up and implementation are still lagging behind. To tackle the challenge of real-world use cases and applications, especially for SMEs, this book captures the most important steps, from conceptualization to deployment, with a strong focus on industrial smart services.

The book benefits from both founded research background and multifold practical experience of leading researches and practitioners in the files of services and AI. The content of the book utilizes the experience of the authors and their institutions from more than 100 application-oriented research, industry, and consulting projects in the field of smart services. Particular emphasis is placed on the practical comprehensibility and applicability of the approaches presented.

Grasping the Terminology: Smart Services, Smart Service Systems, and Cyber-Physical Systems

Dominik Martin, Niklas Kühl, and Maria Maleshkova

Abstract During the past years, we can observe a rise of the concepts service systems, smart service systems, and cyber-physical systems. However, distinct definitions are either very broad or contradict each other. As a result, several characteristics appear around these terms, which also miss distinct allocations and relationships to the underlying concepts. Thus, in order to achieve a common understanding of the terminology used within this book, this chapter defines the concepts of service systems, smart service systems, and cyber-physical systems as well as related characteristics.

1 Introduction

As businesses become interconnected, new opportunities and challenges arise for collaboration and co-creation (Chen et al. 2012; Davenport and Harris 2017). Different concepts, such as (smart) service systems (Spohrer et al. 2017; Maglio 2014) and cyber-physical systems (Gunes et al. 2014) emerge and strive to allocate, structure, and explain phenomena in the field of digitally interconnected systems. However, these concepts are often used synonymously (Maglio 2014; Gölzer et al. 2015) or contradict each other (Gunes et al. 2014; Barile and Polese 2010)—which can lead to confusion and misunderstandings among practitioners and researchers. As a clear distinction of those concepts and related characteristics fosters common understanding, we aim to define services, smart services as well as distinct service

---

This chapter is based on the paper Martin et al. (2019).

D. Martin (✉) · N. Kühl
Karlsruhe Institute of Technology (KIT), Karlsruhe, Germany
e-mail: martin@kit.edu; kuehl@kit.edu

M. Maleshkova
University of Bonn, Bonn, Germany
e-mail: maleshkova@cs.uni-bonn.de

© Springer Nature Switzerland AG 2020
M. Maleshkova et al. (eds.), *Smart Service Management*,
https://doi.org/10.1007/978-3-030-58182-4_2

systems, smart service systems, and cyber-physical systems. To approach this topic, we perform a structured research to identify commonly used definitions. We consolidate the insights and define each concept on this basis. Based on this, we intend to overcome boundaries to other disciplines and allow for a common understanding as well as, accordingly, to accelerate new research and development in these areas.

The remainder of this chapter is structured as follows. First, we present theoretical foundations of services, smart services, systems, socio-technical systems, and system-of-systems. Second, we analyze the (smart) service systems and cyber-physical systems concepts in isolation and then summarize them through a conceptualization. Finally, we present a discussion followed by a conclusion.

2 Foundational Concepts

This section provides an overview of the terminology related to (smart) service systems and cyber-physical systems. In particular, it introduces the concepts services, smart services, socio-technical system, system, and system-of-systems.

2.1 Services and Smart Services

The term *service* has multiple, very heterogeneous meanings. It is often used in everyday life and also in specific domains such as the computer science, medical, or economic ones (Vargo and Lusch 2004). For this book, the two relevant definitions are in terms of *economic services* and of *IT services*. Economic services are intangible, as in they are not manufactured, transported, or stocked, they are perishable—they "disappear" after completely delivered to the customer, and they are variable, since exactly the same service cannot be repeated twice in terms of for instance the time, location, circumstances, conditions, etc. A service is an exchange or a transaction between a seller and a buyer or a provider and a consumer, which does not have the primary objective to transfer physical goods, e.g., products. Economic services are frequently described as the non-material equivalent of a good. All of these service characteristics hold also for smart services, since they are a specific type of service, that also relies on IT services for its realization.

IT services are services that are made available to one or more customers or service consumers by an IT service provider. An IT service uses information technologies and supports the business processes of the customer. It consists of a combination of actors (persons), processes, and technologies and is commonly defined by stating what is expected to be delivered, by whom, and in what quality as part of a Service-Level-Agreement (SLA). Similarly to economic services, all characteristics of IT services also hold for smart services, since they rely on information technologies for their implementation.

The heterogeneity of the definition of *smart services* is very similar to the one for services. Currently, we can distinguish three main groups of definitions. First, smarts services understood as *cognitive services* that use artificial intelligence technology and methods in order to implement a technical solution that can learn, improve, and perform in an "intelligent" manner. These services usually rely on machine learning approaches and focus on supporting learning, self-improving, or optimization functionality. They are able to grasp (i.e., cognition) the current state of data, processes, businesses, etc. and act accordingly.

Second, smart services understood as *adaptable and user-centric services*. These are services that take the user as a co-creator and co-designer of the final results. They adapt to different customer needs and provide flexibility for reacting to different situational or requirement circumstances. The "smartness" aspect is realized by offering specific services for specific needs and abandoning the "one fits all" approach.

Finally, smart services as defined in the context of *Industry 4.0 services* and as understood in this book. Smart services are IT services that are based on a connection between the physical and the digital world. They aim to optimize and upgrade the value creation and economic efficiency by relying on the integration provided by Industry 4.0 and new technology developments. Furthermore, smart services are user-centered and cover a scope that goes beyond a single company. They are usually industry specific and are facilitated by the integration of data, processes, value chains, and even business models. In terms of technology, smart services are highly dependent on the availability of data and integrated system and sensors. Naturally, these three groups of definitions have some overlaps. For instance, a smart service, as understood in the context of Industry 4.0 can be realized via analytics or machine learning approaches, i.e., via a smart service understood as cognitive service. In some cases smart services are also implemented via services that automatically adapt to user preferences, and recognize and support user needs.

2.2 Socio-Technical Systems

The term *socio-technical system* is often used to describe complex systems consisting of several interacting components (Baxter and Sommerville 2011). Originally, however, the term was used to describe a set of people and related technologies that are structured in a certain way to produce a specific result (Bostrom et al. 1977).

A *system* is generally referred to as a "collection of components organized to accomplish a specific function or set of functions" (Boulding 1956, p. 73). Boulding (1956) particularly stresses the system boundaries which delimit a system and determine which parts belong to a system and which to the environment. In an open system, interactions can take place with the environment, whereas in an isolated system no interactions can take place (Standards Coordinating Committee of the Computer Society of the IEEE 1990). Interactions can be both the exchange of information (from an Information Systems (IS) viewpoint) (Standards Coordinating

Committee of the Computer Society of the IEEE 1990) and the exchange of mass or energy (from a nature science viewpoint) (Sagawa 2013). Particularly complex open systems consisting of multiple parts that perform complex interactions with each other and with the environment are widely spread in reality (von Bertalanffy 1950). In order to categorize (smart) service systems and cyber-physical systems and form a better understanding of these terminologies, the basic concepts socio-technical systems and system-of-systems are introduced.

According to Cartelli (2007), a socio-technical system consists of two components (subsystems): The technical subsystem represents assets such as machines and equipment, as well as processes and tasks that are responsible for the conversion of input resources into outputs. The social subsystem is made up of people (such as employees) who are structured in groups and have assigned certain roles to operate, control, and use the components of the technical subcomponent. Cartelli (2007) emphasizes the facet of knowledge, which is "socially constructed and developed in the interactions among people" (Cartelli 2007, p. 3), as part of the social subsystem and its value for a socio-technical system.

Both subsystems are "jointly independent, but correlative interacting" (Bostrom et al. 1977, p. 17) in order to pursue and adapt to goals in the socio-technical system's environment and are therefore not separable from each other due to their manifold dependencies (Baxter and Sommerville 2011).

2.3 Systems-of-Systems

A *system-of-systems* has—like a typical system—interdependent components operating together to accomplish a certain common goal (Gideon et al. 2005). Unlike a typical system, the components of a system-of-systems are themselves systems (Maier 1998). According to Maier (1998) a system-of-systems is an "assemblages of components that are themselves significantly complex, enough so that they may be regarded as systems and that are assembled into a larger system" (Maier 1998, p. 269). However, Maier names two limitations: First, the components must be operationally independent. That is, if a system-of-systems is broken down into its components, they must be able to fulfill their original purpose independently. Second, the component systems can not only work independently of each other, they do so as well. Thus, the subsystems maintain their operational independence continuously. Gideon et al. (2005) summarize a system-of-systems as a "system build from independent systems that are managed separately from the larger system" (Gideon et al. 2005, p. 357).

3   State-of-the-Art Definitions in Academia

In order to cover relevant and yet established definitions we conduct a systematic literature research in July 2018 and focus on peer-reviewed articles from the field of Information Systems, Service Science, and Computer Science. Overall, we regard an amount of 354 articles, which are selected by reading the abstract in order to exclude unrelated articles. Through forward and backward search, further relevant articles are identified. By completely reading the remaining articles, all in all 110 relevant articles are selected and analyzed in a final step.

The results of the literature search and the analysis of the definitions depicted in each article are summarized in the following sections. In order to provide the reader with a comprehensive picture of the differences and similarities of the definitions, first the concepts are considered individually, before they are compared with each other.

3.1   Service Systems

The concept Service System appears most frequently in the results of our conducted literature search. Overall, 64 articles refer to the term Service System. According to Spohrer et al. (2007) a Service System comprises "service providers and service clients working together to coproduce value in complex value chains or networks" (Spohrer et al. 2007, p. 72). Components of a Service System are "people, technology, internal and external service systems connected by value propositions, and shared information" (Spohrer et al. 2007, p. 72) and examples include individuals, firms, and nations. Based on this article, Spohrer et al. (2007) and Maglio (2014) synthesize the definition and formulate: "Service systems are value-co-creation configurations of people, technology, value propositions connecting internal and external service systems, and shared information (e.g., language, laws, measures, and methods)" (Maglio et al. 2009, p. 18). Examples include cities, businesses, nations, as well as individuals as the smallest representative of a service system and world economy as the largest (Maglio et al. 2009).

The majority of articles adopt this definition (Maglio 2014; Barile and Polese 2010; Maglio et al. 2009; Baekgaard 2009; Edvardsson et al. 2011; Jaakkola and Alexander 2014; Zhou et al. 2014), while others phrase it slightly different, but in principle remain faithful to the overall message (Kleinschmidt et al. 2016; Kleinschmidt and Peters 2017; Ralyté et al. 2015; Eaton et al. 2015; Knote and Blohm 2016; Herterich et al. 2016; Brust et al. 2017; Spohrer et al. 2017). Besides the more detailed definitions, some authors like Kleinschmidt and Peters (2017) and Lintula et al. (2017) use shorter and thus less specific descriptions. Böhmann et al. (2014), Dörbecker et al. (2015), and Li and Peters (2016) state that a Service System is a "socio-technical system that enables value co-creation guided by a value proposition" (Böhmann et al. 2014, p. 74), whereas Brust et al. (2017) describe it as "collections of people, technology and interactions" (Brust et al. 2017, p. 8).

However, some authors deviate from this common definition and suggest divergent definitions, such as the one proposed in Höckmayr and Roth (2017): "A service system is composed of multiple entities that interact to co-create value" (Höckmayr and Roth 2017, p. 3). Similarly, Motta et al. (2014) describe a Service System only very abstract as a system which supports business services. Alter (2008, 2011, 2017a,b) refers to work systems and defines service systems as "work systems that produce product/services and that may or may not involve co-production by customers and value co-creation" (Alter 2008, p. 4), while a work system is a "system in which human participants and/or machines perform work using information, technology, and other resources to produce products and services for internal or external customers" (Alter 2008, p. 4). Although some authors like Blohm et al. (2016), Dörbecker and Böhmann (2015) and Matzner and Scholta (2014) use the term Service System and name components as well as properties, but avoid defining it.

In conclusion, we also suggest using the definition according to Maglio and Spohrer (2008) and Spohrer et al. (2007), as it is the most concise and commonly used one, and define service systems for this article as "value-co-creation configurations of people, technology, value propositions connecting internal and external service systems, and shared information (e.g., language, laws, measures, and methods)" (Gideon et al. 2005, p. 18).

3.2 Smart Service Systems

The concept smart service system has the lowest number of hits with only 10 represented articles in the searched outlets and databases. This concept is described by Barile and Polese (2010), Maglio (2014), and Medina-Borja (2015) as an extension of the Service System concept containing self-management capabilities. Barile and Polese (2010) define: "Smart service systems may be intended as service systems designed for a wise and interacting management of their assets and goals, capable of self-reconfiguration (or at least of easy inducted re-configuration) in order to perform enduring behavior capable of satisfying all the involved participants in time" (Barile and Polese 2010, p. 31).

According to Maglio (2014), smart service systems are "capable of self-detection, self-diagnostic, self-corrective, or self-controlled functions through the incorporation of technologies for sensing, actuation, coordination, communication, control, and more" (Maglio 2014, p. 1). By automating and self-managing systems, high costs and security risks caused by humans can be reduced, which can lead to improved offers or even new ones (Maglio 2014).

Beverungen et al. (2019) state that smart service systems are service systems, "in which smart products are boundary-objects that integrate resources and activities of the involved actors for mutual benefit" (Beverungen et al. 2019, p. 6).

According to the authors Maglio and Lim (2016) as well as Medina-Borja (2015), such a system is even "capable of learning, dynamic adaptation, and decision making based upon data received, transmitted, and/or processed to improve its response to a future situation" (Maglio and Lim 2016, p. 2), which can be done by integration of sensing, actuation, and communication technologies. In addition, Maglio and Lim (2016) describe that big data analytics can contribute to the innovation of smart service systems by "embedding human knowledge and capabilities in technologies to serve human purposes for effective value co-creation" (Maglio and Lim 2016, p. 3). De Santo et al. (2011) also emphasize the capability of such a system to learn and to "simultaneously optimizing the use of resources and improving the quality of the services provided" (De Santo et al. 2011, p. 3).

Nevertheless, we recommend using a modification of the definition proposed by Medina-Borja (2015) as it is the most detailed and comprehensive and includes most of the characteristics of the other definitions. Furthermore, it delivers a clear demarcation from service systems: "A 'smart' service system is a [Service] [S]ystem capable of learning, dynamic adaptation, and decision-making based upon data received, transmitted, and/or processed to improve its response to a future situation. The system does so through self-detection, self-diagnosing, self-correcting, self-monitoring, self-organizing, self-replicating, or self-controlled functions. These capabilities are the result of the incorporation of technologies for sensing, actuation, coordination, communication, control, etc." (Medina-Borja 2015, p. 3).

3.3 Cyber-Physical Systems

Hauser et al. (2017) state that research on cyber-physical systems (CPS) no longer takes place only in the disciplines of electronics and computer science, but also extends to other fields such as IS. Therefore, they describe a CPS as the extension of a legacy system with information technology (Hauser et al. 2017). Banerjee et al. (2012) propose also an abstract definition and describe CPS as "systems that use the information from the physical environment, and in turn affect the physical environment" (Banerjee et al. 2012, p. 283). Furthermore, they list examples such as smart electricity grid and unmanned aerial vehicles (Banerjee et al. 2012). Likewise, Gölzer et al. (2015) argue that CPS are "able to communicate with each other, to detect their environment, to interpret available data and to act on the physical world" (Gölzer et al. 2015, p. 1). They also emphasize the capabilities of self-control and self-optimization (Gölzer et al. 2015), while Gruettner et al. (2017) describe CPS as "intelligent networking of people, machines, and industrial processes, which in product components communicate with the production gear by embedded sensors" (Gruettner et al. 2017, p. 1853). Bradley and Atkins (2012) state that CPS "interface physics-based and digital world models" (Bradley and Atkins 2012, p. 60) and emphasize the benefits of integrating physical and computational models.

A formal definition is provided by Burmester et al. (2012) describing a CPS as a "finite state system consisting of several networked components, some of which may be cyber while others are physical" (Burmester et al. 2012, p. 3). Akkaya et al. (2016) identify the challenges of designing a Cyber-Physical System as "complexity, heterogeneity, and multidisciplinary nature" (Akkaya et al. 2016, p. 997), but avoid using a distinct definition. In addition, there are some articles that use the term CPS, but neither describe nor define it (Janiesch and Diebold 2016; Jaskolka and Villasenor 2017; Jin et al. 2014; Tabuada et al. 2014; Venkitasubramaniam et al. 2015). Other authors give examples such as smart grids (Siaterlis and Genge 2011; Yu and Xue 2017), machine-to-machine communication (Gharbi et al. 2014), and data centers (Parolini et al. 2012), but also avoid clear definitions. However, most authors describe CPS basically as a conjunction of computation and physical processes, where there is a mutual influence through observation and control (Derler et al. 2012; Han et al. 2014; Lee 2008; Nuzzo et al. 2015; Poovendran 2010; Rajhans et al. 2014; Wu et al. 2011).

Böhmann et al. (2014) build the bridge to service systems and explain that the availability of data and automation capabilities provided by cyber-physical systems contribute to service system innovation. Matzner and Scholta (2014) also combine the CPS and service systems concepts and define: "[CPS] are service systems that connect physical and cyber elements through global networks" (Matzner and Scholta 2014, p. 1).

Furthermore, Gunes et al. (2014) summarize some aspects of different definitions and define CPS as "complex, multi-disciplinary, physically-aware next generation engineered systems that integrate embedded computing technology (cyberpart) into the physical phenomena" (Gunes et al. 2014, p. 4244), where integration is achieved by the capabilities of "observation, communication, and control [. . .] of the physical system" (Gunes et al. 2014, p. 4244).

Sanislav and Miclea (2012) also recognize the variety of different definitions provided in the existing literature and list several, however, without synthesizing or providing their own.

Ribeiro et al. (2017) and Wu et al. (2011) emphasize the intelligence of such systems and characterize CPS as "intelligent systems that are composed of digital virtual/cyber technologies, software, and physical components, and intelligently interact with other systems across information and physical interfaces" (Ribeiro et al. 2017, p. 6131). Sampigethaya and Poovendran (2013) consider CPS based on applications in aviation and describe mainly benefits and challenges. Also Sztipanovits et al. (2012) and Yao et al. (2016) focus mainly on challenges related to the integration of the various computational and physical elements of CPS.

Furthermore, Wan et al. (2013) describe some characteristics of CPS such as "cyber capability in every physical component" (Wan et al. 2013, p. 1108), close integration, "dynamically reorganizing/reconfiguring" Wan et al. (2013), and "high degrees of automation" (Wan et al. 2013, p. 1108).

We recommend following the definition of the majority of the authors and, thus, we provide an abstract definition: "A Cyber-Physical System is an intelligent system connecting the physical and the digital/cyber world through influence and control using sensors and actuators."

3.4 Summary

This literature review shows that the concepts service system, smart service system, and cyber-physical system are not uniformly defined and also that the differentiation is not always clear. While most authors agree on service systems, smart service systems and CPS in particular are not clearly defined.

By applying an open coding approach, properties of the examined concepts described in the articles are codified. Codes with similar characteristics are clustered and, thus, grouped together in categories (Saldaña 2009). Overall, we identify five categories of properties the concepts service system, smart service system, and cyber-physical system have in common. Table 1 depicts five identified categories components, attributes, actions, structure, and boundaries. The categories components, attributes, and actions include a set of codes resulting from the different views of the articles being analyzed. We consider the most frequently occurring representatives for these three categories.

The key components of all three concepts are frequently mentioned in the definitions within the articles and are also conceptually very clear, especially in the concepts of service system and smart service system. For example, service systems and smart service systems both include people and technology, while in terms of service systems, the term information is very present, data is often referred to in smart service systems. A CPS consists of a cyber part that provides computational capabilities, sensors collecting data, as well as actuators.

A variety of attributes are mentioned across all analyzed articles; however, only the key attributes are listed in Table 1. All three concepts emphasize the interaction between components, but also the interaction with the environment. Likewise, the attribute adaptability appears for all three concepts, although it is not mentioned as often in CPS definitions as the attribute distributed. In addition, the code dynamic is very common in service systems, while a CPS is particularly described as intelligent and smart service systems is capable to learn and make decisions.

Table 1 Conceptualization of (smart) service systems and cyber-physical systems

	Service system	Smart service system	Cyber-physical system
Key components	Information, people, technology	Data, people, technology	Cyber part, sensors, actuators
Key attributes	Interaction, dynamic, adaptive	Interaction, adaptive, learning, decision-making	Interaction, intelligent, distributed
Key actions	Value creation	Sensing, control	Sensing, control
Structure	Complex, people-centered	Complex, self-centered	Complex, data-centered
Boundaries	Open, dynamic	Open, dynamic	Open, partially dynamic

However, a small number of key actions are named, but the ones named are mentioned very frequently. Nearly every article defining a service system names the goal of creating value. For smart service systems and CPS, the actions are not quite as clear, but for both the two most common are sensing and control.

The structure of all three analyzed systems is described as a complex. In addition, service systems focus on people—both as component and user—while smart service systems focus on the system itself and its purpose. CPS are often outlined as data-centered.

All three concepts are considered to be open systems. Furthermore, service systems and smart service systems are able to change dynamically, while for CPS at least the physical part is fixed, but the components of the cyber part can also change dynamically.

4   Interrelations of Concepts

The analysis of the literature on the three concepts shows that service systems can be understood as socio-technical systems (Eaton et al. 2015; Böhmann et al. 2014; Dörbecker and Böhmann 2015; Qiu 2009). In addition, a smart service system is a special kind of a Service System (Barile and Polese 2010; Brust et al. 2017; Maglio and Lim 2016; Lim and Maglio 2018). CPSs, on the other hand, are referred to as a kind of Service System (Matzner and Scholta 2014), but more often characterized as technical systems (Gunes et al. 2014; Herterich et al. 2016; Huang and Dong 2018; Jirkovsky et al. 2017; Kang et al. 2012), which can thus be part of a socio-technical and, thus, part of a (smart) service system.

The analysis also shows that the need for information in service systems is enormous as it acts as a key component. The same applies to data in smart service systems. This data, which can be further processed into information, can be collected by CPS. Thus, by enriching CPS with connectivity capabilities, the need for information/data of (smart) service systems can be met. In addition, intelligent CPS can also serve as a social component to mimic the role of people.

Thus, the concepts service system, smart service system, and CPS are closely interlinked and, therefore, have similar characteristics. All concepts emphasize the interaction between humans and technology and the ability for multi-criteria decision-making. This leads to extremely complex and heterogeneous structures that can dynamically adapt over time.

In addition to components such as humans, technology, or CPS, however, service systems themselves can also be components of service systems. This system-of-system property affects all three concepts. Thus, the system boundaries can be extended by parts of the environment, so that other systems arise.

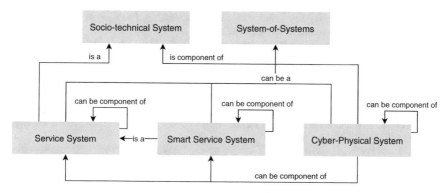

Fig. 1 Interrelations of (smart) service systems and cyber-physical systems

Figure 1 depicts the interrelations of the three considered concepts as well as their connections to socio-technical system and system-of-systems concepts.

5 Conclusion

The concepts of (smart) service systems and cyber-physical systems have been a re-occurring term in research and industry. Aiming for precise definitions, distinctions, and similarities, we apply a thorough literature research and review 110 relevant articles. As a result, we show that especially the concepts smart service system and cyber-physical system are often used in a similar context in different disciplines. The concepts include similar facets and characteristics. However, our research reveals some cases of inconsistent definitions, especially for the concepts of smart service systems and cyber-physical systems. For clarification, we derive suitable definitions from literature and fuse them in a conceptualization. These definitions and concepts may assist researchers in the understanding of the terms and their relationships.

References

Akkaya, I., Derler, P., Emoto, S., & Lee, E. A. (2016). Systems engineering for industrial cyber – physical systems using aspects. In *Proceedings of the IEEE* (Vol. 104, pp. 997 – 1012).

Alter, S. (2008). Service system fundamentals: Work system, value chain, and life cycle. *IBM Systems Journal, 47(1)*, 1–25.

Alter, S. (2011). Metamodel for service design and service innovation: Integrating service activities, service systems, and value constellations. In D. F. Galletta & T.-P. Liang (Eds.), *Proceedings of the International Conference on Information Systems*. Association for Information Systems.

Alter, S. (2017a). Answering key questions for service science. In *Proceedings of the European Conference on Information Systems* (pp. 1822–1836).

Alter, S. (2017b). Service system axioms that accept positive and negative outcomes and impacts of service systems. In *Proceedings of the International Conference on Information Systems* (pp. 1–21).

Baekgaard, L. (2009). Service scenarios - a socio-technical approach to business service modeling. In *Proceedings of the European Conference on Information Systems*.

Banerjee, A., Venkatasubramanian, K. K., Mukherjee, T., & Gupta, S. K. S. (2012). Ensuring safety, security, and sustainability of mission-critical cyber-physical systems. In *Proceedings of the IEEE* (Vol. 100, pp. 283–299).

Barile, S., & Polese, F. (2010). Smart service systems and viable service systems: Applying systems theory to service science. *Service Science, 2(1/2)*, 21–40.

Baxter, G., & Sommerville, I. (2011). Socio-technical systems: From design methods to systems engineering. *Interacting with Computers, 23*, 4–17.

Beverungen, D., Müller, O., Matzner, M., Mendling, J., & Vom Brocke, J. (2019). Conceptualizing smart service systems. *Electronic Markets, 29*, 7–18.

Blohm, I., Haas, P., Peters, C., Jakob, T., & Leimeister, J. M. (2016). Managing disruptive innovation through service systems – the case of crowdlending in the banking industry. In *Proceedings of the International Conference on Information Systems* (pp. 1–15).

Böhmann, T., Leimeister, J. M., & Möslein, K. (2014). Service Systems Engineering. *Business & Information Systems Engineering, 6(2)*, 73–79.

Bostrom, R. P., Heinen, J. S., & Heinen, J. S. (1977). MIS problems and failures: A socio- technical perspective part I: The causes. *MIS Quarterly, 1(3)*, 17–32.

Boulding, K. E. (1956). General systems theory: The skeleton of science. *Management Science, 2*, 197–208.

Bradley, B. J. M., & Atkins, E. M. (2012). Toward continuous state–space regulation of coupled cyber–physical systems. In *Proceedings of the IEEE* (Vol. 100, pp. 60–74)

Brust, L., Antons, D., Breidbach, C. F., & Salge, T. O. (2017). Service-dominant logic and information systems research: A review and analysis using topic modeling. In *Proceedings of the International Conference on Information Systems*.

Burmester, M., Magkos, E., & Chrissikopoulos, V. (2012). Modeling security in cyber-physical systems. *International Journal of Critical Infrastructure Protection, 5(3–4)*, 118–126.

Cartelli, A. (2007). Socio-technical theory and knowledge construction: Towards new pedagogical paradigms? *Issues in Informing Science and Information Technology, 4*, 1–14.

Chen, H., Chiang, R. H. L., & Storey, V. C. (2012). Business intelligence and analytics: From big data to big impact. *Mis Quarterly, 36(4)*, 1165–1188.

Davenport, T., & Harris, J. (2017). *Competing on analytics: Updated, with a new introduction: The new science of winning*. Boston: Harvard Business Press.

De Santo, M., Pietrosanto, A., Napoletano, P., & Carrubbo, L. (2011). Knowledge based service systems. In *System theory and service science: integrating three perspectives in a new service agenda* (pp. 24–39).

Derler, P., Lee, E. A., & Sangiovanni Vincentelli, A. (2012). Modeling cyber-physical systems. In *Proceedings of the IEEE*.

Dörbecker, R., & Böhmann, T. (2015). FAMouS – Framework for architecting modular services. In *Proceedings of the International Conference on Information Systems* (pp. 1–18).

Dörbecker, R., Tokar, O., & Böhmann, T. (2015). Deriving design principles for improving service modularization methods - lessons learnt from the complex integrated health care service system. In *Proceedings of the European Conference on Information Systems* (pp. 0–15).

Eaton, B., Elaluf-calderwood, S., Sørensen, C., & Eaton, B. (2015). Distributed tuning of boundary resources: the case of Apple's iOS service system. *MIS Quarterly, 39(1)*, 217–243.

Edvardsson, B., Ng, G., Min, C. Z., Firth, R., & Yi, D. (2011). Does service-dominant design result in a better service system? *Journal of Service Management, 22(4)*, 540–556.

Gharbi, G., Guermouche, N., & Monteil, T. (2014). Temporal verification of mobile publish/subscribe machine-to-machine communications. In *Proceeding of IEEE International Symposium on a World of Wireless, Mobile and Multimedia Networks* (pp. 2–4).

Gideon, J. M., Dagli, C. H., & Miller, A. (2005). Taxonomy of systems-of-systems. In *Conference on Systems Engineering Research, Institute of Electrical and Electronics Engineers (IEEE)*.

Gölzer, P., Cato, P., & Amberg, M. (2015). Data processing requirements of industry 4.0-use cases for big data applications. In *Proceedings of the European Conference On Information Systems* (pp. 1–13).

Gruettner, A., Richter, J., & Basten, D. (2017). Explaining the role of service-oriented architecture for cyber-physical systems by establishing logical links. In *Proceedings of the ECIS* (pp. 1853–1868)

Gunes, V., Peter, S., Givargis, T., & Vahid, F. (2014). A survey on concepts, applications, and challenges in cyber-physical systems. *KSII Transactions on Internet and Information Systems, 8(12)*, 4242–4268.

Han, S., Xie, M., Chen, H. H., & Ling, Y. (2014). Intrusion detection in cyber-physical systems: Techniques and challenges. *IEEE Systems Journal, 8(4)*, 1049–1059.

Hauser, M., Günther, S. A., Flath, C. M., & Thiesse, F. (2017). Designing pervasive information systems: A fashion retail case study. In *Proceedings of the International Conference on Information Systems* (pp. 1–16).

Herterich, M. M., Eck, A., & Uebernickel, F. (2016). Exploring how digitized products enable industrial service innovation – An affordance perspective. In *Proceedings of the European Conference on Information Systems*.

Höckmayr, B., & Roth, A. (2017). Design of a method for service systems engineering in the digital age. In *Proceedings of the International Conference on Information Systems* (pp. 1–23).

Huang, X., & Dong, J. (2018). Reliable control policy of cyber-physical systems against a class of frequency-constrained sensor and actuator attacks. *IEEE Transactions on Cybernetics, 48(12)*, 3432–3439.

Jaakkola, E., & Alexander, M. (2014). The role of customer engagement behavior in value co-creation: A service system perspective. *Journal of Service Research, 17(3)*, 247–261.

Janiesch, C., & Diebold, J. (2016). Conceptual modeling of event processing networks. In *Proceedings of the European Conference On Information Systems*.

Jaskolka, J., & Villasenor, J. (2017). Identifying implicit component interactions in distributed cyber-physical systems. In *Proceedings of the HICSS* (p. 10).

Jin, J., Gubbi, J., Marusic, S., & Palaniswami, M. (2014). An information framework for creating a smart city through internet of things. *IEEE Internet of Things Journal, 1(2)*, 112–121.

Jirkovsky, V., Obitko, M., & Marik, V. (2017). Understanding data heterogeneity in the context of cyber-physical systems integration. *IEEE Transactions on Industrial Informatics, 13(2)*, 660–667.

Kang, W., Kapitanova, K., & Son, S. (2012). RDDS: A real-time data distribution service for cyber-physical systems. *IEEE Transactions on Industrial Informatics, 8(2)*, 393–405.

Kleinschmidt, S., Burkhard, B., Hess, M., Peters, C., & Leimeister, J. M. (2016). Towards design principles for aligning human-centered service systems and corresponding business models. In *Proceedings of the International Conference on Information Systems* (pp. 2–11).

Kleinschmidt, S., & Peters, C. (2017). Towards an integrated evaluation of human-centered service systems and corresponding business models: A systems theory perspective. In *Proceedings of the ECIS* (pp. 3060–3070).

Knote, R., & Blohm, I. (2016). It's not about having ideas - It's about making ideas happen! Fostering exploratory innovation with the intrapreneur accelerator. In *Proceedings of the European Conference on Information Systems*.

Lee, E. A. (2008). Cyber physical systems: Design challenges. In *2008 11th IEEE International Symposium on Object and Component-Oriented Real-Time Distributed Computing* (pp. 363–369). Washington: IEEE Computer Society.

Li, M. M., & Peters, C. (2016). Mastering shakedown through the user: The need for user-generated services in techno change. In *Proceedings of the European Conference on Information Systems*.

Lim, C., & Maglio, P. P. (2018). Data-driven understanding of smart service systems through text mining. *Service Science, 10(2)*, 154–180.

Lintula, J., Tuunanen, T., & Salo, M. (2017). Conceptualizing the value co-destruction process for service systems: Literature review and synthesis. In *Proceedings of the Hawaii International Conference on System Sciences* (pp. 1632–1641).

Maglio, P., & Lim, C.-H. (2016). Innovation and big data in smart service systems. *Journal of Innovation Management, 4(1)*, 11–21.

Maglio, P. P. (2014). Editorial column — Smart service systems. *Service Science, 6(1)*, i–ii.

Maglio, P. P., & Spohrer, J. (2008). Fundamentals of service science. *Journal of the Academy of Marketing Science, 36(1)*, 18–20.

Maglio, P. P., Vargo, S. L., Caswell, N., & Spohrer, J. (2009). The service system is the basic abstraction of service science. *Information Systems and e-Business Management, 7(4 SPEC. ISS.)*, 395–406.

Maier, M. W. (1998). Architecting principles for systems of systems. *Systems Engineering, 1(4)*, 267–284.

Martin, D., Hirt, R., & Kühl, N. (2019). Service systems, smart service systems and cyber-physical systems—What's the difference? Towards a unified terminology. In *14. Internationale Tagung Wirtschaftsinformatik 2019 (WI 2019), Siegen, Germany, February 24–27* (pp. 17–31).

Matzner, M., & Scholta, H. (2014). Process mining approaches to detect organizational properties in cyber-physical systems. In *Proceedings of the European Conference on Information Systems*.

Medina-Borja, A. (2015). Editorial column—smart things as service providers: A call for convergence of disciplines to build a research agenda for the service systems of the future. *Service Science, 7(1)*, ii–v.

Motta, G., You, L., Sacco, D., & Miceli, G. (2014). Mobility service systems: Guidelines for a possible paradigm and a case study. In *Proceedings of 2014 IEEE International Conference on Service Operations and Logistics, and Informatics* (pp. 48–53).

Nuzzo, P., Sangiovanni-Vincentelli, A. L., Bresolin, D., Geretti, L., & Villa, T. (2015). A platform-based design methodology with contracts and related tools for the design of cyber-physical systems. In *Proceedings of the IEEE* (Vol. 103, pp. 2104–2132).

Parolini, L., Sinopoli, B., Krogh, B. H., & Wang, Z. K. (2012). A cyber-physical systems approach to data center modeling and control for energy efficiency. In *Proceedings of the IEEE* (Vol. 100, pp. 254–268).

Poovendran, R. (2010). Cyber-physical systems: Close encounters between two parallel worlds. In *Proceedings of the IEEE* (Vol. 98, pp. 1363–1366).

Qiu, R. G. (2009). Computational thinking of service systems: Dynamics and adaptiveness modeling. *Service Science, 1(1)*, 42–55.

Rajhans, A., Bhave, A., Ruchkin, I., Krogh, B. H., Garlan, D., Platzer, A., & Schmerl, B. (2014). Supporting heterogeneity in cyber-physical systems architectures. *IEEE Transactions on Automatic Control, 59*, 3178–3193.

Ralyté, J., Khadraoui, A., & Léonard, M. (2015). Designing the shift from information systems to information services systems. *Business & Information Systems Engineering, 57(1)*, 37–49.

Ribeiro, F., Rettberg, A., Pereira, C. E., & Soares, M. S. (2017). A model-based engineering methodology for requirements and formal design of embedded and real-time systems. In *Proceedings of the HICSS* (pp. 6131–6140).

Sagawa, T. (2013). *Thermodynamics of information processing in small systems*. Springer Theses. Tokyo: Springer Japan.

Saldaña, J. (2009). *The coding manual for qualitative researchers*. Cambridge: Cambridge University Press.

Sampigethaya, K., & Poovendran, R. (2013). Aviation cyber-physical systems: Foundations for future aircraft and air transport. In *Proceedings of the IEEE* (Vol. 101, pp. 1834–1855).

Sanislav, T., & Miclea, L. (2012). An agent-oriented approach for cyber-physical system with dependability features. In *Proceedings of 2012 IEEE International Conference on Automation, Quality and Testing, Robotics* (pp. 356–361).

Siaterlis, C., & Genge, B. (2011). Theory of evidence-based automated decision making in cyber-physical systems. In *2011 IEEE International Conference on Smart Measurements of Future Grids (SMFG) Proceedings* (pp. 107–112).

Spohrer, J., Maglio, P., Bailey, J., & Gruhl, D. (2007). Steps toward a science of service systems. *Computer, 40(1)*, 71–77.

Spohrer, J., Siddike, M. A. K., & Kohda, Y. (2017). Rebuilding evolution: A service science perspective. In *Proceedings of the Hawaii International Conference on System Sciences* (pp. 1663–1672).

Standards Coordinating Committee of the Computer Society of the IEEE (1990). IEEE Standard Glossary of Software Engineering Terminology.

Sztipanovits, J., Koutsoukos, X., Karsai, G., Kottenstette, N., Antsaklis, P., Gupta, V., Goodwine, B., Baras, J., & Wang, S. (2012). Toward a science of cyber-physical system integration. In *Proceedings of the IEEE* (Vol. 100, pp. 29–44)

Tabuada, P., Caliskan, S. Y., Rungger, M., & Majumdar, R. (2014). Towards robustness for cyber-physical systems. *IEEE Transactions on Automatic Control, 59(12)*, 3151–3163.

Vargo, S. L., & Lusch, R. F. (2004). The four service marketing myths: Remnants of a goods-based, manufacturing model. *Journal of Service Research, 6(4)*, 324–335.

Venkitasubramaniam, P., Yao, J., & Pradhan, P. (2015). Information-theoretic security in stochastic control systems. In *Proceedings of the IEEE* (Vol. 103, pp. 1914–1931).

von Bertalanffy, L. (1950). An outline of general system theory. *The British Journal For Philosophy Of Science, 1(2)*, 134–165.

Wan, J., Chen, M., Xia, F., Li, D., & Zhou, K. (2013). From machine-to-machine communications towards cyber-physical systems. *Computer Science and Information Systems, 10(3)*, 1105–1128.

Wu, F. J., Kao, Y. F., & Tseng, Y. C. (2011). From wireless sensor networks towards cyber physical systems. *Pervasive and Mobile Computing, 7(4)*, 397–413.

Yao, J., Xu, X., & Liu, X. (2016). MixCPS: Mixed time/event-triggered architecture of cyber – physical systems. In *Proceeding of IEEE*.

Yu, X., & Xue, Y. (2017). Beyond smart grid—a cyber–physical–social system in energy future. In *Proceedings of the IEEE* (Vol. 105, pp. 2290–2292).

Zhou, Z., Lin, Y., & Yue, F. (2014). Service-dominant logic for exploring modular business service system. In *Proceedings of 2014 IEEE International Conference on Service Operations and Logistics, and Informatics* (pp. 108–112).

Industrial Maintenance in the Digital World

Michael Vössing and Niklas Kühl

Abstract For most industrial goods, markets have become global and highly competitive. Manufacturers, whose products are reaching the maturity phase of their life cycles, have to differentiate their offerings through complementary services (e.g., maintenance, repair, and overhaul). Driven by changing customer demand and the widespread adoption of cyber-physical systems, maintenance providers are pursuing performance or facilitator contracts as well as condition- and prediction-based maintenance policies to differentiate their offerings. However, many companies struggle to adapt their processes and develop sustainable offerings—even though these changes could address the principal-agent problem associated with maintenance outsourcing. This chapter outlines why innovation in industrial maintenance requires an integrated approach that leverages these opportunities simultaneously and how this approach addresses the principal-agent problem associated with maintenance outsourcing.

1 Introduction

Manufacturers of industrial goods increasingly supplement their product offerings with supplementary services—commonly known as industrial services (Gitzel et al. 2016). These services have become essential sources of profit, differentiation, and growth for companies (Baines et al. 2011; Oliva and Kallenberg 2003; Penttinen and Palmer 2007). On average, companies generate more than half of their profits with services (Strähle et al. 2012). Typically, logistics and transport constitute a significant share of the costs associated with the delivery of these services. Accordingly, improving service operations has a direct impact on profitability (Sörensen et al.

This chapter is based on the paper Vössing (2019).

M. Vössing (✉) · N. Kühl
Karlsruhe Institute of Technology (KIT), Karlsruhe, Germany
e-mail: voessing@kit.edu; kuehl@kit.edu

© Springer Nature Switzerland AG 2020
M. Maleshkova et al. (eds.), *Smart Service Management*,
https://doi.org/10.1007/978-3-030-58182-4_3

23

2008). Companies rely on field service planning systems—specialized information systems that support the scheduling and dispatching of resources to spatially distributed customers. These systems are utilized in a variety of industries, such as telecommunications (Cordeau et al. 2010), in-home health care (Begur et al. 1997), aircraft operations (Safaei et al. 2011), or industrial manufacturing (Paz and Leigh 1994). As outlined by Fitzgerald and Kruschwitz (2014), the digital world is transforming processes by connecting companies, customers, and machines in new ways. So far, few scholars have explored how companies can leverage these opportunities to improve service operations (Agnihothri et al. 2002; Belvedere et al. 2013). However, they predict that "in the near future every company will base most operational decisions on data" (Cohen 2018, p. 1709). In this chapter, we examine service operations in the context of industrial maintenance (i.e., maintenance, repair, and overhaul of industrial machinery). As outlined by Waeyenbergh and Pintelon (2002), in this context the opportunities of emerging technologies (i.e., technology-push) are complemented with changing customer expectations (i.e., market-pull):

- *Market-pull* refers to the increasing demand for performance or facilitator contracts—also known as output-based, outcome-based, or usage-based contracts (Hypko et al. 2010; Kim et al. 2007; Ng et al. 2013).
- *Technology-push* refers to the widespread adoption of digital technologies. Specifically, cyber-physical systems and advanced analytic capabilities (Lee et al. 2015) are enabling manufacturers to develop condition- and prediction-based maintenance policies (Herterich et al. 2015).

However, Manufacturers struggle to find business models that make these contracts sustainable and to sell these offerings to their customers because they are not intrinsically valuable without a noticeable reduction of machinery downtime (Oliva and Kallenberg 2003). These observations align with the statements of Legner et al. (2017), which highlight that companies struggle to adjust their work routines, processes, and structures to the changing environment.

In this chapter, we outline how maintenance services are currently delivered (cf. Sect. 2.1) and discuss why the established processes constitute a problem for both customers and providers (cf. Sect. 2.2). Further, we reflect on the opportunities arising from changing market forces (cf. Sect. 3.1) and digital technologies (cf. Sect. 3.2). Finally, we challenge the assumptions that determine how maintenance services are currently delivered and outline how they should be delivered (cf. Sect. 4). We provide a new perspective on maintenance contracts and policies by emphasizing that they are deeply intertwined. Accordingly, we highlight why companies need to redesign their service operations processes and adapt their business models to compete in the digital world.

2 Fundamentals of Industrial Maintenance

Following the principles for problematization outlined by Alvesson and Sandberg (2011), we examine selected studies as a means to identify the major assumptions underlying the studied domain. We, further, present the principal-agent problem as a theoretical lens for investigating the challenges providers and customers face.

2.1 Definition of Industrial Maintenance

In many industries, companies rely on physical assets (i.e., machinery). To preserve the availability of these assets *maintenance services* are needed.

- The term *maintenance services* refers to those "activities [aimed] at keeping an item in or restoring it to, the physical state considered necessary for the fulfillment of its production function" (Geraerds 1985, p. 5).

Traditionally, companies conducted these activities independently after purchasing an asset. However, today companies typically outsource them to service providers (Campbell 1995; Martin 1997). The delivery of maintenance services is referenced under a variety of terms (Fraser et al. 2015). Building on the work of Pintelon and Van Puyvelde (2013), we refer to three dimensions:

- *Maintenance actions* are the building blocks of maintenance services. They can be divided into corrective actions that refer to those activities that restore assets from a non-operational to an operational condition and preventive actions that refer to activities that control asset degradation (Pongpech et al. 2006).
- *Maintenance policies* specify the underlying mechanisms that trigger maintenance actions. Scholars have extensively tried to categorize these policies. Commonly run-to-failure, time-based, usage-based, and condition-based maintenance policies are referenced (Garg and Deshmukh 2006; Tsang 2002).
- *Maintenance contracts* govern the contractual relationship between maintenance providers and customers.

The latter are closely linked to maintenance concepts (e.g., total productive maintenance) and utilize maintenance policies to achieve specific objectives. Martin (1997) and Tsang (2002) describe three primary types of maintenance contracts that vary in the complexity of the contract, its duration, and the size of the maintenance knowledge the customer retains:

- *Work package contracts*—sometimes referred to as cost & margin or time & material contracts—are based on the transactional exchange of value.
- *Performance and facilitator contracts*, on the other hand, describe long-term partnerships between providers and customers based on the delivery of contractually agreed outcomes.

While the specifics of these contracts differ, we refer to them together due to their shared focus on co-creating value. The presented maintenance contracts and policies have been explored extensively in the last decades. However, research indicates that while the theoretical knowledge is vast, empirical evidence is rare. Theory, therefore, is often decoupled from the practical application (Fraser et al. 2015). In practice, many companies primarily rely on run-to-failure and time-based maintenance policies as well as work package contracts (Martin 1997; Tsang 2002).

2.2 Principal-Agent Problem of Industrial Maintenance

As outlined by Krinsky and Mehrez (1989) as well as Murthy et al. (2013), the relationship between maintenance customers and providers constitutes a principal-agent problem. The theory describes a conflict of interest in relationships where one party is expected to act in another's best interest (Murthy and Jack 2014). Based on the assumption that all parties try to maximize their own utility, the theory emphasizes that in contractual relationships incentives are needed to limit the divergence of self-interest (Jensen and Meckling 1976). The theory provides an empirically testable perspective on problems of cooperative effort (Eisenhardt 1989). It is used to determine contracts that address issues complicating these relationships. For example, when participants do not put in the agreed-upon effort because their objectives differ (Murthy and Jack 2008). As a result, the rules governing the relationship have to be adjusted so that the self-interested and rational choices of the agent and principal align—commonly by introducing monetary incentives. Performance-based incentives are a viable means to achieve this goal.

Today, maintenance services are generally priced by adding a margin to the costs accrued by the provider when delivering the service. This constitutes an agency problem as the self-interests of both parties are not aligned (see Fig. 1). The customer desires machine availability—which entails a reduction in the amount of required service—while the provider seeks to maximize revenue. Accordingly, the provider has little incentive to improve the availability of the machinery, as the revenue is dependent on the number of served customer requests and not

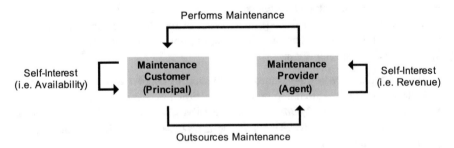

Fig. 1 Principal-agent problem of industrial maintenance, based on Murthy et al. (2013)

on the accomplished service level. Additionally, risks are unevenly distributed as customers bear the financial risk associated with breakdowns (i.e., repair costs and downtime). As a result, work package contracts are "prone to wastage, inefficiency, and duplicated effort" (Tsang 2002, p. 14). While the majority of academic literature focuses on the normative aspects of these problems (i.e., how to structure contracts and design appropriate incentive structures), this work explores how the agency problem can be addressed by redesigning service operations (Jensen and Meckling 1976).

3 Opportunities in Industrial Maintenance

In this section, we introduce two phenomena that are challenging the identified assumptions of how maintenance services should be delivered. Specifically, we highlight that the expectations of customers are changing (i.e., market-pull) and that digital technologies (i.e., technology-push) are enabling providers to develop more complex service offerings (Breidbach et al. 2018).

3.1 Market-Pull: Maintenance and Asset Outsourcing

Since the early 1970s, companies have been outsourcing maintenance services to service providers (Pongpech et al. 2006). Today, industrial machinery is even more complicated, and even simple maintenance actions require specialized knowledge. Hence, for many companies outsourcing maintenance service to external providers is a valid alternative to self-provisioning as maintenance activities are increasingly considered a secondary competence (Smith 2013). Outsourcing allows companies to concentrate their resources on core competencies and minimize the economic risk associated with uncertain failure rates and, thus, unpredictable demand for maintenance services over the lifetime of machines (Campbell 1995). The outsourcing of maintenance services is typically accompanied by a shift from the transactional purchase of services (i.e., work package contracts) toward the purchase of long-term service contracts (i.e., performance or facilitator contracts) (Mcilwraith et al. 2011).

Asset outsourcing is an extension of this phenomenon. Due to rising investment costs, companies increasingly do not want to own their assets but instead lease them or pay for their usage (Pongpech et al. 2006). Accordingly, maintenance contracts are emerging that are based on the sale of performance (i.e., performance or facilitator contracts) and incorporate penalties for the downtime of machinery to incentivize maintenance providers (Ng et al. 2009). These contracts fundamentally restructure the risks, responsibilities, and costs associated with asset ownership (Baines et al. 2007). While these new types of maintenance contracts have not yet been adopted widely, their advantages for providers and customers can already be observed in the context of IT infrastructure management (Ahamed et al. 2013), aircraft turbine maintenance (Pongpech et al. 2006), and the provisioning of commercial printers (Takeda and Kosaka 2016). Ultimately, these contracts benefit customers by incentivizing maintenance providers to design more reliable products and improve their service operations processes (Kim et al. 2007). However, they also benefit providers by increasing workforce utilization, differentiating their offerings, and generating continuous income streams. Further, retaining ownership of their machinery enables manufacturers to collect unique information on product usage and degradation (Baines et al. 2007).

3.2   Technology-Push: Cyber-Physical Systems

The term cyber-physical systems (CPS) refers to physical assets that are equipped with sensors and microprocessors to collect data and communicate this data to other connected systems (Thoben et al. 2017). Their widespread adoption in the manufacturing industry is referred to as the fourth industrial revolution to reflect its potential to revolutionize all industrial processes. CPS are closely linked to concepts such as the Industrial Internet of Things (Atzori et al. 2010), smart manufacturing (Thoben et al. 2017), and smart service systems (Beverungen et al. 2019). Initially, these systems were developed to automate manufacturing processes and address demand with high variability and small lot sizes. However, in the context of maintenance outsourcing, they enable manufacturers to collect data from machinery located at customers' locations. As noted by Bektas et al. (2014), in dynamic and stochastic planning problems—which include field service planning in the context of industrial maintenance—there is a "strong incentive to exploit and integrate [...] information on [...] future events" (Bektas et al. 2014, p. 300). CPS allow manufacturers to collect vast amounts of data from their customers to predict the behavior of individual assets (e.g., degradation). Therefore, CPS play an essential role in the servitization of the manufacturing industry (Herterich et al. 2015). These systems enable the development of advanced product-service offerings (Ardolino et al. 2018) and can align the perspectives of customers and providers on value creation (Beverungen et al. 2019). More specifically, maintenance providers can leverage the collected data to develop condition- and prediction-based maintenance policies.

4   Industrial Maintenance in the Digital World

Companies often do not utilize these opportunities. Many manufacturers focus on supplying equipment to customers and providing the necessary maintenance services. This self-image is characterized by a reliance on run-to-failure and time-

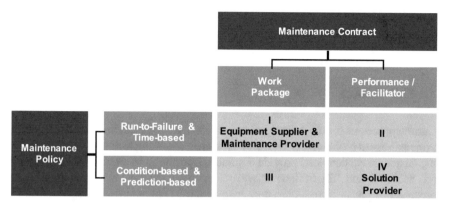

Fig. 2 Feasibility of provider roles based on the combination of maintenance contract and policy

based maintenance policies as well as work package contracts (cf. Fig. 2, I). However, changing customer expectations and emerging technologies are enabling new maintenance contracts and maintenance policies (cf. Sect. 3). Nonetheless, the relationship between maintenance providers and customers remains mostly unchanged as companies struggle to leverage these opportunities.

Equipment suppliers and maintenance providers have little incentive to adopt these maintenance contracts and policies individually (cf. Fig. 2, II and III). As long as companies rely on run-to-failure and time-based maintenance policies, they have little incentive to offer performance or facilitator contracts that would penalize them for unavailable machinery—simply because these contracts would tie their revenue to the availability of their customer's machinery (cf. Fig. 2, II). Similarly, work package contracts, which imply cost- and margin-based pricing, do not incentivize maintenance providers to develop and offer their customers condition- and prediction-based maintenance policies to increase the availability of their machines because their revenue is primarily based on serving the highest number of service requests (cf. Fig. 2, III). Innovation, therefore, requires a simultaneous adoption of condition- and prediction-based maintenance policies as well as an overhaul of established maintenance contracts (cf. Fig. 2, IV). A variety of recent research complements this analysis. Kowalkowski et al. (2015) outline multiple growth trajectories for manufacturing companies. Unfortunately, Kowalkowski et al. (2015) and others use different terminology to discuss similar phenomena. To integrate these relevant contributions, we adopt the term *solution provider* to unify these concepts (Helander and Möller 2008). Ardolino et al. (2018) and Field et al. (2018) note that emerging technologies are fundamentally transforming how services are delivered. Research shows that even though companies evaluate these contracts by adapting their business model, many ultimately remain *equipment suppliers and maintenance providers*. While the requirement to pursue these opportunities simultaneously hinders innovation, it provides a unique opportunity for maintenance providers to differentiate their offerings. Solution providers can focus on the interests of their customers (e.g., machinery availability) and, thus, notably increase the value of maintenance outsourcing.

5 Conclusion

Current processes for the delivery of maintenance services (cf. Sect. 2.1) constitute a principal-agent problem (cf. Sect. 2.2). However, emerging technologies and changing customer expectations provide a unique opportunity to overcome this problem (cf. Sects. 3.1 and 3.2). Maintenance providers often continue to rely on established processes because introducing new maintenance contracts (e.g., performance or facilitator contracts) and policies (e.g., condition- and prediction-based policies) individually is not viable. However, performance or facilitator contracts fundamentally require cyber-physical systems—and vice versa (cf. Sect. 4). Becoming a *solution provider* allows companies to leverage these opportunities and generate vast benefits for themselves and their customers.

References

Agnihothri, S., Sivasubramaniam, N., & Simmons, D. (2002). Leveraging technology to improve field service. *International Journal of Service Industry Management, 13(1)*, 47–68.

Ahamed, Z., Inohara, T., & Kamoshida, A. (2013). The servitization of manufacturing: An empirical case study of IBM corporation. *International Journal of Business Administration, 4(2)*, 18–26.

Alvesson, M., & Sandberg, J. (2011). Generating research questions through problematization. *Academy of Management Review, 36(2)*, 247–271.

Ardolino, M., Rapaccini, M., Saccani, N., Gaiardelli, P., Crespi, G., , & Ruggeri, C. (2018). The role of digital technologies for the service transformation of industrial companies. *International Journal of Production Research, 56(6)*, 2116–2131.

Atzori, L., Iera, A., & Morabito, G. (2010). The internet of things: A survey. *Computer Networks, 54(15)*, 2787–2805.

Baines, T., Lightfoot, H., Evans, S., Neely, A., Greenough, R., Peppard, J., Roy, R., Shehab, E., Braganza, A., Tiwari, A., Alcock, J. R., Angus, J. P., Bastl, M., Cousens, A., Irving, P., Johnson, M., Kingston, J., Lockett, H., Martinez, V., Michele, P., Tranfield, D., Walton, I. M., & Wilson, H. (2007). State-of-the-art in product-service systems. *Proceedings of the Institution of Mechanical Engineers, 221(10)*, 1543–1552.

Baines, T., Lightfoot, H., & Smart, P. (2011). Servitization within manufacturing: Exploring the provision of advanced services and their impact on vertical integration , *Journal of Manufacturing Technology Management, 22(7)*, 947–954.

Begur, S. V., Miller, D. M., & Weaver, J. R. (1997). An integrated spatial DSS for scheduling and routing home-health-care nurses. *Interfaces, 27(4)*, 35–48.

Bektas, T., Repoussis, P. P., & Tarantilis, C. D. (2014). *Dynamic vehicle routing problems* (2nd ed.). Philadelphia: Society for Industrial and Applied Mathematics.

Belvedere, V., Grando, A., & Bielli, P. (2013). A quantitative investigation of the role of information and communication technologies in the implementation of a product-service system. *International Journal of Production Research, 51(2)*, 410–426.

Beverungen, D., Müller, O., Matzner, M., Mendling, J., & Vom Brocke, J. (2019). Conceptualizing smart service systems. *Electronic Markets, 29*, 7–18.

Breidbach, C., Choi, S., Ellway, B., Keating, B. W., Kormusheva, K., Kowalkowski, C., Lim, C., & Maglio, P. (2018). Operating without operations: how is technology changing the role of the firm? *Journal of Service Management, 29(5)*, 809–833.

Campbell, J. D. (1995). Outsourcing in maintenance management: A valid alternative to self-provision. *Journal of Quality in Maintenance Engineering 1(3)*, 18–24.

Cohen, M. C. (2018). Big data and service operations. *Production and Operations Management, 27(9)*, 1709–1723.

Cordeau, J. F., Laporte, G., Pasin, F., & Ropke, S. (2010). Scheduling technicians and tasks in a telecommunications company. *Journal of Scheduling, 13(4)*, 393–409.

Eisenhardt, K. M. (1989). Agency theory: An assessment and review. *The Academy of Management Review, 14(1)*, 57–74.

Field, J. M., Victorino, L., Buell, R. W., Dixon, M. J., Meyer Goldstein, S., Menor, L. J., Pullman, M. E., Roth, A. V., Secchi, E., & Zhang, J. J. (2018). Service operations: What's next? *Journal of Service Management, 29(1)*, 55–97.

Fitzgerald, M., & Kruschwitz, N. (2014). Embracing digital technology: A new strategic imperative. *MIT Sloan Management Review, 55(2)*, 1–12.

Fraser, K., Hvolby, H.-H., & Tseng, T.-L. B. (2015). Maintenance management models: A study of the published literature to identify empirical evidence. *International Journal of Quality & Reliability Management, 32(6)*, 635–664.

Garg, A., & Deshmukh, S. (2006). Maintenance management: Literature review and directions. *Journal of Quality in Maintenance Engineering, 12(3)*, 205–238.

Geraerds, W. (1985). The cost of downtime for maintenance: preliminary considerations. *Maintenance Management International, 5(1)*, 13–21.

Gitzel, R., Schmitz, B., Fromm, H., Isaksson, A., & Setzer, T. (2016). Industrial services as a research discipline. *Enterprise Modelling and Information Systems Architectures, 11(4)*, 1–22.

Helander, A., & Möller, K. (2007). System supplier's customer strategy. *Industrial Marketing Management, 36(6)*, 719–730.

Helander, A., & Möller, K. (2008). How to become solution provider: System supplier's strategic tools. *Journal of Business-to-Business Marketing, 15(3)*, 247–289.

Herterich, M. M., Uebernickel, F., & Brenner, W. (2015). The impact of cyber-physical systems on industrial services in manufacturing. *Procedia CIRP, 30*, 323–328.

Hypko, P., Tilebein, M., & Gleich, R. (2010). Benefits and uncertainties of performance-based contracting in manufacturing industries. *Journal of Service Management, 21(4)*, 460–489.

Jensen, M. C., & Meckling, W. H. (1976). Theory of the firm: Managerial behavior, agency costs and ownership structure. *Journal of Financial Economics, 3(4)*, 305–360.

Kim, S.-H., Cohen, M. A., & Netessine, S. (2007). Performance contracting in after-sales service supply chains. *Management Science, 53*(12), 1843–1858.

Kowalkowski, C., Windahl, C., Kindström, D., & Gebauer, H. (2015). What service transition? Rethinking established assumptions about manufacturers' service-led growth strategies. *Industrial Marketing Management, 45*(1), 59–69.

Krinsky, I., & Mehrez, A. (1989). Principal-agent maintenance problem. *Naval Research Logistics, 36(6)*, 817–828.

Lee, J., Bagheri, B., & Kao, H. A. (2015). A cyber-physical systems architecture for industry 4.0-based manufacturing systems. *Manufacturing Letters, 3*, 18–23.

Legner, C., Eymann, T., Hess, T., Matt, C., Böhmann, T., Drews, P., Mädche, A., Urbach, N., & Ahlemann, F. (2017). Digitalization: Opportunity and challenge for the business and information systems engineering community. *Business & Information Systems Engineering, 59(4)*, 301–308.

Martin, H. H. (1997). Contracting out maintenance and a plan for future research. *Journal of Quality in Maintenance Engineering, 3(2)*, 81–90.

Mcilwraith, J., Stark, J., & Stark, J. (2011). *Complex engineering service systems. Decision engineering*. London: Springer.

Murthy, D. N. P., & Jack, N. (2008). Maintenance outsourcing. In K. A. H. Kobbacy, & D. N. P. Murthy (Eds.), *Complex system maintenance handbook* (1st ed., pp. 373–393). London: Springer.

Murthy, D. N. P., & Jack, N. (2014). *Extended warranties, maintenance service and lease contracts: Modeling and analysis for decision-making*. London: Springer.

Murthy, D. N. P., Jack, N., & Kumar, U. (2013). Maintenance outsourcing: Issues and challenges. In T. Dohi, & T. Nakagawa (Eds.), *Stochastic reliability and maintenance modeling* (9 ed., pp. 41–62). London: Springer.

Ng, I. C., Ding, D. X., & Yip, N. (2013). Outcome-based contracts as new business model: The role of partnership and value-driven relational assets. *Industrial Marketing Management, 42(5)*, 730–743.

Ng, I. C., Maull, R., & Yip, N. (2009). Outcome-based contracts as a driver for systems thinking and service-dominant logic in service science: Evidence from the defence industry. *European Management Journal, 27(6)*, 377–387.

Oliva, R., & Kallenberg, R. (2003). Managing the transition from products to services. *International Journal of Service Industry Management, 14(2)*, 160–172.

Paz, N. M., & Leigh, W. (1994). Maintenance scheduling: Issues, results and research needs. *International Journal of Operations & Production Management, 14(8)*, 47–69.

Penttinen, E., & Palmer, J. (2007). Improving firm positioning through enhanced offerings and buyer-seller relationships. *Industrial Marketing Management, 36(5)*, 552–564.

Pintelon, L., & Van Puyvelde, F. (2013). *Asset management: The maintenance perspective*. Leuven: Acco.

Pongpech, J., Murthy, D., & Boondiskulchock, R. (2006). Maintenance strategies for used equipment under lease. *Journal of Quality in Maintenance Engineering, 12(1)*, 52–67.

Safaei, N., Banjevic, D., & Jardine, A. K. S. (2011). Workforce-constrained maintenance scheduling for military aircraft fleet: a case study. *Annals of Operations Research, 186(1)*, 295–316.

Smith, D. J. (2013). Power-by-the-hour: the role of technology in reshaping business strategy at Rolls-Royce. *Technology Analysis & Strategic Management, 25(8)*, 987–1007.

Sörensen, K., Sevaux, M., & Schittekat, P. (2008). *"Multiple Neighbourhood" search in commercial VRP packages: Evolving towards self-adaptive methods* (pp. 239–253). Berlin: Springer.

Strähle, O., Füllemann, M., & Bendig, O. (2012). *Service now! Time to wake up the sleeping giant*. Munich: Bain & Company

Takeda, M., & Kosaka, M. (2016). Fuji Xerox - manufacturer managed equipment service. In J. Wang, M. Kosaka, & K. Xing (Eds.), *Manufacturing servitization in the Asia-Pacific* (1st ed., pp. 137–154). Singapore: Springer.

Thoben, K.-D., Wiesner, S., & Wuest, T. (2017). "Industrie 4.0" and smart manufacturing – a review of research issues and application examples. *International Journal of Automation Technology, 11(1)*, 4–16.

Tsang, A. H. (2002). Strategic dimensions of maintenance management. *Journal of Quality in Maintenance Engineering, 8(1)*, 7–39.

Vössing, M. (2019). Redesigning service operations for the digital world: Towards automated and data-driven field service planning. In *Proceedings of the 27th European Conference on Information Systems (ECIS)*, Stockholm, & Uppsala, Sweden.

Waeyenbergh, G., & Pintelon, L. (2002). A framework for maintenance concept development. *International Journal of Production Economics, 77(3)*, 299–313.

Part II
Smart Service Design

Introduction to Smart Service Design

Philipp Jussen and Katharina Heeg

Abstract This chapter examines the question of the contribution of smart services for companies and the implications this has for the management of these business models. The chapter starts by outlining the different terminology used to describe smart services and introduces a business-driven view on the digitalization strategy of a company. The characteristic features of digital business models are explained as well as their implications for the management of smart service organizations.

1 Introduction

In 2011, the German economy proclaimed, in a way, its own fourth industrial revolution, the *Industrie 4.0*. This terminological description of the developments around the digital transformation of the industry is mainly the result of two future-oriented projects by acatech (Kagermann et al. 2013, 2015). By coining the term *Smart Service World,* these projects addressed the question of future-oriented business models for digital platforms. Since then, many industrial sectors have seen an expansion and professionalization of customer-targeted digital activities. In addition to the classical service business, which has become a central profit and revenue driver for many industrial companies over the past 20 years, these companies are now expanding their range of services to include digital offerings. This chapter examines the question of what strategic contribution smart services can make for companies and what implications this has for the management of these business models.

P. Jussen (✉)
Schaeffler Monitoring Service GmbH, Herzogenrath, Germany
e-mail: philipp.jussen@schaeffler.com

K. Heeg
Institute for Industrial Management (FIR) at RWTH Aachen University, Aachen, Germany
e-mail: Katharina.heeg@fir.rwth-aachen.de

© Springer Nature Switzerland AG 2020
M. Maleshkova et al. (eds.), *Smart Service Management*,
https://doi.org/10.1007/978-3-030-58182-4_4

2 What Are Smart Services?

For a better understanding, this chapter begins with a description of the characteristics of *smart services*. Smart services are services which aggregate and process data stemming from digitally networked physical objects (so-called smart products) and generate added value based on this data. This added value can be, for example, the intelligent control, adaptation, and optimization of smart product functions. However, the collected data can also be used for other purposes (DIN 2019). In science and practice, numerous terms are used partly synonymously, partly in differentiation with changing meanings. These terms include remote services, Internet-based services, digital services, and databased services. Table 1 shows how the three most commonly used terms differ.

To better understand this book, an overview of the characteristic features of smart services is necessary. Data is the central resource of smart service business models. Access to this data is therefore of crucial importance in the development of the business model. The fact that this data originates from networked physical objects, for example digitally connectable production plants, determines the use cases. Another characteristic of smart services is thinking in platform business models.

Smart services are also characterized by thinking in platform employment models. The smart service provider often tries to take on a manufacturer-neutral position regarding the smart product that provides the basis for the service. There are several reasons for this. On the one hand, the smart service providers try to address the largest possible installed base of machines and systems. On the other hand, the positioning often also serves the purpose of occupying a dominant role in the digital ecosystem of the value chain. This is the reason why, for example,

Table 1 Typical features of different terms for digital services (Husmann 2020)

	Product-related services	IT-based services	Smart services
Interaction form during service provision	Physically	Physically	Digitally
Type of service provision	Physically	On-premise	On-demand
Scalability	Low	Low	High
Connectivity	None	Via the customer's internal network	Via Internet to the provider
Service type	Descriptive	Descriptive	Predictive/prescriptive
Origin of the data/reference object	Single physical product	Single physical product	Multi-vendor products/entire value chain
Example	On-site repair	On-site condition monitoring	Self-optimization of production

machine tool manufacturers also connect machines from competing manufacturers on their digital platforms.

A third essential characteristic of smart services is the fact that they aim to make databased predictive and prescriptive statements and offer services that are based on these statements. This characteristic is often referred to as the smartness of digital services.

3 Smart Services as Part of a Digitalization Strategy

From a strategic point of view, smart services can have different meanings for a company and take on several roles within a company strategy. In order to define these roles, companies need to decide on their digitalization strategy. It is important to note that a digitalization strategy in the context of this chapter is primarily a business strategy and not a technology one. In order to define a clear focus for it, companies must understand the underlying digital technologies (cloud & edge, big data, etc.). However, understanding possible new business models, their mechanisms, and possible effects on one's own value creation system as well as the market in which the company is located plays an even more decisive role. Based on the assumption that the company in question is not a new start-up but a company that already pursues existing business activities apart from a possible smart service offering, the typical components and roles of smart services within the company's digitalization strategy can be distinguished as illustrated in Fig. 1.

The illustration shows that first of all, smart services can be used for internal improvement. Although the focus of this is often on customer processes or contact points, the actual goal of using smart services is often linked to a cost reduction for the company providing the service. Although the range of smart service technologies is used for this purpose, this is not a business model transformation. Typical goals of the use of smart service technologies for internal optimization purposes are the reduction of throughput times or quality improvement. A typical example is the offer of an online portal for ordering spare parts with digitally integrated order processing. Here, a wide range of potential can be leveraged by using smart services and additional competitive advantages can be generated. The demand for spare parts can be predicted precisely due to the improved data

Fig. 1 Levels of a digitalization strategy

Typical customer targets:

- Increase of machine availability (OEE, output, quality, etc.)
- Reduction of machine operating costs (downtime costs, consumption costs, etc.)
- Optimization of LCC of the machine (extension of service life, etc.)
- Optimization of the integration of the machine into adjacent processes
- Optimization of the machine's operability

Typical challenges on the supplier side:

- Technical challenges
  - Access and connectivity
- Organizational challenges
  - Design of the portfolio of machine/product, service and smart service
  - Drafting of contracts
  - Integration of smart services in your own processes

Fig. 2 Customer goals and provider challenges when complementing existing business areas with smart services

availability for example, and, based on this, warehouse inventory can be optimized. However, the actual business model, selling spare parts, does not change. Likewise, the use of smart services is usually not charged directly to the customer in the form of a revenue model.

A second level of a digitalization strategy can be the expansion of existing business areas. Especially in the everyday practice of industrial companies, it can often be observed that existing product and service offerings are expanded by digital offerings. Because of these additional services, the customer receives an added value on top of the use of the product or the existing service. Although digital services often generate additional revenue for the provider, the focus is not on building the most profitable smart service business possible. Rather, the smart services support the existing product and service business. Further provider goals are the increase of customer loyalty and the generation of data providing information about the customer's product use, which, in return, can be used for further development. Figure 2 summarizes the typical goals customers and service providers have in mind when deciding to include smart services in their existing portfolio.

A typical example for these kinds of smart services in an industrial context are networked machines and plants, the data of which is used for quality improvements or machine failure prediction. This is often achieved with the help of additional smart services, which are offered by the plant manufacturer based on IoT technologies via a digital channel (web-based dashboard or app). From a provider's point of view, there are more challenges to overcome than just the development of specific smart services because, for example, the new digital service offerings always need to be considered as part of a portfolio in combination with already existing products and services. Service bundles are often put together to provide the customer not only with individual digital services, but a combination of physical and digital ones.

A third digitalization strategy level is the development of new business areas, separated from the existing product and service business. This business strategy focuses on the creation of an independent, profitable smart services business. Independence in this context means that it does not have to be subordinated to an existing product or service business. From a supplier's point of view, this strategy element

Fig. 3 Typical models for implementing elements of a digitalization strategy

also serves as an opportunity for diversification. In the same way, the knowledge of customer needs in one's own ecosystem can be used to realize additional customer added value in addition to the classic core business. One example for this is the company 365farmnet. It is a subsidiary of the agricultural machinery manufacturer CLAAS, but operates independently on the market. The focus of 365farmnet's range of services is not the digitally networked agricultural machine, but rather the provision of digital solutions for farm management. Customers can purchase these without having to own a CLAAS agricultural machine.

The fourth level of a digitalization strategy can be considered as a specialization of the previously mentioned third one. Its business strategy is aimed at gaining access to digital control points in ecosystems with highly scalable business models based on smart services, and, consequently, gaining a dominant position on the market. This is usually achieved in combination with platform business models. The special features of this strategy are explained in the following section of this chapter on digital business models.

With regard to the digitalization strategy and the role of smart services, it is important to point out that the various areas of application typically determine the way in which companies implement the services. Figure 3 illustrates the typical models for implementing the elements of a digitalization strategy. While programs and organizational mechanisms for the optimization of the company's own processes often already exist, the company must consider new forms of financing for the usually very risky introduction of digital business models. Likewise, the strategic level often determines the type of service offering from the very beginning. For example, smart services that are offered as a supplement to existing products and services are usually placed on the market with the same brand name and are connected tightly to the existing business in terms of the organizational structure. When smart services are offered with the aim of moving into entirely new business areas that are independent of the existing product and service business, however, they often receive a new brand name or are made part of a new legal entity.

4   Digital Business Models

The term *digital business models* is used widely and often in many different ways in the context of digitization. This inflationary use means that it is usually unclear, both in practice and in science, which special features characterize these business models. A frequently used terminology approximation emphasizes the technologies that are used to implement the business model (Meinhardt and Popp 2018). Business models are often described as digital if they provide databased services for the customer, have a digital customer interface, or simply rely on digitalized processes. However, the characteristic features, especially the often disruptive character of digital business models, are not emphasized by this definition. This is why the following part of this chapter presents the characteristic features of digital business models. Once these are explained, it becomes clear why the development and management of these business models presents companies with very special challenges.

In order to understand digital business models, it is useful to illustrate what their strategic goals are first, completely independent of the technology used. Figure 4 presents these goals and their interdependencies. There are two aspects that need to be emphasized at this point. Digital business models are successful on the market mainly because of two key competitive advantages: scalability and forecasting ability. It is the strategic task of the digital business model management to achieve these competitive advantages. Although both can also be desirable for companies with a classic tangible assets business model, they can reach so-far unknown extents when digital technologies and entirely digital services are involved. Scalability means that the company is able to roll out new services to a large number of users within a very short time. Among other things, this requires a short-cycle release capability, which in turn can be achieved if the business model is designed to be as independent as possible and does not rely on physical assets. Forecasting capability means gaining unique insights from (mass)data and using them to achieve superior performance and added value for the customer. For this purpose, it is necessary to obtain access to this data both technically and contractually. Crucial basic requirements for achieving these characteristics are a networked infrastructure consisting of networked users, networked physical assets, and working in digital ecosystems with open interfaces.

Fig. 4 Interdependencies of digital business models

4.1 Scalability

From the beginning, digital business models aim to adopt a dominant market position in order to control or even change market mechanisms. To accomplish this, it is necessary that a critical mass of a relevant target market obtains the services of a company—as quickly as possible. Right from the start, digital business models are designed in such a way that a large number of customers can use the services as quickly as possible. Many examples from the B2C sector have shown that even short-term profit targets are often subordinated to this goal. All available capital is invested in growth and innovation, often over a period of several years. With the infrastructure that is available in the B2C sector today, which means smartphones connected via the Internet, there is the unprecedented possibility of reaching many hundreds of millions of potential users with new services and business ideas within a very short time. Users are often already registered with a customer account and payment data, so that the administrative effort is minimal. Within minutes, new apps can be downloaded, tested, and deleted again. A well-known statistic shows the scalability of apps by comparing the time required until a technology or product reaches 50 million users. While inventions such as the personal computer or mobile phone still needed 14 or 12 years to reach this number, the Pokemon Go App, for example, only needed 19 days (Desjardins 2018). In the B2C area, the mass distribution of smartphones provides the relevant infrastructure of networked people for the scalability of digital business models. At the same time, it can be observed that more and more machines, systems, and objects are being networked. This includes cars or machine tools as well as trackable logistics objects (e.g., containers) or measuring stations that collect and send data in an agricultural field for months without an external power supply. This so-called *Internet of Things* benefits from steadily decreasing costs for data acquisition and networking technology and decreasing electricity requirements for networking. If the element of the connected human is added to this concept, one can refer to it as the so-called *Internet of Everything*.

However, scalability is not only a consequence of allocating capital to growth-promoting measures. Instead, scalability also requires very short innovation cycles in order to convert identified customer needs into new or improved services at high frequency and to deliver these to the user in the form of new functions. This potential of the feature, known as release capability, is especially present in the digital world. Physical products or rather their physical properties and functions can often only be adapted or changed after the customer's purchase with considerable effort—if at all. In any case, it is often associated with very unpleasant side effects for the customer. Software is subject to these restrictions to a much lesser extent. New functions or adjustments can be rolled out automatically at the push of a button. Web-based services do not even need updates, which can be perceived as annoying, for example in the case of app updates on smartphones. Further requirements for a high scalability are:

- *Independence from physical assets:* Digital business models are usually not limited to individual manufacturers of physical assets, but try to offer comprehensive services.
- *Independence from physical resources:* In order to achieve scalability of the service provision, digital business models also rely on independence from physical resources. Required resources are purchased as a service from third parties (e.g., cloud infrastructure) only to the extent that is necessary to provide the service.
- *Independence from regional restrictions:* Even though the actual market launch of digital business models often means that several regions are conquered one after the other, digital business models are not limited by language or other regional specifics.
- *Easy access for customers:* Companies that pursue a digital business model make it as easy as possible for their customers to access their services. This concerns organizational, legal, or financial hurdles as well as usability.

4.2   Forecasting Ability

In terms of actual performance, the ability to forecast represents the central competitive advantage of digital business models. This is where the actual added value for the customer is created. Due to digital networking, the amount of data generated and available doubles approximately every 12 months. With the help of this data and steadily decreasing costs for storage space and computer performance, more and more use cases for the use of this data are becoming economically interesting. This progress is accompanied by a permanent further development and automation of the procedures of machine learning and artificial intelligence.

Digital business models generate added value from data for customers in many different ways. Creation of added value can range from the possibility of comparing several options for action (e.g., provider comparison portals), to the aggregation and visualization of data (e.g., IoT platforms), to the automation of actions and transactions (e.g., P2P lending portals). Technologically, this usually requires a software-defined data platform that can aggregate and manage data from different sources and make it available for analysis. If data originating from the physical world is used, digital business models also need to answer the question of how this data can be generated technically and economically. Finally, data access must also be ensured both organizationally and, above all, contractually. There are two ways for companies to gain access to mass data. Direct data transactions are one option, which means the data providing customer receives a direct service promise based on this data in return. Another option is to use data that is the by-product of another service provision. In this case, the customer does not explicitly receive added value in return for his data, but obtains another service first. In the B2C context, end customers often still allow the use of their data by simply agreeing to the general terms and conditions of a provider of a free service. In the B2B sector, however, most companies are very much aware of the issue of access and use of their data and attach importance to clear contractual regulations.

5 The Challenge of Managing Smart Services

The described characteristics of smart services and digital business models result in specific challenges for their management. They also explain why the development and provision of smart services and the adoption of digital business models are associated with great changes, especially for established companies with a traditional business model.

- *Radical customer focus:* Although customer orientation is, in principle, a core characteristic of any good corporate management, smart services require a completely new and in-depth approach to the customer. It is no longer enough to only understand the technical challenges the customers are facing. It is much more important to understand processes and procedures as well as the needs, experiences, and preferences of individuals in detail in order to be successful with smart services.
- *Thinking in ecosystems:* To understand the market and customer situation as well as the company's own service provision, it is necessary to think in ecosystem patterns. Ecosystems are often designed specifically for digital business models. These can be, for example, partner companies of the smart service provider, which extend the scope of services or use the provider's customer access.
- *Short-cycle innovation:* In order to be successful with smart services, it is necessary to translate customer needs into new services and to introduce them to the market with a high frequency. This requires early involvement of the customer and the early testing of new services together, as well as thinking in minimum viable services. This means that the service development is initially limited to core functions and those services that are of interest to the customer. They are introduced to the market first. Afterward, the range of functions and services is expanded gradually, based on initial market experience.
- *Importance of the market launch:* Just like customer orientation, the ability to successfully manage the market launch can be an advantage for any company. In the case of smart services, however, two special features give special significance to the market launch. First, due to the mostly agile development approach and thinking in minimum viable services, the market launch takes place at a very early stage in the development and product life cycle. Whereas the market introduction processes for classic business models are often designed with a specific launch date in mind and are subject to a linear process, it is advisable to take on an agile approach for the market introduction of smart services. Second, with smart services, the transaction numbers per customer are often relatively low, at least at the beginning of the customer relationship. This, together with the digital nature of the underlying business models, often makes it necessary to rely

on new (digital) forms of marketing and distribution in order to keep the costs of customer acquisition in reasonable proportion.

Overall, it becomes clear that the use of smart services and the transition towards digital business models are accompanied by numerous potentials and monetary profit prospects, but also at the same time pose a number of great challenges for companies. To overcome these hurdles, it is necessary to agree to restructurings and work on competence expansions to ensure successful smart service management.

References

Desjardins, J. (2018). *How long does it take to hit 50 million users?* Retrieved April 29, 2020, from https://www.visualcapitalist.com/how-long-does-it-take-to-hit-50-million-users/

DIN. (2019). *DIN SPEC 33453 development of digital service systems.* Berlin: Beuth.

Husmann, M. (2020). *Erfolgsfaktoren bei der Markteinführung im Maschinen- und Anlagenbau.* Aachen: Apprimus Verlag.

Kagermann, H., Wahlster, W., & Helbig, J. (2013). *Recommendations for implementing the strategic initiative INDUSTRIE 4.0 (final report).* Edited by et al. acatech – National Academy of Science and Engineering e.V. Retrieved June 21, 2020, from https://www.acatech.de/wp-content/uploads/2018/03/Final_report__Industrie_4.0_accessible-1.pdf

Kagermann, H., Riemensperger, F., Leukert, B., Hoke, D., Schuh, G., Scheer, A.-W., et al. (2015). *Smart service welt. Recommendations for the strategic initiative web-based services for businesses (final version long report).* Edited by et al. acatech – National Academy of Science and Engineering e.V. Retrieved June 21, 2020, from https://www.acatech.de/wp-content/uploads/2018/03/BerichtSmartService2015_LANGVERSION_en.pdf, checked on 6/21/2020.

Meinhardt, S., & Popp, K. M. (2018). Digitale Geschäftsmodelle. In *HMD – Praxis der Wirtschaftsinformatik* (Vol. 55, pp. 229–230). Wiesbaden: Springer.

Smart Service Engineering

Benedikt Moser and Marcel Faulhaber

Abstract This chapter presents Smart Service Engineering as a development approach for a customer-centric and highly iterative development of smart services. It outlines the development of data-based services in an industrial context, starting with the development of a strategy, followed by the iteration of prototypes, and finally leading to the successful market launch.

1 Challenges in the Development and Market Launch of Smart Services

The successful development and market launch of smart services poses a great challenge for many industrial companies (Dreyer et al. 2018). While companies have been successfully developing and selling physical products for many decades, these processes present companies with greater challenges in connection with industrial services and solution systems, which consist of products and services combined. New digital offerings present new service components and allow companies to supplement and expand their existing portfolio to offer their customers the best possible solution to their problems.

A central factor for the successful development and market launch of smart services is the identification of customer needs and the fast creation of adequate solutions for them. However, identifying the needs in advance and designing tailor-made solutions is often not common practice in business. This is because only once the smart service is used, questions referring to the benefit of the service for the customer and the interaction of the two are answered. Therefore, the goal of every smart service development must be to achieve the earliest possible service market launch in the form of a *minimum viable service* (Ries 2017). The aim is to implement the first version of a benefit-generating service instead of a full-blown solution, to

B. Moser (✉) · M. Faulhaber
Institute for Industrial Management (FIR) at RWTH Aachen University, Aachen, Germany
e-mail: benedikt.moser@fir.rwth-aachen.de; marcel.faulhaber@fir.rwth-aachen.de

© Springer Nature Switzerland AG 2020
M. Maleshkova et al. (eds.), *Smart Service Management*,
https://doi.org/10.1007/978-3-030-58182-4_5

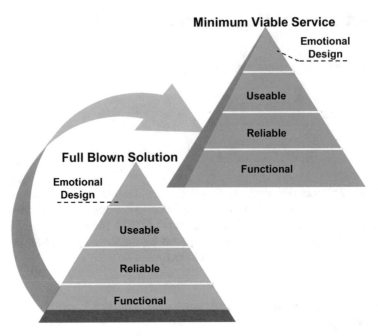

Fig. 1 Development of a minimum viable service

learn quickly from the customer's usage phase, and to use these learnings to develop the service further (see Fig. 1).

The results of industry benchmarking we conducted previously show that top performers in the field of smart services can develop new services up to six times faster than the average competitor. On average, this leads to 80% higher sales growth in the service area (Dreyer et al. 2018; Jussen and Frank 2018; Moser et al. 2018). The first step of the development of a *minimum viable service* is to focus only on the core functionalities of the smart service. This is followed by an in-depth analysis of customer feedback and customer behavior (usage data), which is used for an iterative development process to create new functionalities. This approach makes it possible to reduce the time to market of the smart service in its basic functionality/configuration and allows for a faster adaptation of new extended functionalities to the respective market conditions. The initial development of core functionalities triggers only small investments, as the degree of complexity is kept to a minimum and focused on the actual customer problem.

In comparison to traditional products and services, this approach aims to accomplish the market entry and achieve releases of new functionalities at a higher frequency. This is a distinguishing feature when compared to tangible goods, where new features and functionalities can often only be introduced to the market via a new product generation or at a very high cost. Due to their digital components, smart services have particularly high potential for agile development processes. The high frequency of iterations makes it possible to develop smart services continuously and adapt them to changing customer needs. This idea of constant renewal and further development while focusing on identified customer needs is a central requirement criterion for a process model for the successful development and market launch of smart services.

2 Smart Service Engineering

As described in the previous chapter, the successful development and market launch of smart services poses great challenges for industrial companies. A central challenge is to harmonize the various target dimensions, such as the time required for the service development, the target cost framework, and the desired service quality. The fact that the individual target dimensions are interdependent means that successful smart service development, like any other development project, faces a conflict of these dimensions. However, the dimension *time to market* is of the utmost importance for the development of smart services. The development process of smart services relies on fundamental assumptions about customer needs. Besides, they are underlying constant change in the digital age. Subsequently, companies need to validate their smart services at an early stage in the market to manage their efforts effectively and efficiently to meet the customer needs best (Kuehl 2016). The development of physical products, in particular, is currently characterized by development cycles that take several years. Intending to reach the customer faster, these development periods need to be shortened. To achieve this, it is necessary to ensure the best possible quality, which meets the customer's requirements but only requires a manageable capital investment.

To meet these challenges, the *Smart Service Engineering Process Model* represents an approach to develop smart services in highly iterative cycles with a strong focus on the customer. The model also includes the successful launch of the new service on the market. A shift in the structure of target variables, which could be observed recently, justifies this approach (Wissentschaftliche Dienste Deutscher Bundestag 2016). In the course of the ongoing digitalization, the time required for the development and marketing of a new smart service has gained dramatically in importance in recent years. Today, development processes are expected to be shorter but, at the same time, remain within a fixed budget. To keep up with this development, *Smart Service Engineering* is based on existing concepts such as the *lean start-up approach* usually applied when founding (digital) companies and *DevOps* as a successful approach in software development (Naidu 2015). *Smart Service Engineering* was developed and validated together with industrial companies and represents a proven method for the development of smart services, which will be explained in more detail in the following chapters.

Figure 2 shows the *Smart Service Engineering* model. It consists of three successive elements, which contain different key tasks. The transition between these elements is fluid, enabling and facilitating an iterative process. The overall aim is to repeat this process several times, to achieve the result in the form of a

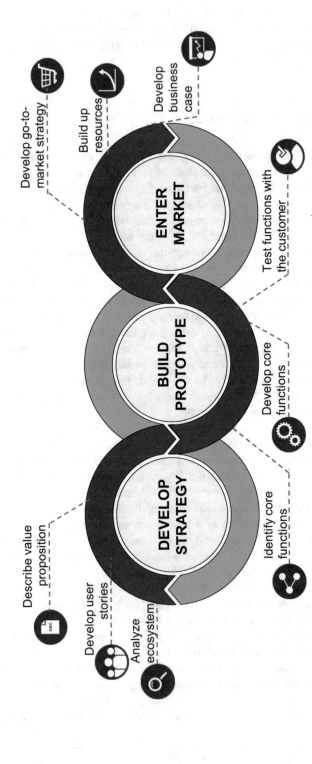

Fig. 2 Smart Service Engineering

marketable smart service as quickly as possible. This can be achieved by focusing on a development that is as close as possible to customer needs.

The logical order of the activities implies that the main tasks for a quick market launch are easy to identify. In the model's sub-element *develop strategy,* the company's ecosystem is analyzed to allow for the strategic placement of the company. Also, the digital service offering needs to be located strategically. By developing user stories to describe possible usage scenarios of the smart service, hypotheses on the service benefit and business cases can be derived, formulated, and prioritized. Based on these hypotheses, the core functionality for the desired customer group can also be defined.

The derivation and definition of the core functionalities of the smart service can be transferred seamlessly to the phase of a prototype implementation. The aim is to develop a prototype providing the beneficial functionality the central customer requirements ask for. This requires the prioritization of development activities. All in all, the development takes place with the help of agile methods for the realization and implementation of the core functionalities. These core functionalities are used to obtain feedback in direct exchange with the customers on the functionality and benefits of the service. This feedback serves as a basis for initiating a continuous improvement process (Ries 2017).

The subsequently renewed process loop is necessary to plan the market entry and to build up the necessary resources for the long-term success of the smart service. Since the core functionality has already been validated in exchange with the customer, the service can be rolled out and the market can be conquered. This requires a viable business model, the details of which can still be adapted during the course of the market launch (e.g., the pricing model). It also becomes apparent that a roadmap can support the successful market entry of smart services. To realize this roadmap, it is required to establish organizational resources and processes. In most companies, the service and sales department represents an integral part of this activity, as it is usually the central interface for customer contact. Not only does it ensure that experience value and feedback find their way back to the company due to the exchange with customers, but it also makes sure that new functionalities and offers are communicated. This ensures the long-term operation and success of the smart service. To provide deeper insights into the individual tasks for each Smart Service Engineering phase, they are examined in more detail below.

2.1 Developing the Strategy

The goal of the first sub-element "develop strategy" is to derive a *plan of action* for the strategic positioning of the company in its surrounding ecosystem. Based on an in-depth understanding of the potential customers, the company environment, industries, markets, and competitors, initial ideas for potential value propositions are derived, as shown in Fig. 3. These must eliminate existing pain points the customer has. It must be ensured that the planned smart service will provide an actual benefit

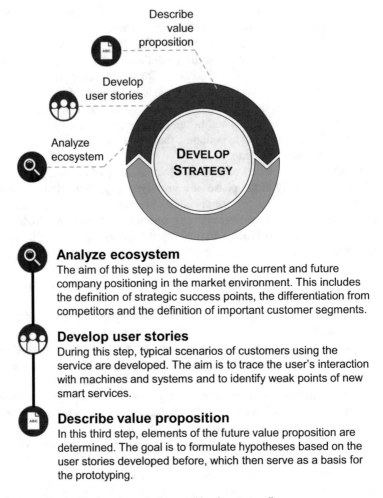

Analyze ecosystem
The aim of this step is to determine the current and future company positioning in the market environment. This includes the definition of strategic success points, the differentiation from competitors and the definition of important customer segments.

Develop user stories
During this step, typical scenarios of customers using the service are developed. The aim is to trace the user's interaction with machines and systems and to identify weak points of new smart services.

Describe value proposition
In this third step, elements of the future value proposition are determined. The goal is to formulate hypotheses based on the user stories developed before, which then serve as a basis for the prototyping.

Fig. 3 Smart Service Engineering sub-element "develop strategy"

to the customer. The procedure for this is primarily deductive. A suitable service offering is derived from an identified explicit strategy. Due to the iterative character of this strategy development phase, however, *market pull concepts* can also be developed, and their strategic fit can be checked later on.

This point of the Smart Service Engineering process requires a definition of strategic success factors for the entire company concerning smart services as well as a detailed definition of customer pains that the service is supposed to address. Ideally, these pains describe problems that many potential customers have and for which there are no solutions available yet. This step also determines the customer segments that will be important in the future. Typical application scenarios, so-called user stories, are developed together with customers and users. This requires a clear understanding of the user's interaction with machines and systems, as well as the value-providing integration of the smart service. With the help of typical user stories, existing shortcomings in the use of machines and systems or services are recorded and analyzed, to build a consistent customer experience in the form of a customer journey. For each promising user story, the corresponding value proposition is formulated for the individual customer and user segments. They are prototypically implemented and validated as part of the next step of Smart Service Engineering. The following sub-steps of the element develop strategy and the corresponding methods are described further in the following chapter.

2.2 Analyzing the Ecosystem

By determining the current and the desired future positioning of a company in the market, it is possible to derive a trading strategy (Anderson and Markides 2007). The clear pursuit of this strategy ensures that the goals are reached, while also serving as the overall basis for decision-making during the entire process of Smart Service Engineering (Immonen et al. 2016). The strategic analysis can be differentiated according to (company-) internal and external focal points. In the course of the external analysis, relevant competitors are identified and the data context within the relevant ecosystem is examined. The questions that are to be answered at this point include the following:

- Who already collects data along the value chain under consideration?
- Who offers services in this ecosystem that could be enriched by providing data?
- Which systems, standards, and IT landscape already manage data in the ecosystem under consideration?

In addition to traditional strategic instruments, leading companies use tools to find answers for these questions, such as ecosystem mappings, system modeling, role analyses, customer exploration, field analyses at the customer's site, and value network representations (Borgmeier et al. 2017). Many conventional strategic analysis frameworks can easily be applied to the context of smart services (Leimeister 2020). However, the scope of the observations is inevitably shifting and expanding, because value creation is increasingly taking place in hybrid value networks and less in traditional linear value chains (Randhawa and Scerri 2015; Rabe et al. 2017).

In contrast to the analysis of external market environments, the analysis of internal factors aims at identifying existing competencies and potentials (what can we do particularly well?) to meet external market requirements better, and, ideally, faster and more efficiently than the competition. In the area of industrial management of services, it is a well-known strategy to define strategic success positions of the company and compare them directly with competitors of an existing market (Pümpin and Amann 2005). However, smart services make fundamentally different demands than physical services when it comes to the potential level of a service organization (Pöppelbuß and Durst 2017), especially with regard to the processing of *Smart Data*. Digital core competencies for the handling of data are acquisition, transmission, aggregation, synchronization, and multimodal information provision (Schuh et al. 2017a). To position the company successfully in a digital ecosystem, it is required to adjust its strategic orientation in an iterative procedure. Transparency of existing digital service landscapes and relevant skills serves as the starting point for the efficient use of resources (what do we already have, what can we reuse?) (see Beverungen et al. (2018)), while the strategic orientation (at what point of the value-added network do we provide which services best?) can be further developed in the course of *Smart Service Engineering* at a low cost, based on user as well as overall market feedback.

To obtain a comprehensive picture of the value network the company works in, it is first necessary to identify the relevant market players and quantify the relevant transactions in the market environment (money, goods, data, etc.). Figure 4 illustrates the steps during which such an analysis of the ecosystem or value network can take place.

The first iteration focuses on the company-internal analysis of internal customers and suppliers. The goal is to create internal value within the company. The analysis represents a general view of the company as a whole and shows potentials in internal processes as well as in the field of automation. The second iteration details the value network by analyzing the transactions of the company, the suppliers, and the customers. This iteration often identifies potentials in the automation and digitalization of the customer interface or interaction.

The third iteration includes an expansion of the scope of observation concerning the customer and supplier market, in which the perspective is broadened to include the entire value-added network, allowing the new market and sales potentials to be uncovered. The fourth and final iteration examines other players in the market and their value creation networks. The goal is to identify possible highly scalable or platform-like approaches that represent a potential disruption of the entire market or value network.

By determining the position in the company's value-added network and identifying the transaction flows, a target corridor can be derived, which defines the greatest potential for internal optimization or new revenue sources. The quantitative analysis of the value-added network makes it possible to understand the later developments and their effects on the system by using key figures. This also makes it possible to quantify success (Immonen et al. 2016). For this purpose, it must be defined which criteria are used to measure success. The result of this analysis is a specific idea of how the smart service can be integrated into the ecosystem and what benefits it provides, or which pain points it can resolve. Depending on the customer group, these can be monetary benefits or non-monetary gains such as higher customer satisfaction. The decisive factor regarding the positioning in the ecosystem is differentiation from the competition and the solving of real customer problems.

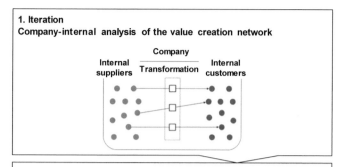

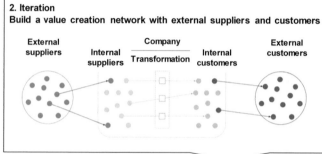

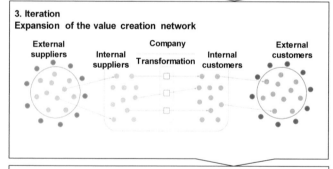

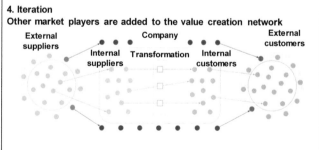

Fig. 4 Example of an ecosystem analysis

2.3 Developing the User Story

The result of the ecosystem analysis is the identification of those customer segments that are to be addressed primarily and which are the basis for the user stories that are to be developed in the following. The user stories reflect the typical service application scenarios of users within the customer segments and illustrate how smart services can improve these scenarios (Edvardsson et al. 2012; Anderl et al. 2016). Concerning the development of smart services, the focus is particularly on the interaction of users with machines and equipment, which takes place within the framework of typical jobs and roles that are representative of the addressed segment. This phase does not aim at a purely descriptive recording and formalization of activities, but rather at a deep understanding of user behavior. The understanding of the so-called *pains and gains* of individual users within the customer segments may already be partially available, depending on the level of the ecosystem analysis, but most probably not on the level of the actual interaction of users with their environment. The activities for capturing precisely these customer interactions and problems can be classified in close analogy to the customer view of the *Value Proposition Canvas* according to Osterwalder et al. (2014).

In general, needs, dissatisfaction, and process flows can be identified with different methods of qualitative market research. The most common methods are interviews and focus groups. Both are especially suitable for services that are already familiar to the customer. They are used to create a basic understanding of the customer (Leimeister 2020). However, as a basis for innovation processes in the product and service context, they have certain shortcomings, as deeper needs, which are yet unknown to the customer, cannot be identified (Matthing et al. 2004). For this reason, a user-centered user story creation needs to capture the actual user processes in great detail beyond customer interviews. Standardized and non-standardized process analyses and models, such as *UML, BPMN, OMEGA* (Rabe et al. 2017), or a *Customer Journey Map,* can function as a documentation tool, as well as *Job Shadowing* (see Redlich et al. (2018)). The latter is the interaction-free observation of users during the execution of their activities.

User stories formally serve to identify value gaps in the previously recorded user experience (Roy et al. 2009), and the resulting derivation of potentials for smart services. User stories are designed from the perspective of fictitious users and describe their goals or wishes as well as the expected outcome (von Engelhardt et al. 2018). The focus on existing, urgent, and well-described user pain points as the starting point of *smart service engineering* guarantees a customer-centered perspective for the entire development process. User stories are the starting point for agile development and must be created with the involvement of potential customers. They should also take into account the technological and organizational capabilities of the company. At this point, users cannot often foresee or articulate developments and innovations (von Hippel 1986), so that the room for solution possibilities is already limited at the beginning of the development. The ideas generated at this point often serve as impulses "to enrich existing concepts or to create completely new ways" (von Engelhardt et al. 2018). The development of the possible solution is initially independent of its ultimate feasibility. Therefore, the user stories refer exclusively to the technical problem of the user or customer segments and explicitly do not describe a technical solution. For example, time-consuming technical discussions tend to be moved from the process and are dealt with later, which distinguishes the method of user stories from use cases. Use cases, as a guiding target image, harbor two dangers that conflict with the elementary principles of *smart service engineering*. In comparison to user stories, use cases detail the solution to be developed and the type of customer interaction on a functional level in advance, even before feedback is collected from customers for the first time. The open innovation and learning approach is compromised, and in the worst case, the innovation team works toward an optimal fulfillment of an already defined solution. The high level of detail before going through agile iteration loops leads to a delay, because too much time is spent on answering the *what* and *how*, while the question of *why* remains unanswered (see Hastie and Wick (2014)).

User stories take on the important function of acting as an interface between the user's requirements of the system and the solution scenarios (Haab et al. 2019). User stories can be compared easily, which visualizes the approaches and process sequences for using the smart service in the application domain. For this purpose, the users, the tools, the organization as well as the environment, the tasks, and the relationships between the individual elements should be identified and established. To illustrate the usability of the smart service, the creation of *user storyboards* is useful (see Fig. 5).

User storyboards comprise the defined and elaborated user stories and form the customer journey. This enables conclusions to be drawn about the underlying purchase decision processes (Anderl et al. 2016). As a key marketing instrument, the customer journey can also highlight points of contact between the end customer and supplier. This method provides a clear picture of the user's interaction with machines and systems. Observations are obtained by recording the actions of the worker with the machine on-site. Thus, weak points of the interaction can be determined, which can further be used to define weak points of the smart service as well.

2.4 Defining the Value Proposition

The preceding step generates an understanding of perceived problems and pain points of the potential customer or user groups and derives an overall vision of the application of smart services. In the following step of *smart service engineering*, value propositions must be formulated. The problems are abstracted, and prelim-inary value propositions are developed based on knowledge of the capabilities of the company or the value network. At the end of the phase, it must be clear how smart services resolve these problems and pain points and what value the customers gain. The detailed observation of users serves as input for the formation of the value

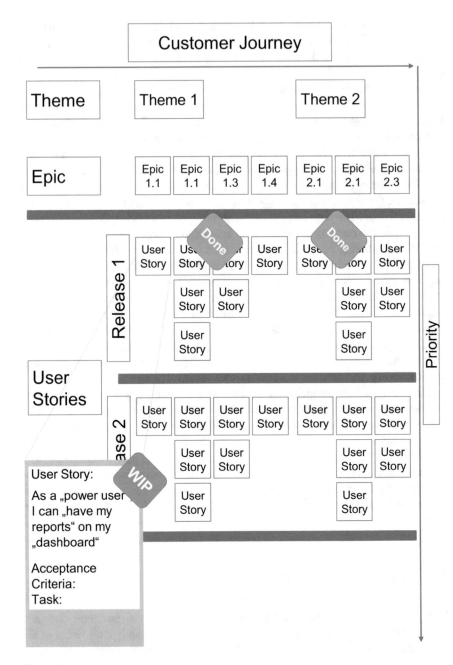

Fig. 5 Example of a user storyboard

proposition. While the user story only implicitly defines the customer needs the service solution should meet, these needs must be made explicit with the value proposition. To ensure that these are always directly related to the solution space created by the user story, the so-called *Voice of the Service* is defined (Stich 2018; Schuh et al. 2017b). Serving as an orientation point for the development, it defends the identified basic requirements against changing internal and external influences or resistance until these are either confirmed or falsified by corresponding hypothesis tests (see Fig. 6).

Based on the previously identified user groups, their characteristics, and their user stories, the value proposition is now being formulated. With the help of value proposition design, customer needs can be visualized much more precisely and corresponding hypotheses about the service's beneficial properties can be derived (Osterwalder et al. 2014). As already described in the previous sections, a multitude of stakeholders can be involved in the provision of a service, who, like different customer segments, must be addressed with their canvas models (Pöppelbuß and Durst 2017; Osterwalder et al. 2014). This is particularly the case in the B2B context of smart services. While using the *Value Proposition Canvas*, the patterns of value creation are used and put into an application framework that makes it easier to combine the customer segment with the value proposition of the smart service. On the customer side, the customer tasks (customer job(s)) and the respective gains and pains are discussed. The goal is to relieve the pain of the customer by providing him with an adequate solution (*pain relievers*) and to create valuable gains (with the help of the *gain creators*). The *Value Proposition Canvas* is shown in Fig. 7. Additionally, to sharpen or validate the assumptions about the characteristics of the user and customer segments, persona analyses can be carried out. This means that a more in-depth understanding of the needs can be achieved by describing fictitious representative actors within the segments in keywords (see Redlich et al. (2018), von Engelhardt et al. (2018)).

This step aims to formulate a usage hypothesis, which forms the basis for the following prototype phase. These hypotheses are prioritized for targeted addressing of the users. The core functionalities of the smart service are then determined based on this hierarchy. Prototyping is then used to check the technical feasibility of the smart service and to verify the hypotheses that have been established and their accuracy. In this way, the benefits of the smart service are validated and, if necessary, extended to come as close as possible to solving the customer's problem.

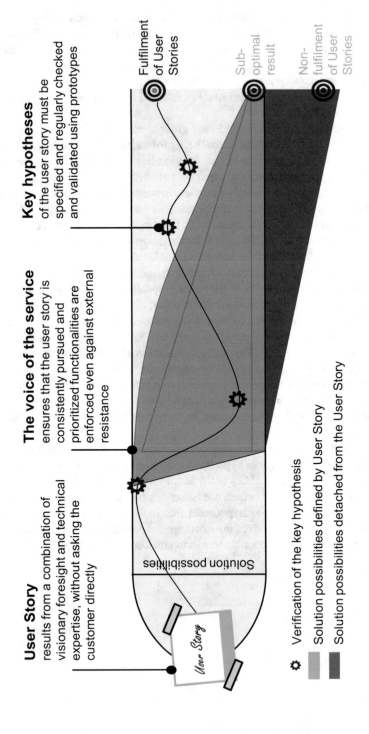

Fig. 6 User stories as a key element of smart service engineering

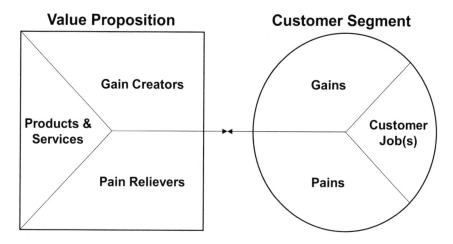

Fig. 7 Value Proposition Canvas (Osterwalder et al. 2014)

3 Conclusion

Based on the first element of *smart service engineering*, the last chapters explained how a strategy for smart services can be developed. The three sub-elements *analyzing the ecosystem, designing user stories,* and *defining value propositions* were discussed. The developed value propositions now serve as input to enter a prototyping phase in the next element of *Smart Service Engineering* and to validate the designed value propositions with the customer at the end of this element.

References

Anderl, E., Schumann, J. H., & Kunz, W. (2016). Helping firms reduce complexity in multichannel online data: A new taxonomy-based approach for customer journeys. *Journal of Retailing, 92*(2), 185–203. https://doi.org/10.1016/j.jretai.2015.10.001.

Anderson, J., & Markides, C. (2007). Strategic innovation at the base of the pyramid. *MIT Sloan Management Review, 49*(1), 83.

Beverungen, D., Lüttenberg, H., & Wolf, V. (2018). Recombinant service systems engineering. *Business & Information Systems Engineering, 60*(5), 377–391.

Borgmeier, A., Buchholz, C., & Grohmann, A. (2017). Lessons Learned und Vorgehensweise zum Aufbau von Smart Services. In A. Borgmeier, A. Grohmann, & S. F. Gross (Eds.), *Smart Services und Internet der Dinge: Geschäftsmodelle, Umsetzung und Best Practices: Industrie 4.0, Internet of Things (IoT), Machine-to-Machine, Big Data, Augmented Reality Technologie* (pp. 263–286). München: Carl Hanser Verlag GmbH.

Dreyer, S., Zeren, J., Lebek, B., et al. (Eds.). (2018). *Critical success factors for introducing smart services: A supplier's perspective.* Lüneburg: Multikonferenz Wirtschaftsinformatik.

Edvardsson B, Kristensson P, Magnusson P et al. (2012) Customer integration within service development—A review of methods and an analysis of insitu and exsitu contributions. zTechnovation 32(7–8): 419–429. doi: https://doi.org/10.1016/j.technovation.2011.04.006.

Haab, H., Bieber, D., & Elfert, P. (2019). Zwischen Interaktionsarbeit und Service-Engineering – Auf dem Weg zu einem integrativen Ansatz in der Dienstleistungsforschung. In V. Stich, J. H. Schumann, D. Beverungen, et al. (Eds.), *Digitale Dienstleistungsinnovationen* (Vol. 10, pp. 49–71). Berlin, Heidelberg: Springer.

Hastie, S., & Wick, A. (2014). *User stories and use cases – Don't use both!* Retrieved September 9, 2018, from https://www.batimes.com/articles/user-stories-and-use-cases-dont-use-both.html

Immonen, A., Ovaska, E., Kalaoja, J., et al. (2016). A service requirements engineering method for a digital service ecosystem. *Service Oriented Computing and Applications, 10*(2), 151–172. https://doi.org/10.1007/s11761-015-0175-0.

Jussen, P., & Frank, J. (2018). *Whitepaper Datenbasierte Dienstleistungen: Mit datenbasierten Geschäftsmodellen in der produzierenden Industrie erfolgreich sein.*

Kuehl, N. (2016). Needmining: Towards analytical support for service design. In T. Borangiu, M. Dragoicea, & H. Nóvoa (Eds.), *Exploring services science* (Vol. 247, pp. 187–200). Cham: Springer.

Leimeister, J. M. (2020). *Dienstleistungsengineering und -management: Data-driven Service Innovation/Jan Marco Leimeister* (2nd ed.). Berlin, Heidelberg: Springer Gabler.

Matthing, J., Sandén, B., & Edvardsson, B. (2004). New service development: Learning from and with customers. *International Journal of Service Industry Management, 15*(5), 479–498.

Moser, B., Jussen, P., & Kampker, A. (2018). *Smart service engineering: An agile approach to develop data-driven services.* Frontiers in Service, Austin, TX.

Naidu, M. S. (2015). Changing scenario of testing paradigms using DevOps – A comparative study with classical models. *Global Journal of Computer Science and Technology, 15*(2), 23–27.

Osterwalder, A., Pigneur, Y., Bernarda, G., et al. (2014). *Value proposition design. Strategyzer series.* Hoboken, NJ: Wiley.

Pöppelbuß, J., & Durst, C. (2017). Smart Service Canvas – Ein Werkzeug zur strukturierten Beschreibung und Entwicklung von Smart-Service-Geschäftsmodellen. In M. Bruhn & K. Hadwich (Eds.), *Dienstleistungen 4.0* (pp. 91–110). Wiesbaden: Springer Fachmedien.

Pümpin, A., & Amann, W. (2005). *Kernkompetenzen aufbauen und umsetzen* (1st ed.). Bern: Haupt Verlag.

Rabe, M., Kühn, A., Dumitrescu, R., et al. (2017). Impact of smart services to current value networks. *Journal of Mechanical Engineering, 13*(2), 10–20.

Randhawa, K., & Scerri, M. (2015). Service innovation: A review of the literature. In R. Agarwal, W. Selen, G. Roos, et al. (Eds.), *The handbook of service innovation* (pp. 27–51). London: Springer.

Redlich, B., Becker, F., Fischer, S., et al. (2018). Das DETHIS-Verfahren: Design Thinking für das Service-Engineering in kleinen und mittleren Unternehmen. In V. Stich, J. H. Schumann, D. Beverungen, et al. (Eds.), *Digitale Dienstleistungsinnovationen* (pp. 73–88). Berlin, Heidelberg: Springer.

Ries, E. (2017). *Lean Startup: Schnell, risikolos und erfolgreich Unternehmen gründen* (5th ed.). München [Ann Arbor, MI]: Redline Verlag [ProQuest].

Roy, R., Shehab, E., Tiwari, A., et al. (2009). The servitization of manufacturing. *Journal of Manufacturing Technology Management, 20*(5), 547–567.

Schuh, G., Stich, V., & Basse, F. et al. (2017a). Change request im Produktionsbetrieb. In WZL an der RWTH Aachen, Fraunhofer IPT (Eds.), *Internet of production für agile Unternehmen.* (pp. 111–127). Aachen: Apprimus.

Schuh, G., Diels, F., Ortlieb, C. et al. (2017b). Agile Produktentwicklung. In WZL an der RWTH Aachen, Fraunhofer IPT (Eds), *Internet of Production für agile Unternehmen* (pp. 31–49). Aachen: Apprimus.

Stich, V. (2018). *Smart services entwickeln* (Vol. 21). Aachen: Aachener Dienstleistungsforum.

von Engelhardt, S., Enstahler, J., Giechen, J.-H. et al. (2018). *Smart Service Welt Innovationsbericht 2018 – Begleitforschung Smart Service Welt*. Retrieved August 30, 2018, from https://vdivde-it.de/de/publikation/smart-service-welt-innovationsbericht-2018

von Hippel, E. (1986). Lead users: A source of novel product concepts. *Management Science, 32*(7), 791–805.

Wissentschaftliche Dienste Deutscher Bundestag. (2016). *Zur Diskussion um die Verkürzung von Produktlebenszyklen*. Retrieved December 9, 2019, from https://www.bundestag.de/resource/blob/438002/42b9bf2ae2369fd4b8dd119d968a1380/wd-5-053-16-pdf-data.pdf

Smart Service Prototyping

Jan Hicking

Abstract This chapter is dedicated to prototyping, one of the steps of the Smart Service Engineering Cycle. It includes three phases: realizing core functionalities, developing core functionalities, and testing functionalities with customers. In order to realize prototypes successfully, methodical aspects of rapid IoT prototyping are used.

First of all, this chapter explains the motivation behind rapid prototyping and provides an introduction to the approach. The concept of rapid IoT prototyping is based on the idea of developing short-cycle solution variants on the basis of benefit hypotheses or benefit promises and user stories focusing on them. The aim is to achieve data acquisition, aggregation, linkage, processing, and finally visualization by developing it in a vertically integrated manner. Once this is accomplished, the prototype can be evaluated with customers, which also makes it possible to put the benefit hypotheses to the test. Finally, the collected customer feedback can be incorporated more quickly into the development process of new prototype versions, leading to a continuous improvement of the user experience as well as a constant focus on prioritizing the user. Another component of rapid IoT prototyping is working and thinking in terms of minimum viable products (MVP), i.e., solutions that do not meet all of the defined requirements in the first iteration, but are nevertheless already functional.

1 Introduction to Rapid IoT Prototyping

In the field of engineering sciences, rapid prototyping includes all processes that enable the production of three-dimensional objects by joining material layers at a constant thickness (Hackney 2003, p. 105). In principle, physical, virtual, and hybrid prototypes can be distinguished, but rapid prototyping only addresses the

J. Hicking (✉)
Institute for Industrial Management (FIR) at RWTH Aachen University, Aachen, Germany
e-mail: jan.hicking@fir.rwth-aachen.de

© Springer Nature Switzerland AG 2020
M. Maleshkova et al. (eds.), *Smart Service Management*,
https://doi.org/10.1007/978-3-030-58182-4_6

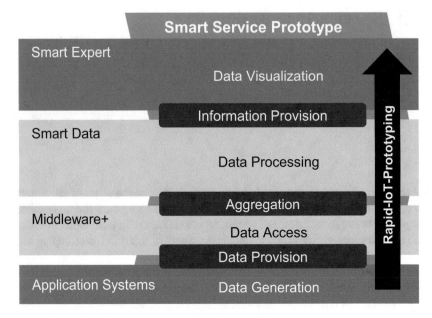

Fig. 1 Sketch of rapid IoT prototyping (Brecher et al. 2017)

construction of prototypes with physical components (Bertsche and Bullinger 2007, p. 4). In the context of networking physical assets such as machines, plants, and production goods and the associated development of intelligent products or cyber-physical systems, the overall concept of rapid prototyping is expanded.

Rapid IoT prototyping is a procedure used to digitally connect production assets at a high speed, to generate data, and to transfer the assets to the Internet of Things (Mazzei et al. 2018, pp. 439–442).

The result of rapid IoT prototyping is a data-based prototype. It includes the networking with operational application systems, which for example provide event data, as well as physical objects, such as machines or material carriers. The various data sources can be accessed via a middleware. Subsequently, simple logical operations or complex methods of machine learning are used for data processing. Finally, users are provided with information generated from the data. A prototype in the context of rapid IoT prototyping is a digital breakthrough from data acquisition through data aggregation and processing to information provision at user level. This is illustrated in Fig. 1.

2 Prototyping

The goal of the second sub-element *prototyping* is the conception, development, and evaluation of a solution module in the form of a prototype, which is created based on a previously defined benefit hypotheses. In the context of smart services,

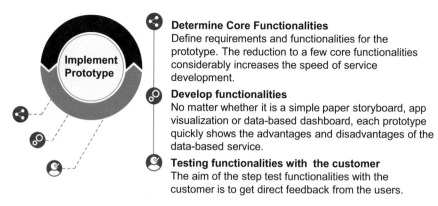

Determine Core Functionalities
Define requirements and functionalities for the prototype. The reduction to a few core functionalities considerably increases the speed of service development.

Develop functionalities
No matter whether it is a simple paper storyboard, app visualization or data-based dashboard, each prototype quickly shows the advantages and disadvantages of the data-based service.

Testing functionalities with the customer
The aim of the step test functionalities with the customer is to get direct feedback from the users.

Fig. 2 Smart Service Engineering sub-element: prototyping

the prototype can be based exclusively on software, but can also contain physical elements.

Rapid IoT prototyping is used as an accompanying method in smart service engineering (Fig. 2). The sub-steps of the element *prototyping* are described in more detail below.

2.1 Determine Core Functionalities

In order to quickly develop a first smart service prototype, the core functionalities must be defined. Based on user stories and the formulated benefit hypotheses, it must be determined what type and form of MVP is to be developed. Because smart services increasingly contain physical components that are considered as data sources, the physical components are of particular importance in the context of rapid IoT prototyping because they are used to generate the necessary data basis (Kampker et al. 2017). For this purpose, the following additional questions must be answered in advance:

- What networking activities must be performed on physical components?
- What data-based added value can be derived from the benefit hypothesis?

The actual design of the first phase shall be illustrated by providing the example of a mechanical engineering company at this point. In a multi-stage process, couplings are built from machine elements as assemblies that are used in large machines or plants to connect shafts with each other. During one of the steps of this process, mobile welding units are distributed over the entire production hall and used as needed. Often, these devices are not available at the production station when the process step requires them. In order to reduce the effort of searching and obtaining one of the units, production staff need to know when and where the devices are used. To obtain this information, Bluetooth low-energy beacons were used and attached to the devices. The beacons send a signal every 30 seconds, which is transmitted via the network. On a simple HTML interface, the employees could now see in which section of the hall the device is located. To achieve rapid IoT prototyping, it was crucial to define what information the production employees really required and make it the very basis of the prototype.

This example makes clear that users of rapid IoT prototyping have to know exactly what kind of information or data-based added value they wish to obtain with the help of the prototype. The information requirements for the feasibility of a solution can be defined based on the specific functions of the user story. The exact information requirement is project-specific. Taxonomies or reference architectures of intelligent products from science as well as best practice examples of smart services from industry serve as orientation. In the following, we will use another example to show how to determine the required information demand.

This second example describes the prototypical digitalization of a mechanical engineering product. The product is used to compensate for excess energy in moving systems and has a braking effect when used. The aim is to digitalize the product in such a way that a product failure is detected when it occurs and a message is sent to the producer to quickly provide the customer with a replacement product. In order to realize this digitalization project, it is important to know which information can be used to report the product failure. The following questions must be answered:

- Which data can be collected from the product by using sensors?
- Which combination of which data leads, when aggregated, to the provision of the information of product failure?

In this project, product failure could be determined by measuring the acceleration and the force acting on the energy compensator. By using sensor technology, these two factors had to be recorded and the resulting data processed. An edge computer was used, which made it possible to evaluate the sensor data directly and transmit the information of a machine overload to a web interface.

In order to answer the questions listed above in general, it may be helpful to examine various components of a cyber-physical system (CPS). They consist of different components that have to be taken into account during the prototypical development (see Fig. 3).

Essential components of a CPS are transmission technologies and the corresponding IT infrastructure. Without these components, networking is not possible and no data transmission can be mapped. The technology cluster *IT Infrastructure* represents hardware and software components a CPS communicates with. These include, for example, servers, databases, and other peripheral devices. It can be understood as a basic element that ensures the exchange, storage, and transport of data and information in the sense of information processing.

The technology cluster *transmission technologies* is equally important. It enables the transmission of data and information so that captured raw data is transported from the source to the point of data processing. These technologies include wired and wireless mobile radio technologies such as GPRS, GSM, LTE, 5G, Bluetooth,

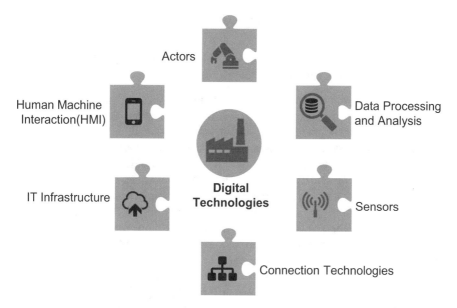

Fig. 3 Technology cluster of cyber-physical systems (Jordan et al. 2017)

and wireless LAN. They differ primarily in range, frequency, and latency. When building a prototype, it is therefore important to pay attention to the amount of data to be transmitted in what time and at what distance. The determination of these characteristics already excludes some technologies in advance.

What is special about the concept of CPS is the ability of a system to absorb and interact with the environment. The technology cluster *sensor technology* enables a CPS to acquire raw data and create a virtual image of the environment. The choice of sensors is determined by the characteristics of the physical principle of action, the type of detection, and, if necessary, the type of material and the application distance.

The technology cluster *actors* enables a CPS to physically intervene in a process. Just like a robot, the adaptation of detailed planning at the level of production machines can also be understood as intervention.

The technology cluster *human–machine interface* ensures that a CPS can interact and communicate with humans. When selecting such interfaces, attention must be paid to the interaction surface, the degree of interaction, and the human senses to be addressed. A well-known example of such an interface is a solution using *augmented reality*.

In the age of artificial intelligence, the last technology cluster *data processing and analysis* is of particular importance. It enables a system to derive its own options for action on the basis of available data. The main selection criterion is the computing capacity that can be made available in sufficient quantity when using IoT platforms.

In connection with physical components, physical design limits must be taken into account.

- How can data transmission be arranged without Internet connection?
- How can the energy supply of a mobile object be designed?

Therefore, all relevant design restrictions that may affect the data acquisition at the physical object must be considered. If the restrictions described below are looked into in great detail at the beginning, core functionalities have to be derived according to the results of the assessment. For example, there may not be a local and open WiFi available to transfer field data from an object. Consequently, the core functionality of sending field data using other techniques must be formulated.

The consideration of possible restrictions in early project phases minimizes the potential of errors during the utilization phase of the prototype. For example, restrictions of the *available space* for housing the sensor technology to be implemented represent a major challenge. Furthermore, the *environmental conditions*, such as humidity, temperature, and light incidence, have to be examined and adapted with regard to the technical restrictions of the sensor components. These conditions can be actively tested within the rapid IoT prototyping. In order to guarantee a continuous data flow, a *continuous power supply* of the sensory components is necessary. The further processing of the collected data in downstream institutions causes restrictions especially with regard to the design. The *degree of isolation* determines the possibilities for the acquisition of relevant sensor data and data transfer. For example, design restrictions prevent the ability to collect data of relevant technical components that have a significant impact on the functionality of the product. Furthermore, the degree of shielding limits the possibilities for transmitting relevant sensor data. *Ensuring information security* is a central challenge in data acquisition and processing. For IoT applications, the component with the lowest security level determines the quality of information security of the overall system. This means that all conventional security mechanisms, such as IT security to protect the components and communication and network security to protect the data, must be guaranteed for IoT applications (Schaumüller-Bichl and Kolberger 2016).

The most relevant design restrictions are listed in Table 1.

Table 1 Important design restrictions

#	Design restriction	Description
1	Available space	Must be considered for physically embossed prototypes
2	Environmental conditions	Must be considered for prototypes that are exposed to the environment
3	Continuous power supply	Must be considered for mobile prototypes
4	Degree of isolation	Must be taken into account when considering the Internet connection
5	Ensuring information security	For example, important for the transfer of personal data

2.2 Develop Functionalities

Companies today are provided with various options for developing functions that facilitate data processing to create added value and, consequently, facilitate the provision of a smart service. In the context of rapid IoT prototyping, companies have to choose between a scalable and industrial-strength solution and an open source one. Many commercial providers offer scalable payment models, such as pay-per-use models, so that costs increase with increasing data volume or processing power. The use of IoT platforms or software-defined platforms represents an industry-compatible solution. Companies should be aware that not every IoT platform supports the freely configurable development of functions. The criterion of an open development environment is of particular importance in this context (s. Stich et al. 2018, p. 31). In this respect, it is important to distinguish between vendor-specific and completely open development environments. It is important to note that classic software development kits (SDKs) in particular are included in vendor-specific development environments (s. Stich et al. 2018, p. 35). In addition to this possible solution, the use of *low-code platforms*, such as NodeRed, is another approach to aggregating the measured data (Bouveret 2017). These enable the user to aggregate data in a targeted manner without programming knowledge. Thus, *low-code platforms* are suitable for the efficient and cost-effective construction of prototypes. Due to their low complexity, their use is limited to the first iteration stage of a set of functions. For further iteration stages, the development of specific codes has to be initiated. The properties of the underlying data model, such as flexibility and extensibility, and the product-specific architecture must be taken into account in the design of the program code. If it is already clearly established during the first step that the development of complex code is increasingly involved, the use of software-defined platforms is recommended in early project phases. On the one hand, these platforms ensure cross-domain access to current data and, at the same time, enable real-time evaluation of the data using analytics procedures. On the other hand, the use of a central data source ensures the truth of the data, since wrong decisions are avoided by data redundancy (Schuh et al. 2017). The concern about lock-in effects at an early stage is justified. Companies should consider early on the transferability from the selected platform to another.

Not all functionalities have to be developed independently. Some of them, such as device and ID management, are provided by industry-standard development platforms. Here, special attention has to be paid to the supplier and the scope of services offered by the supplier. However, development tasks can also be outsourced to partners. This is cost-dependent, so that this in- or outsourcing decision must be made on the basis of service costs and development costs as well as taking into account their own capacities.

Finally, prototyping sensors are used to create a prototype structure that fulfills the determined design restrictions. The implementation of hardware-based MVP is more costly and time-consuming than in the case of software-based approaches. To compensate for this disadvantage, Barros points out that it is crucial to focus the design on only one function (Barros 2013). This can be extended by additional functions during each iteration loop.

An essential aspect of setting up an MVP is the design of a simple but effective architecture. Porter and Heppelmann dedicate a contribution to this topic by presenting a generic architecture for intelligent products linked to smart services. A presentation adapted for the user is illustrated in Fig. 4. Since companies have to use technologies for the development of necessary functions, technology clusters are assigned to individual architecture components, which are to be taken into account. For users of rapid IoT prototyping, it is recommended to pay special attention to the technology clusters sensors, transmission technology, and IT infrastructure for the first sprints (see Fig. 3). While the sensor technology supports the data acquisition significantly, the IT infrastructure serves to design the location of data storage and the location of data analysis. As described above, the IT infrastructure can be designed using an IoT platform. Finally, transmission technologies represent an essential networking element that transmits raw data on the one hand and analysis results on the other hand, thus enabling an intelligent product with a smart service. Many times, aspects regarding information security are not taken into account during the prototype phase. It makes sense, however, to consider information security nevertheless in order to achieve a high scalability. Networked objects and the associated data-based service are particularly vulnerable. It must be ensured that the data transmission path from an object to a platform located on

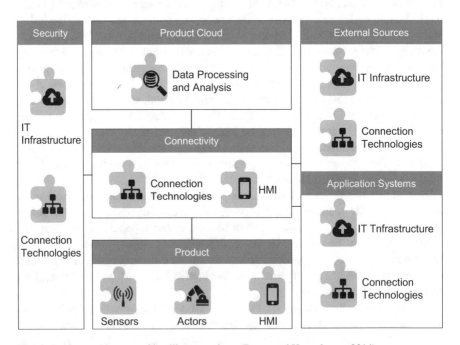

Fig. 4 Product architecture of intelligent products (Porter and Heppelmann 2014)

the Internet is generally secure. The point of attack is rather the source where data originates and the place where data is stored: the networked object and the platform. Only the networked object must be clearly protected by means of restricted local access rights, rights, and user management. However, the transmission path is also a target for cyber-attacks. The BSI basic protection offers many important tips on how the information security of networked systems can be guaranteed. However, companies must also be aware that the design of information security depends on the application and the framework conditions it contains.

2.3 Testing Functionalities with the Customer

As a final step, the developed prototype is tested with the customer in a clearly defined test scenario. The construction of such a scenario creates the opportunity to vary the test conditions discretely and traceably. Structural elements such as a morphological box are suitable for modeling a test scenario with clearly measurable test conditions.

Figure 5 shows a fictive testing scenario with several test dimensions. In this test scenario, the developed prototype has to reach each acceptance criterion in each test dimension. By way of example, any test user can understand the prototype's functions. Else, the given feedback of any user has to be taken into account and the prototype has to be improved in a next development step.

UML-supported activity diagrams are used to narrow down the scenario, making the test procedure efficient in terms of the *lean concept*. The Unified Modeling Language (UML) is a graphical modeling language for specification, design, documentation, and visualization of software and other systems. The subsequent sprint to develop the prototype further is initiated by the final documentation of the test results. At the same time, the results obtained are directly incorporated into the improvement of the prototype in order to incrementally develop a benefit-optimized and product-related result. In contrast to a software-based MVP, hardware-based prototypes cannot be verified by simple A/B testing. Therefore, the requirements for the test procedure are more complex. Consequently, in order to determine real

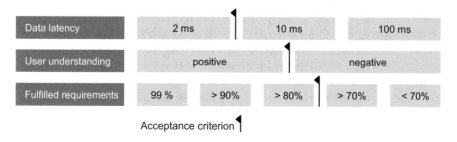

Fig. 5 Fictive test scenarios

user feedback, several prototypes with different approaches have to be presented to a selected group of users. Simplifying the sprints by limiting them to one main function reduces the number of variants, making the test phase more efficient and cost-effective. Finally, it is recommended to carry out rapid IoT prototyping projects with key customers at an early stage and to test the developed prototypes in a real user environment early on.

3 Application of Rapid IoT Prototyping

Rapid IoT prototyping enables companies to digitally connect their physical production plants and assets very quickly, collect data, and transfer it to the Internet of Things. The following project with one of the oldest family-run companies in Germany shows how rapid IoT prototyping can work. As an example, they equipped a conventional production machine without any digital assets in a way that made it possible to collect and use data in a short amount of time – the machine was successfully connected to the Internet of Things and the company was prepared for digital transformation.

Increasing competitive pressure and an antiquated machine park posed great challenges for the company, because quality and craftsmanship, former unique selling points, can no longer ensure long-term economic success. In order to counteract this, it was agreed to develop new data-driven services and to open up new business areas by means of machine connectivity. The large investments, both in terms of time and money, as well as the overall high project risk are required to develop new business activities and can be reduced by the rapid IoT prototyping approach. Due to cooperation with a platform-providing company and the company's own technicians, it was possible to finish the project in just 8 weeks.

During the first sprint, the project participants faced the challenge of selecting a suitable combination of technological components in the sensor technology cluster. This selection was based on the results of a requirements analysis. During the next step, the selected sensor technology and an IoT platform could be connected without any difficulties so that data could be generated. During a second sprint, different positions and the use of different sensors were tested and a final configuration was determined, which resulted in an improved prototype. During the last sprint, the final configuration of the prototype was agreed on and built. In this sprint, a copy of the punching machine was equipped with prototypical sensors and networked within a very short time. With the help of an IoT platform, the recorded data could be visualized on a dashboard and prepared for management purposes. In a matter of a few weeks and just three sprints, it was demonstrated that a previously fully mechanical machine can be updated prepared for the challenges of data-driven services with a low time and cost budget.

This project deliberately focused on a few selected core functionalities in order to achieve a functional prototype very fast. Due to this decision, the rapid IoT prototyping approach was successful and implemented fully, from raw data

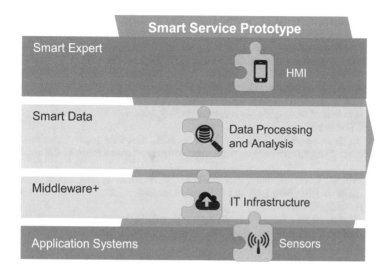

Fig. 6 Classification of technology clusters in the Internet of Production

acquisition to the storing and processing of data and the display of the relevant information on a dashboard (see Fig. 6).

Rapid IoT prototyping, as the example demonstrates, proves to be an adequate method to transfer benefit hypotheses defined during early phases of the Smart Service Engineering Development into prototypical solutions in a structured way and to involve the customer at an early stage of development and the step of result verification.

References

Barros, M. (2013) Here's how to make hardware startups more than just a fad. *Wired.*

Bertsche, B., & Bullinger, H.-J. (2007). *Entwicklung und Erprobung innovativer Produkte - Rapid Prototyping: Grundlagen, Rahmenbedingungen und Realisierung [Online]*. Berlin, Heidelberg: Springer.

Bouveret, C. C. (2017, December 13). Was steckt hinter den buzzwords low-code und rapid application development? *ComputerWoche.*

Brecher, C., Klocke, F., Schmitt, R., & Schuh, G. (Eds.). (2017). *AWK Aachener Werkzeugmaschinen-Kolloquium 2017 Internet of Production für agile Unternehmen.* Apprimus: Aachen.

Hackney, P. M. (2003). The development of three-dimensional printing techniques for 'concept modellers' to competitive rapid prototyping systems. In A. E. W. Rennie, D. M. Jacobson, & C. E. Bocking (Eds.), *Third National Conference on Rapid Prototyping, Tooling, and Manufacturing. 20–21 June 2002 Centre for Rapid Design and Manufacture Buckinghamshire Chilterns University College, High Wycombe, UK. National Conference on Rapid Prototyping, Tooling, and Manufacturing (3, 2002, High Wycombe)* (1st ed.). Bury St Edmunds: Professional Engineering Publication.

Jordan, F., Bernardy, A., Stroh, M., Horeis, J., & Stich, V. (2017). Requirements-based matching approach to configurate cyber-physical systems for SMEs. In *Proceedings of PICMET 2018 - Portland international conference on Management of Engineering and Technology: Technology management for the interconnected world* (pp. 1–7). Portland, OR: IEEE.

Kampker, A., Frank, J., & Jussen, P. (2017, May 1). Digitale Vernetzung im Service. *WiSt - Wirtschaftswissenschaftliches Studium, 46*, 4–11.

Mazzei, D., Baldi, G., Montelisciani, G., & Fantoni, G. (2018). A full stack for quick prototyping of IoT solutions. *Annals of Telecommunications, 73*(7–8), 439–449. https://doi.org/10.1007/s12243-018-0644-5.

Porter, M. E., & Heppelmann, J. E. (2014). How smart, connected products are transforming competition: Spotlight on managing the internet of things. *Harvard Business Review, 1912*(11), 64–88.

Schaumüller-Bichl, I., & Kolberger, A. (2016). IoT als Herausforderung für die Informationssicherheit. *e & i Elektrotechnik und Informationstechnik, 133*(7), 319–323. https://doi.org/10.1007/s00502-016-0427-5.

Schuh, G., Hoffmann, J., Gruber, M., & Zeller, V. (2017). Managing IT complexity in the manufacturing industry – An agenda for action. *Journal of Systemics, Cybernetics and Informatics: JSCI, 15*, 44–52.

Stich, V., Hoffmann, J., & Heimes, P. (2018). Software-definierte Plattformen: Eigenschaften, Integrationsanforderungen und Praxiserfahrungen in produzierenden Unternehmen. *HMD Praxis der Wirtschaftsinformatik, 55*(1), 25–43.

Capturing the Value: How to Charge
for Smart Services

Tobias Enders and Ronny Schüritz

Abstract The emergence of smart services across industry sectors has transformed the way service providers co-create value with their customers. While the development of a smart service requires substantial effort in itself, a critical step is oftentimes neglected in the process: defining a sustainable revenue model. Key decisions need to be made on setting a price and choosing a revenue mechanism that defines how customers are charged (e.g., subscription, pay per use). This chapter provides guidance to organizations on selecting a revenue mechanism that fits the needs of the smart service and the customer situation. Furthermore, this section sheds light on the reasons why customers hesitate to pay for smart services in the first place and what practices services providers can apply to overcome those hesitations.

1 Introduction

The exploitation of data and analytics represents a way for organizations to stay innovative and ahead of the competition (LaValle et al. 2011). By leveraging their acquired capabilities in the fields of data and analytics, firms create new products and services to gain a competitive advantage (Davenport 2013). While most organizations focus on purely internal analytics and data usage scenarios, e.g., to automate and to support decision-making processes, others turn these resources and capabilities into a monetary value by offering smart services to external clients. By doing so, an organization may pursue a multitude of objectives: for instance, the smart service may be a lever to support and enhance the sale of another one of the

This chapter is based on the papers: Enders et al. (2019), Enders et al. (2020), Schüritz et al. (2017a).

T. Enders (✉) · R. Schüritz
Karlsruhe Institute of Technology (KIT), Karlsruhe, Germany
e-mail: tobias.enders@kit.edu; ronny.schueritz@kit.edu

firm's products and is therefore only sold in a bundle. In an alternative scenario, companies start offering smart services as stand-alone offerings to amend their entire business model and establish new revenue streams in the process (Wixom and Ross 2017).

Through the process of servitization, which also extents to the launch of smart services, companies have found a way to create mutual value with their customers (Neely 2008). Being observed across most industry sectors, smart service providers contribute their analytical and professional expertise to interact with their customers in a newly created digital ecosystem. Augmented by the customers' resources—mostly in the form of data—value is co-created that providers aim to capture, i.e., turn into a monetary benefit.

While the development of a smart services is a complex endeavor in itself, it also requires defining a suitable revenue model as part of the overall business model (Chesbrough and Rosenbloom 2002; Johnson et al. 2008; Teece 2010), a process that is often underappreciated by organizations that approach datatization as the next step in their servitization journey (Schüritz et al. 2017b). This chapter sheds light on the challenges that organizations are facing in the process of capturing the value upon launching smart services. In particular, the following key aspects will be addressed: (1) Understanding the reasons why customers may hesitate in adopting smart services. (2) Exploring ways to overcome customer hesitations and turn service value into monetary benefit. (3) Understanding the broad range of direct and indirect revenue models that can be applied to smart services. (4) Focusing on factors that influence the design of the revenue model (Schüritz et al. 2017a; Enders et al. 2019, 2020).

1.1 Understanding the Challenges of Launching and Monetizing Smart Services

Service providers suffer from the slow adoption of smart services in the market and customer's hesitations to pay for them (Enders et al. 2020). Understanding the reasons that cause slow service adoption is critical to develop approaches to address those. The reasons identified in a study show strong parallels to obstacles generally observed in broad change management situations. Those obstacles relate to change resistance in firms to adopt and introduce this new kind of service. In the following sections, the factors contributing to change resistance are outlined, and it is explained how this inhibits the launch and successful monetization of smart services from a provider perspective.

1.1.1 Routine Seeking

Organizations aim for stability in their routines. Especially companies with a long history rely on established processes on their daily operations. Bound by their falsely perceived dependency on legacy systems, organizations reject the introduction of innovative services by pointing to smoothly running processes. Changing market conditions and customer demands, which could be addressed by smart services, are oftentimes neglected by the management. Drawing parallels to human behavior, the introduction of smart services triggers changes within the organization (i.e., a deviation from routines), which may lead to fear of losing control. Not only do smart services call for the adjustment or creation of new processes, but also for the acceptance of new revenue models. While especially historically grown companies are used to one-time payments for a purchase (e.g., for a tangible asset or labor services), smart services may require entering into a service contract that demands a regular (e.g., monthly, quarterly) payment. A subset of ERP systems in operation today do not allow re-occurring (service) payments to be processed that, e.g., depend on a usage parameter. This shortcoming poses a challenge to service providers, which they cannot actively influence. The change in payment routines may therefore spark (emotional) fear and eventually lead to rejection of smart services altogether.

1.1.2 Cognitive Rigidity

Rigid organizational structures oftentimes lead to narrow-mindedness and cognitive rejection of innovation. A peculiarity of this phenomenon is that employees prefer to apply acquired skills over and over again; however, with the introduction of smart services, new skills may be required. The "threat" of having to invest time and effort to learn new skills lets employees reject the innovative service while creating a negative atmosphere and spirit in the entire workforce. Furthermore, customers are having a difficult time to understand the value that a smart service adds to their organization. This trait of skepticism puts the service provider in a spot to prove the value added and how their solutions are superior to those of competitors.

1.1.3 Emotional Reaction to Imposed Change

Emotional reaction or stress is usually associated with human behavior; however, a similar form of uneasiness can be observed in organizations. In the context of smart service and its adoption and implementation, the operations of various departments may be affected. This form of imposed changes to the organization induces stress on various levels. For example, customers are concerned about a possible lock-in effect where they cannot terminate the service without disruption to their business operations. This is owed to the fact that smart services are oftentimes deeply embedded within the IT and process of the customer's operations to exploit their full potential. Customers, however, value flexibility in changing service providers in case of a disappointing service experience.

Since smart services oftentimes demand the transfer of data to the service provider for analysis, customers are concerned about data security and privacy. Once the data has left the customer's firewall, the data may be exposed to external threats and possible data misappropriation. Given the sensitive nature of this concern, stress is induced on an organizational level, which may inhibit smart service adoption.

1.1.4 Short-Term Focus

Organizations show a strong short-term focus in the decisions they make. This is partially owed to external stakeholder demands but also in the way that employees are incentivized. When it comes to smart services, their implementation may require a considerable amount of time and effort, which contradicts entrepreneurial aspirations for a short-term return on investment. Setting up smart services may even trigger the need for new IT infrastructure, which may be costly and as such may be an additional obstacle for organizations with a strong short-term focus. Few customers embrace the introduction of smart services as a way to leave a legacy system behind and migrate to a new, more scalable platform. This may, in part, also be owed to the aforementioned concerns around data security and privacy when considering data migration to a cloud environment. It can be concluded that organizations prefer certain short-term gains over long-term profits—even if those may be higher—which hinders the adoption of smart services.

In order to capture the value of smart services in the external market, one needs to understand the reasons why customers hesitate in the adoption process. By addressing those hesitations, the process of service adoption may be accelerated and thus creates the basis for smart service providers to charge for the service and establish new revenue streams in the process.

1.2   How to Address Hesitations for Smart Service Adoption

While understanding the reasons that influence smart service adoption is a critical first step, the next section turns to solution approaches. For this purpose, four exemplary practices that organizations have successfully applied to drive adoption of smart services in the market are introduced.

1.2.1   Transparent Revenue Model

Entering into a contract for smart services may be perceived as risky to customers since payment models deviate from what they are used to. While historically purchase decisions mostly involved one-time payments to the supplier, service contracts require the customer to commit to multiple payments over a period of time. This paradigm shift requires service providers to offer transparent revenue models to ease the transition for their customers. In a B2B setting, purchase decisions may involve multiple management levels. It is therefore of relevance to understand the decision-making criteria on each level and to potentially offer various revenue models for one and the same service to meet customer expectations.

Smart services offer a multitude of revenue models, which are described later in this chapter. For simplification purposes of this chapter, a revenue model is defined as a combination of a revenue mechanism and pricing scheme. On the one hand, a study finds that customers perceive a subscription-based mechanism as the most simple to understand since it incurs a fixed and plannable fee to be paid on a regular basis. On the other hand, pay-per-use models increase transparency of the level of service usage. When pricing a smart service, customers value a tier model for various levels of demand. This incentivizes the customer to increase service usage and may lead to increased profits on the provider side due to low costs incurred in scaling a smart service.

1.2.2 Starting Small

The scope of functionalities of a smart service can inhibit or accelerate its adoption process. Hence, for customers to get familiar with the service, a limited scope is advisable. This allows that trust into the performance and added value of the service can grow. Starting on a small scale further limits the financial exposure for the customer and eases the decision to try the service. As trust builds up, additional and more complex features can be offered to the client. Empirical evidence suggests that offering multiple service packages with varying scope allows customers to self-select and choose the solution that meets their needs. A growing level of trust and access to customer data—within the scope of the contract—also comes at an advantage for the service provider: by closely monitoring service transactions, the provider can derive insights, learn about customer pain points, and offer better tailored solutions in the future.

1.2.3 Value-Based Selling

Customers enter into a service contract with a provider if they believe that there is a net benefit. For the contract to close, the provider must clearly outline the added value created by the service and understand if this is also perceived by the customer. Since the value perception varies from customer to customer, it is of utmost importance to showcase what problem is being solved and the benefit derived.

Clearly outlining the unique selling proposition of the service and highlighting its superiority toward competitors' offering allows providers to put a stake in the ground. Given the intangibility of a service, customers value the definition of key performance indicators (KPIs) that show the added value to their business. This allows tracking the value added over time. A value-based selling approach is not to be mixed up with a value-based pricing strategy, which proposes charging different prices for the same service to different customers. Value-based selling rather aims for articulating the value that the smart service generates, which is not necessarily the same as the monetary benefit it creates and therefore an indication of the price.

The use of show cases and reference clients that faced a similar issue as the potential client has proven to go a long way. Customers develop a better understanding of how the smart service creates a benefit in a given situation. Furthermore, providers may be able to highlight the efficiency gains driven by the service and therefore aid business case calculations on the customer side.

1.2.4   User Experience

The perceived simplicity of using a smart service plays a key role in the adoption process. One instrument for ensuring an easy and intuitive use is the user interface that can simplify the daily work of the end user of a smart service. If enough attention is not paid to these requirements, the adoption process may be negatively impacted. Therefore, the requirements of various stakeholders such as end users and purchasing departments need to be taken into account early during the design and development process of the service. Methods such as design thinking aid in better understanding the needs of the customer and the development of prototypes.

Further advantages, which result from an intuitive user experience, facilitated by an appealing design, are strengthening the users' emotional binding to the service, the acceleration of the employees' training, and a reduction of stress due to seamless integration of the service into daily routines. Thus, it is recommended to conduct extensive testing with the (end) users of the service to identify design errors early, to understand how they use the service, and finally to avoid disappointed customers.

1.3   Picking from a Broad Range: Revenue Mechanisms for Smart Services

The development of smart services creates cost that needs to be recouped by the provider. Companies therefore need to define how they want to capture some of the value they have created for the customer. There are manifold options for companies to monetize smart services; some of them are more indirect for the customers while others charge the customer directly for the service (cf. Fig. 1) (Schüritz et al. 2017a).

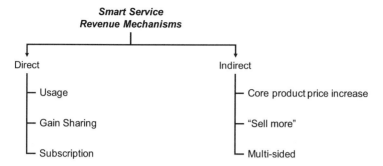

Fig. 1 Smart service revenue mechanisms (own illustration)

1.3.1 Direct Revenue Mechanisms

Direct revenue mechanisms capture the value from smart services by directly charging the customer for the offered service. Such an approach for capturing value is most likely chosen when the smart service is a clearly distinct stand-alone service or can be additionally purchased as an add-on to an existing product or service. The most common direct revenue mechanisms for smart services are *subscription models, usage fee models, and gain sharing models.*

In subscription models, the most commonly found direct revenue model for smart services, customers pay a periodically recurring fee to have access to the smart service. Such models can be used over a fixed period of time (e.g., annual contract) or with more flexible short-term contracts. Subscription models are also commonly used with different feature differentiation models, meaning a customer can chose between different subscription models that vary in respective features or limitations (e.g., "basic" vs. "professional"). The differentiation of these models is most often based either on functionality or on volume. Functionality limitations in smart services usually limit the functionality in a basic tier by e.g. not offering support, cutting back on offered analytical methods, or missing APIs to other services. Volume-based limitations in smart services can be introduced in different ways such as the request the user can make to the service, the amount of data which can be processed, the number of devices (e.g., phones, sensors) that can be added to the service, the number of users that can use the service, or the number of customers that can be analyzed with the service.

Providers that choose a usage fee model charge the customer based on the usage of the smart service. The usage can be determined in different ways such as volume of analyzed data, the amount of customer queries, channels, or requests, as well as the number of accesses granted.

Smart services are supposed to create value for the customer. If the value can be exactly determined, measured, and quantified by both the provider and the customer, a *gain sharing model* can also be an attractive revenue mechanism for smart services. In such cases, the provider is paid a certain fee or percentage based on the success of the smart services and the value created for the customer.

1.3.2 Indirect Revenue Mechanisms

Indirect revenue mechanisms capture the value from smart services not by charging directly for the service, but instead identify other ways to gain a monetary benefit.

Smart services that are bundled with other products and services and may even be an indistinguishable part of the product or service are more difficult to be charged directly. Therefore, companies tend to choose to *raise the price* of the core product or service to recoup some of the cost that was created by the smart service. In some cases, the business case may also be justified by the assumption that due to the additional smart service, the provider is able to *sell more* of the product or service through different means. In some cases, the additional sales are generated through a higher wallet share, which means the existing customer base is willing to purchase more of the product due to the additional value of the smart services. The additional value of the smart service can also stimulate new customers and generate more sales. Further, smart services enable an additional direct touchpoint with the customer. This touchpoint enables the provider to better qualify and guide the customer, understand the context of usage, and enable a better usage of the product.

The digital nature of smart services also allows companies to engage in new multisided mechanisms. In such cases, a smart service is not charged directly nor is the value captured by the bundled product or service, but instead new revenue stream is identified. This new revenue stream can be *advertisement* that is offered to the customer of the smart service. Revenue may be generated through one-time advertising fees for each issued advertising, through the establishment of a subscription model for an advertiser, or through the integration of a brokerage fee. To achieve a higher customer satisfaction, resulting in higher earnings, the service provider of the smart service utilizes data to enable targeted or personalized advertising. The provider of the smart service may also value access to customer data very highly which can be another stream of income for the provider. The gained data can be used to improve their products or services and better understand the customer or in some cases even sold to third parties. While customers do not have to pay extra for the service or endure advertisements, they accept the service provider to work with their data. Multi-sided models such as advertising and "pay with data" are mostly used in smart services offered in a B2C setting rather than a B2B one. However, as smart services evolve over time, so might their revenue models.

1.4 Factors Influencing the Design of the Revenue Model

Designing a revenue model is a critical part of releasing new offerings to market as it describes the process of capturing the value of the offering. In some cases, the revenue model may even decide if the offering becomes a success. There are two key decisions the service provider has to make: how (revenue mechanism) and how much (price) to charge the customer. How to set one or multiple price points is a complex question to answer that depends on a variety of factors and is addressed in separate literature. In the following sections, guidance is given on how to pick the revenue mechanism for a smart service.

There are four factors that influence the decision-making process for a revenue mechanism: service characteristics, provider interests, customer interests, and market factors (Enders et al. 2019). The revenue mechanism is chosen for a specific service, which is described by certain characteristics. These specific characteristics itself have an influence on the choice of the revenue mechanism. Further, both provider and customer have individual interests and preferences regarding the revenue mechanisms that influence the decision-making process. Finally, provider and customer interact in the context of an industry or market, which has an influence on the selection of the revenue mechanism as well.

1.4.1 Service Characteristics

Smart services rely on data as their key resource and analytics to provide value to customers. The services offered, however, may substantially differ from each other: for instance, there are heavy equipment manufacturers that start providing monthly usage reports to the operator of the machines for predictive maintenance purposes or a mobile phone network operator that provides targeted advertising services based on customer movement data. The nature of these offerings in itself can differ substantially and have an influence on the selection of the revenue mechanism. There are two characteristics that play a role in the decision-making process: the usage pattern and the level of integration with a core product or service.

The usage pattern describes the frequency with which the customer actually uses the offering, which is often defined by the service itself, for instance, an alarm service of machinery that has to continuously monitor and process data in order to detect abnormalities. Hence, the smart service is provided continuously and adds value not just at a certain point in time. The choice of the revenue mechanism should therefore reflect that value for the customer is created on a continuous basis. In contrast, where the value of a service is usually derived from using it occasionally, e.g., generating a quarterly report on energy consumption from a utility provider, other revenue mechanisms may be more appropriate to use (e.g., usage-based).

Further, the integration with the core offering influences the choice of the revenue mechanism, i.e., the extent to which the smart features are integrated with a core product or service. Smart services may be provided as a stand-alone service such as a navigation app on the smartphone or integrated with a core product or service such as system status monitoring for an elevator. A high level of integration between the smart service and the core offering makes it often difficult to distinguish the value created through the smart service from the one created through the core product or service. In such cases, services are often not charged separately and more likely to be charged indirectly through the revenue stream of the core product or service. With a decrease in the level of integration between the core offering and the smart service, there is an increase in the likelihood that an additional and therefore separate revenue mechanism for the smart service can be chosen by the provider.

1.4.2 Provider and Customer Interests

Undisputedly, the provider of a product or service has an interest in capturing the value created by their offerings—not just to cover the costs but to create a sustainable business model with attractive profits. On the other side, customers that benefit from the offering and see the value created are willing to pay for it. Therefore, the interests and preferences of the provider and the customer have an influence on the selection of the revenue mechanism. There are four dimensions—economical, relationship, capability, and common practices—within this group of factors that influence the choice of the preferred revenue model. Economic objectives describe how financial targets that the provider and the customer deem relevant to their business strategy can influence the selection of a revenue mechanism. The relationship perspective between the two parties focuses on the level of trust and therefore supports or inhibits the implementation of certain mechanisms. Based on technical and knowledge capabilities, particular revenue mechanisms are enabled or prevented. Further, common practices outline habits and preference of the provider and customer for a revenue mechanism design.

Economical While overarching financial objectives of organizations include the maximization of profits or revenues, operational targets can influence the selection of the revenue mechanism for smart services. Depending on how the management sets these targets, certain models are more advantageous to implement than others. The choice of the revenue mechanism therefore depends on the financial objective: some organizations have a strong focus on ensuring that they have a quick and reliable return on investment since the setup of smart services may require substantial upfront investments. Others may value the ability more strongly to plan future cash flows with certainty; organizations therefore may prefer mechanisms that have a fixed payment schedule (i.e., subscription model). In addition, providers need to ensure that running costs (e.g., server infrastructure) are covered; this is especially relevant for smart services that require to be available around the clock. Examples include the availability of a dashboard or an alert service. Subscription models are an example of a revenue mechanism that allows the provider to cover these running costs with a high level of certainty while, e.g., usage-based models could lead to a gap in the revenue stream since they are less predictable.

Customers prone to risk avoidance may have an increased need for spending money in a very conscious way; i.e., customers only want to pay for the service when it is needed. A usage-based model is an example of a mechanism that supports this objective.

Relationship The way the provider and customer regard and behave toward each other defines their business relationship. It is in the interest of the provider to build a long-lasting relationship in order to maximize the customer's lifetime value. The level of trust between the business partners is one factor that influences the strength of the relationship. Building trust into the provider to deliver the service in quality comes over time and sometimes requires the provider to give away a service for free at first before being able to charge for it. The quality of the relationship, hence, enables or inhibits the use of certain revenue mechanisms. For example, a performance-based revenue mechanism may only be applied if there is a high level of trust since it may require exchanging sensitive information on operational KPIs between provider and customer.

Service providers are given a choice: they may treat customers fairly and build a trusted relationship to ensure ongoing revenue streams or follow a strategy to extract the maximum amount of revenue and profit from the client while accepting that it may not return for repurchase.

Capabilities The complexity of a revenue mechanism and its initial setup, implementation, and monitoring can vary broadly. Simple mechanisms, such as a subscription, are often better received and understood by the customer compared to more complex constructs (e.g., performance-based models). Furthermore, a lack of availability of knowledge and tools to implement the more complex models further limits the selection of revenue mechanisms. Therefore, the existing capabilities on provider as well as customer side enable limit or restrict the implementation of revenue mechanisms.

Smart services offered by the provider support one or multiple business processes on the client side. In order to set up more complex revenue mechanisms, the client has to have a good understanding of how the smart service interacts with its processes and how to measure the value created. If this is not possible, more simple revenue mechanisms should be applied.

Common Practice There are three levels at which habits and common practices influence the choice of the revenue mechanism: individual, organizational, and industry.

On an *individual* level, one can observe that personal preferences of the person in charge of making strategic revenue mechanism decisions play a role. The person may transfer personal experience into the business environment and require a particular mechanism to be applied. Within an *organization*, there is a tendency to apply the same revenue mechanism for new smart services as has been done for existing ones. On the one hand, capabilities and processes for the implementation of existing revenue mechanisms are likely to be already in place and, therefore, a smooth implementation can be ensured. The introduction of a new model, on the other hand, may require the definition and implementation of new processes, which creates additional risk. On an *industry* level, customers expect the availability of certain mechanisms as a consequence of being common practices. The shift of common practices and therefore the preference of customers within an industry can also require the provider to introduce new and unproven revenue mechanisms, for instance, the customers' intent to shift the risk of service fulfillment and success toward the provider. An example of a revenue mechanism that helps achieve this objective is the performance-based one since the provider only gets paid in case of proven success. Failure of a provider to offer a revenue mechanism that enables the shift of risk toward the provider side may inhibit the sale of the service altogether.

1.5 Market Factors

While provider and customer are most directly involved in the value creation and value capture of the smart service, they do not interact in a vacuum. There can be additional players involved that have an influence on the selection of the revenue mechanism. The behavior of competitors can urge the provider to offer one revenue mechanism over another. Further, the collaboration with partners in an ecosystem may require the provider to align its revenue model design with that of other players.

Competitors While it is often difficult to compare smart services between providers due to their unique and new character, bidding situations sometimes allow us to observe what competitors offer. In addition, some revenue mechanisms may be more frequently used than others. Being able to offer a revenue mechanism that is not common (e.g., performance-based) in a particular setting or industry may be recognized as a competitive advantage since special capabilities are often needed for its implementation.

Partners Not all providers of smart services may have the internal capabilities to develop and run a service on their own (e.g., providing hosting and connectivity services) and, hence, are forced to collaborate with contractors. Therefore, the provider is urged to pick a revenue mechanism that ensures a continuous cash flow (e.g., subscription model) to cover ongoing obligations toward its own contractors. Many services nowadays are sold through third-party platforms. These platforms may further constrain the revenue mechanisms that are eligible to be used with the end customer of the smart service. Finally, offering bundled offerings with a sales partner may further constrain the choices since the strategy needs to be aligned with other parties' expectations.

1.6   Conclusion

Capturing value from smart services is essential for organizations to ensure economic feasibility. However, identifying the right way is difficult. Organizations need to define a direct or indirect mechanism that not just fits its service but is also in line with their own interests, their customers' interest, and a variety of individual market factors—all that, while overcoming customer hesitations to pay for smart services in the first place. Nevertheless, our research has shown that taking all of these factors into account and rigorously developing a value capture mechanism is essential for sustainable success of a smart service.

1.7   Outlook

Just as smart services and their functionalities mature, so do the revenue models that accompany them. This chapter sheds light on some of the facets that providers of smart services need to pay attention to. However, there are additional factors that need to be taken into account: for instance, customer acquisition costs (CAC) may be higher from what companies have experienced in the past and therefore have a significant impact on profitability. Furthermore, while this chapter has addressed the choice of a revenue mechanism as part of the revenue model, smart service providers also need to determine the right price for the service that the market accepts. Given the fact that providers may offer several services at once, an overall portfolio pricing strategy is advisable to reflect the dynamics of the market and changing customer demands.

References

Chesbrough, H., & Rosenbloom, R. S. (2002). The role of the business model in capturing value from innovation: Evidence from Xerox Corporation's technology spin-off companies. *Industrial and Corporate Change, 11*(3), 529–555.

Davenport, T. H. (2013). Analytics 3.0. *Harvard Business Review, 91*(12), 64.

Enders, T., Schüritz, R., & Frey, W. (2019). Capturing value from data: Exploring factors influencing revenue model design for data-driven services. In *Proceedings of 14th international conference on Wirtschaftsinformatik* (pp. 1724–1738).

Enders, T. et al. (2020). Igniting the spark: Overcoming organizational change resistance to advance innovation adoption – The case of data-driven services. In *Proceedings of 10th International Conference on Exploring Service Science*.

Johnson, M. W., Christensen, C. M., & Kagermann, H. (2008). Reinventing your business model. *Harvard Business Review*, (December), 1–10.

LaValle, S., et al. (2011). Big data, analytics and the path from insights to value. *MIT Sloan Management Review, 52*(2), 21–31.

Neely, A. (2008). Exploring the financial consequences of the servitization of manufacturing. *Operations Management Research, 1*(2), 103–118.

Schüritz, R., Seebacher, S., & Dorner, R. (2017a). Capturing value from data: Revenue models for data-driven services. In *Proceedings of the 50th Hawaii international conference on system sciences*.

Schüritz, R. et al. (2017b). Datatization as the next frontier of Servitization – Challenges of organizational transformation. In *Proceedings of 38th international conference on information systems*.

Teece, D. J. (2010). Business models, business strategy and innovation. *Long Range Planning, 43*(2–3), 172–194.

Wixom, B. H., & Ross, J. W. (2017). How to monetize your data. *MIT Sloan Management Review, 58*(3), 10.

Market Launch of Smart Services

Tobias Leiting, Maximilian Schacht, and Jana Frank

Abstract This chapter addresses the market launch and sales of smart services. It opens with an introduction of the new challenges that the market launch of smart services creates for companies. Then follows the discussion of a four-phase approach to the market launch of smart services. Subsequently, successful practices are presented for this approach along eight design fields of the market launch.

1 Challenges During the Market Launch of Smart Services

For the successful management of smart services, the go-to-market phase is crucial, which is why this chapter is dedicated to it. The expansion of a service portfolio with smart services leads to numerous challenges for companies. This is one reason why only 16 to 39 percent, depending on the use case, of manufacturing companies currently realized the potential of smart services (Bullinger et al. 2015, p. 8). One of the biggest challenges for companies is the successful market launch of the smart service. Studies and surveys estimate that the share of smart services that are taken off the market again within the first year after their initial introduction is significantly higher (over 50%) than the share of traditional products that are pulled off the market (approx. 35%) or traditional services (approx. 43%) (Irlbeck 2017; Demirkan et al. 2015). This deficit can be traced back to the unique characteristics of smart services that lead to novel challenges for the sales department. Smart services require a higher degree of interdisciplinary cooperation, have shorter life cycles, require and include access to internal and external data, are more complex due to the necessary process integration at the customer's site, and require more intensive education and persuasion of the customer (Kampker et al. 2018, p. 186; Baumbach 2014).

T. Leiting (✉) · M. Schacht · J. Frank
Institute for Industrial Management (FIR) at RWTH Aachen University, Aachen, Germany
e-mail: tobias.leiting@fir.rwth-aachen.de; maximilian.schacht@fir.rwth-aachen.de; jana.frank@fir.rwth-aachen.de

© Springer Nature Switzerland AG 2020
M. Maleshkova et al. (eds.), *Smart Service Management*,
https://doi.org/10.1007/978-3-030-58182-4_8

According to a study by acatech, smart services in mechanical and plant engineering have so far been used primarily to realize internal potential instead of being marketed as an external service offering and for generating sales (Kagermann et al. 2018).

The market launch of smart services includes the phase from the initial market entry to the ramp-up and growth phase on external markets (Lenfle and Midler 2009, p. 165). According to current studies, companies fail at the beginning of the market launch mainly due to low adoption rates of the service innovation by customers. This can be attributed in part to the insufficient provision of intra-organizational capacities, insufficiently developed willingness on part of the company's employees and customers, and inter-organizational coordination problems (Töytäri et al. 2018; Klein et al. 2018). Often, the focus of product management is on the development of smart services (Geum et al. 2016; Kim et al. 2016), while the go-to-market strategy and sales are neglected. For this reason, the following section presents a phase-oriented go-to-market approach for the market launch of smart services. In addition to different fields of action, this model also contains factors that contribute to the success of the individual market launch steps.

The aim of the approach is to support companies in successfully addressing and organizing their smart services sales process by taking appropriate measures in the relevant fields of action.

2 Phases of the Smart Service Market Launch: From Piloting to Successful Scaling of Smart Services

The process model for the market launch of a smart service is based on the characteristics of smart services and enables the sales department to address the requirements of the customers. The model distinguishes between different phases of the go-to-market, which is necessary because, for numerous steps, a set of sub-goals must be fulfilled before they can be carried out (e.g., collection of the data basis, acquiring potential customers, and organizing responsibilities). The phase-based go-to-market model can be divided into four consecutive steps of piloting, market entry, standardization, and scaling (Fig. 1).

The model starts with the pilot phase, in which the smart service functions, as well as the sales process and service integration, are prototypically tested, validated, and improved in cooperation with the customer. This is helpful because the benefits and possible improvement potential of smart services often only become tangible when they are implemented at the customer's site. In-depth testing will, therefore, enable rapid adaptation and further development of the most important functions of the smart service. In this important initial phase of the smart service sale, the foundations for later sale phases are built. The development and product management teams are in charge during this phase. Close and open-minded partners with whom a trusting relationship exists are selected as test customers. Possible performance adjustments can be carried out particularly easily in this phase, due to

Phase	Characteristic			
	Goal	**Data**	**Sales**	**Customers**
Piloting	Validate and **improve** the **product** in cooperation with pilot customers	**No** customer **data** available	Directed by **development team**/smart service and product management	ca. **0 – 5**
Market entry	Transfer from development department to **sales department** and **first commercial success**	**First** customer **data** (sales and technical data) available	Directed by **development team** and **first sales representatives**	ca. **5 – 15**
Standardization	**Optimize/ standardize** the sales organization and increase commercial success; reduction of the effort	**Meaningful** customer **data** (sales and technical data) available	Directed by **sales employees/sales teams**	ca. **15 – 100**
Scaling	**Reduction** of **marginal costs**, making use of **economies of scale** and high **efficiency**	**Structuring** and **analysis** of the data And derivation of decisions	Directed by **sales employees/sales teams** or **independent department**	**More than 100**

Fig. 1 Phases of the smart service sales process (own figure)

the release capability of the smart service. Within this phase, one can already collect customer data on the benefits of the used smart services.

Once the functionality and benefits of the smart service have been validated together with trial customers during the pilot phase, the actual market launch follows. This phase aims to achieve initial commercial success by selling the smart service, with the involvement of sales departments and employees. The data and information collected during the piloting phase can be accessed to align the planned sales activities with the customer's requirements. Furthermore, in this phase, success stories are generated and worked out, which can be used as a basis for further orientation of the sales department. Often, the first sales successes of the smart service are complicated further by uncertainty about the value proposition for the sales staff, which leads to high communication efforts to explain the technical advantages of the service.

During the standardization phase, the aim is to learn from the first successful sales as well as the difficulties the sales representatives experienced and derive standard measures for the entire organization.

Once the standardization phase is complete, the scaling of the smart service can follow. The successfully standardized smart service can be scaled to all relevant markets and potential customers with low marginal costs. During this phase, all sales processes to be scaled must be automated as much as possible. This ensures high efficiency and thus lowers the costs for customer acquisition. To achieve this, a large amount of available data can be used to optimize the smart service as well as to improve sales activities. Depending on the corporate strategy, sale activities can also be outsourced and handed over to another department.

3   Smart Service Sales Framework

In addition to the division of the four phases piloting, market entry, standardization, and scaling, the activities during the market launch can be divided further into different fields of action, which are shown in the smart service sales framework (Fig. 2). This subdivision enables companies to address measures specifically in the fields of action in which they face the greatest challenges.

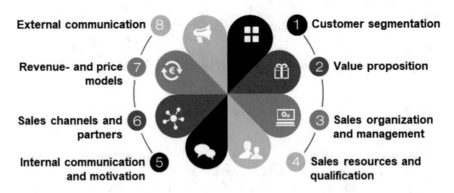

Fig. 2 Smart service sales framework showing the fields of action of sales procedures for smart services (own figure)

Customer segmentation is used to identify different customer target groups that can be approached with the same sales strategy when selling smart services due to similar characteristics. Segmentation of potential smart service customers can be more detailed than segmentation for traditional service customers because more data is available. Because smart services allow precise conclusions to be drawn about customer's usage behavior, customers can be segmented and addressed accordingly.

The *value proposition* is the central value the smart service provides for the customer. When selling the service, it must be communicated what added value the service generates for its customers. All stakeholders on the customer side and in the company must recognize a clear benefit coming from the smart services. This is particularly challenging because smart services often only unfold their true benefit after the service has been implemented successfully and is used by the customer.

Sales organization and management, the next field of action, includes the organizational integration of the sales of smart services into a company as well as the management of sales processes. In this step, the organizational unit that is responsible for smart service sales is built and integrated into the existing product or service sales structure or a unit separate from the conventional product and service business. In addition to this, clear sales processes, targets, and responsibilities are defined.

The prerequisites to ensure successful selling of smart services are defined as part of the field of action *sales resources and qualification*. The training and qualification of sales staff should provide employees with professional, social, and personal skills concerning the requirements for selling smart services. As smart services differ from traditional services and ask for in-depth digital expertise, existing staff should be trained and the recruitment of new staff should be considered as well.

Internal communication describes the communication of the sales department with other departments involved in the smart service, which ensures sales success. Many times, the employees involved are not even aware of the goals the company is pursuing with the new service offering and how these are to be implemented. Clear communication of objectives and incentives can motivate sales employees, so this field of action should not be neglected.

The *sales channels and partners* describe the interfaces between the company and customers. Due to the immateriality of smart services, new distribution channels such as digital platforms can be used to sell them. Because the personal direct exchange is still necessary to build confidence and offer consultation in complex cases, a mix of sales channels must be combined and orchestrated.

The chosen *revenue and price models*, which are explained in detail in Sect. 4.7, determine the form and amount of remuneration for the performance delivered by the smart service. For classic services, a non-recurring fee that is based on the execution costs is usually agreed upon after the service has been provided. Because smart services focus on customer benefit, the revenue models do so as well. Smart services also enable continuous billing due to the continuous provision of services.

In the field of *external communication*, the communication of the service portfolio to the customer is designed. Similar to internal communication, external communication also requires a strategy to demonstrate the explicit added value of smart services.

4 Successful Smart Service Market Launch

To market smart services successfully, it is necessary to link the various phases from pilot testing to successful scaling and the fields of action described above. Factors influencing the success of the phases as well as the fields of action are presented below (Fig. 3).

4.1 Customer Segmentation

In the piloting phase, the smart services should be carried out with trusted customers of the service provider, who are particularly open to digital services and, ideally, use them already (Jussen et al. 2019, p. 385). To this end, the most relevant focus markets and customers with potential are identified by analyzing existing customer data. In addition to classic criteria, segmentation can also be based on aspects such as digital maturity, technological readiness, cooperativeness, and established trust between provider and customer. Stakeholder mapping is used to analyze the customer's buying center to identify the structure and distribution of roles (Newcombe 2003, p. 841). With the help of the characterization of the individual actors involved, it is possible to adjust the value proposition and the actual offer to

Fig. 3 Linkage of the fields of action with the market launch phases (own figure)

be as convincing as possible, leading the buying center to decide to purchase the service or start a joint pilot (ibid.).

For the phase of the actual market entry, it is recommended to choose a market that promises high success due to its own sales organization and customers. In this phase, particularly digitally affine customers with high digital maturity are to be addressed. To identify customers, both the Industry 4.0 Maturity Assessment and the Technology Readiness Index (TRI) can be used to evaluate customers in terms of digitization and openness to new technologies (Schuh et al. 2017, p. 14).

> The **Industry 4.0 Maturity Index** determines the digital maturity based on a holistic approach that considers the entire company of the customer, not just the buying center. It assesses the fields of resources, information systems, culture, and organizational structure and classifies them into one of six ranks, being (in ascending order) computerization, connectivity, visibility, transparency, predictability, and adaptability. This provides a segmentation of the customers and enables the service provider to create suitable sales strategies for each maturity rank.

For the derivation of customer profiles, the creation of personas for specific customer segments is useful (Hou et al. 2020). They can be developed using contextual interviews, statistical analysis, and surveys. Focused on these customer types, sales strategies can be addressed in the best possible way and customer requirements can be evaluated.

For standardization of the sales process, the volumes of data generated by customers due to their smart service use can be used for further analysis. Also, data can be taken from customer relationship management (CRM) systems, where additional data about customers can be found. Based on this broad database, it is possible to analyze which customer segment is interested in which type of service (Salesforce 2019) and to track which customers are already using the smart service regularly and successfully and which are not. This makes it possible to identify customers who need additional advice or support. Furthermore, further development potential can be derived from user behavior and user feedback (Poeppelbuss and Durst 2019, p. 326).

In the final phase of scaling, a large customer database allows for further systematic decisions in customer segmentation. Now, customers can be segmented in regard to their requirements as well as based on their buying potential. In this way, possible upselling potentials for existing customers can be identified and the overall customer satisfaction can be determined. Furthermore, performance tracking can be utilized to evaluate how successfully a customer uses a smart service. Potentially dissatisfied customers can thus be identified and existing shortcomings can be compensated.

4.2 Value Proposition

During the piloting phase, the smart service value proposition will be validated and adapted. This can be achieved, for example, based on feedback from partners or lead user workshops. By using the so-called *Smart Service Canvas*, the value proposition can be identified and presented in a structured way (Poeppelbuss and Durst 2019, p. 327). The canvas particularly highlights the fit between value-added components and customer needs. Another possibility is to make use of a proof of value, which tests assumptions about the value of the smart service solution continuously and can be used to compare it with the customer's objectives (Martinez et al. 2018, p. 31). By involving the pilot partners, for example, utilizing co-financing or a preliminary agreement, it is also possible to prove the interest of the partners financially.

To master the market entry phase, a sales guideline can be developed for the sales staff to help them address the previously identified customer segments. This so-called playbook contains the description of the personas as well as use cases for a context-based description of the smart services. By using these use cases, which have been selected for each customer segment, sales staff can communicate the benefits of the smart services to the customer. Another factor of success is the development of a guide that answers frequently asked questions (FAQs) from customers and provides further background information.

Based on the customer data resulting from the benefit-specific customer segmentation, the individual value proposition of the smart service can be specified for each segment during standardization. By using data of comparable customer types as part of a benefit calculation, it is possible to estimate, quantify, and visualize the achievable benefit to provide a specific and clear basis of a decision to the customer (Liddy et al. 2016, p. 1). It is particularly promising to present this data to the customer in a context-specific manner using data storytelling.

> **Data Storytelling** uses customer data to illustrate the impact of smart services on key performance indicators. This requires access to existing customer data that can be used to calculate performance indicators such as Overall Equipment Efficiency (OEE). By comparing these figures with similar companies, an awareness of where the company stands is created. The comparison allows quantifying the potential for improvement through the use of smart services. By converting this improvement potential into monetary benefits, it is possible to demonstrate the benefits of using Smart Services to the customer in a promising way.

Even in the scaling phase, the value proposition must continue to be communicated to the customer tangibly. To ensure that the customer is always in the clear about the service purchased, the performance achieved by the smart service and the associated benefits must be automatically visualized and compared to similar customer types using dashboards and benchmarks. Also, suggestions for services that have helped similar customers can be made for defined customer segments. To objectively quantify the benefits of the smart service for the customer, it should also be possible to automatically quantify these benefits in monetary terms based on the performance data.

4.3   Sales Organization and Control

During the piloting phase, sales are primarily handled by the development and product management teams, who closely accompany the customer. The work is based on a pilot contract with clearly defined goals, which will culminate in the testing of both the smart service and the sales processes. Often, a minimum viable service that is working but reduced to the very essential functions is continuously tested and adjusted together with the customer (Moogk 2012, p. 24). This requires processes for identifying customer benefits, analyzing the collected data, and processing feedback, as well as a trial phase of a few months. At the end of the pilot process, the smart service is converted into a subscription or license that can be sold.

In the market entry phase, the smart service is provided by the sales organization. Especially in production engineering, a smart service is often offered as an addition to existing product and service offerings. Based on the corporate strategy and the capabilities and resources of the existing sales organizations, a decision must be taken whether smart service sales will be integrated into existing product or service sales organizations or whether it will be carried out by a separate organization instead. New roles need to be defined to carry out the sales process, such as a portfolio manager, who tailors the performance of any physical products, services, and smart services to the customer, or customer success managers, who support the customer in using the service successfully, even after it has been sold (Hilton et al. 2020, p. 364).

A central point of the standardization phase is the creation and implementation of the sales process. By now, the sales process must be equipped with clearly defined roles, responsibilities, and tasks. Furthermore, it must be ensured that the customer is satisfied with the service during the entire contract period and does not cancel but instead renews the existing contract. To fulfill this complex task, the one-face-to-the-customer principle must be expanded to the one-team-to-the-customer principle, in which a sales representative can, if necessary, link the customer with internal specialists who answer questions in a targeted manner. Distribution processes that apply this principle must be developed and rolled out. The focus must be on customer satisfaction and long-term customer relationships (Hilton et al. 2020, p. 362). Furthermore, key figures can be strategically chosen to measure sales success and to adjust activities if necessary (Keck and Ross 2014, p. 341).

A **Customer Success Manager** acts as a partner to the customer during the utilization phase, focusing on improving the customer's value by proactively providing information on optimization potential. His tasks, therefore, include informing his customers about new updates and offers, developing solutions to problems he has identified himself without being asked and being available at all times. His success is measured by the successes of his customers (e.g. higher ROI) which distinguishes him from a regular account manager whose goal is to renew as many contracts as possible.

As the customer base grows, the sales organization must also develop further during the scaling phase. Since a smart service does not develop its benefits as an individual service, but as a solution consisting of a product, service, and smart service, sales must also focus on selling services within a service system as a complete solution. Furthermore, the sales processes for existing customers must be expanded so that they can be offered as individually tailored additional services. The KPIs used to manage the sales organization must be geared toward high customer benefit and long-term customer contracts so that it is clear to employees that these goals are the focus.

4.4   Sales Resources and Qualification

The developers involved in the piloting phase must be trained specifically for sales activities. For those involved, the most important thing is to extend their competence profile and sharpen their focus for specific customer needs and use of the smart service. To ensure a high level of learning success, traditional classroom learning can be supplemented by innovative training strategies such as role-plays with scenarios during which the developers put themselves in the customer's shoes. Missing competencies of sales staff also have to be identified during the pilot phase, to better prepare them for the work within the digital framework of the smart service and enabling them to sell solutions (Koponen et al. 2019, p. 250). For this purpose, competence assessment can be carried out to compare which skills are already available and what kind of competences need to be added (Kauffeld and Lehmann-Willenbrock 2010, p. 28).

In the market entry phase, sales staff must be empowered to successfully sell and implement the smart service and support the customer in its successful use. Therefore, staff members need to be trained both functionally and digitally so that they have an in-depth understanding of all the services on offer, which are linked by the smart services to form an integrated digital solution (Mullen et al. 2006, p. 5). Various training formats are possible, such as internal, external, and digital events as well as a didactically coherent combination of these as part of a so-called blended learning concept (Bohnsack and Margonlina 2019, p. 25). The previously developed guidelines and FAQs, which are based on the information collected with customers during the pilot phase, are further valuable tools for sales success.

Due to the increasing complexity of services and the greater need to build internal interfaces, further professional and methodical training of sales staff is becoming increasingly important in the standardization phase. Furthermore, new roles must be filled by existing and new employees. This is achieved by qualifying employees and targeted recruiting of new talent. The training of employees must also focus on practical elements, such as being able to tell a compelling story based on the advantages of the smart service (Boldosova 2020, p. 132). Furthermore, learning platforms on which employees can train at their own pace and receive information when they need it are becoming more important (Bohnsack and Margonlina 2019, p. 25).

The **70-20-10 Principle** represents a division of the training content into three parts: 10% of knowledge transfer should be provided by traditional classroom-lessons, in which basic skills and tools are taught. Another 20% of knowledge transfer should be based on e-learning, which includes webinars with experts as well as online communities across all hierarchical levels. The other 70% should be learned "on the job" by solving difficult business challenges and demonstrating the value of smart services to customers through collaboration with colleagues. The high level of practical relevance creates an awareness of the need for continuous improvement and thus eliminates a typical blockade attitude that many employees experience when it comes to selling digital services.

Scaling the sales process for smart services requires a large number of personnel, which includes and requires both new employees and experienced experts. For example, service engineers could support the sales (Akkermans et al. 2019, p. 5920). As a result, it is important to professionalize the introduction and orientation process to help newly hired employees to become familiar with their tasks and be productive as quickly as possible. At the same time, existing employees should receive continuous further training and incentives should be created to keep employees in the company in the long term. Above all, additional sales roles and employees for after-sales support are necessary, like the previously mentioned customer success manager, to ensure that the customer achieves the greatest possible success with the smart service solution.

4.5 Internal Communication and Motivation

Internal communication in the piloting phase aims to grow enthusiasm for smart services within the company. External best practices can be pointed out early on. They are role models for successful sales, demonstrate the potential of smart services, and act as a motivator for all those involved. During the pilot phase, the communication paths within the development team must be kept short. An internal messenger channel can be used to quickly exchange information within the group (Teckchandani 2018). Channels and subscriptions within the messenger also allow best practice solutions to be exchanged quickly.

By involving sales staff in the market entry phase, details of the technical functions and the value proposition of the smart service must also be communicated in a comprehensible way to members of staff who have not been involved until now and work decentralized and mobile. For purposes of internal communication, success stories from the previous pilot phase or demonstrators are particularly useful. For employees to become aware of the relevance of smart service sales, clear goals must be set in the form of so-called objectives and key results (OKR) (Doerr 2018). Because the sales of smart services aim for long-term success over long periods instead of short-term revenues, measurable success can be achieved by setting targets that are detached from revenues. By awarding particularly successful sales employees, further employee motivation can be achieved (Gallus and Frey 2016, p. 1704). Monetary incentive systems must also be adapted in such a way that sales staff focuses on high customer loyalty and long-term sales. One criterion for bonuses can be, for example, the number of contracts concluded.

In the standardization phase, sales of smart services will be rolled out to all sales employees. Particularly among previously uninvolved employees, an awareness of the importance of selling smart services for the company must be created. To ensure that the sales staff focuses on long-term business, targeted communication of internal goals and the passing on of information are of decisive importance. Taking these objectives into account through incentives leads to a clearer understanding of the importance of selling smart services. Internal communication aims to provide all employees with precisely the knowledge they need to fulfill their tasks. For this purpose, the internal knowledge management must be refined during the scaling phase, so that best practices, information material, and problem solutions are made available quickly for everyone. Also, all sales employees must be trained to offer holistic and customer-oriented solutions instead of single services (Moser et al. 2019, p. 67).

> The phases require different **Incentive Programs**: During market entry, a target-oriented incentive system is very suitable, which rewards for the fact that the first contracts are concluded with customers. During the standardization phase, however, the goal of achieving high sales and margins with the Smart Services moves into focus, which is why the incentive system should be adjusted accordingly. Different rates should be chosen for smart services than for physical components, as these generate higher margins for the provider. The scaling phase also requires incentives for high customer satisfaction, for example through further incentives when an existing contract is extended or when additional services are purchased by the customer.

4.6   Sales Channels and Partners

The piloting phase is dominated by direct sales, which are realized through personal contact with pilot customers by the development team and product managers.

During the market entry phase, direct sales are still the predominant sales method. As of now, sales staff mostly sell the service directly to customers. Developers can be included in the process in case further questions arise that require in-depth expertise. One advantage of direct sales is that it ensures close customer contact and direct feedback loops. Furthermore, providers can make future arrangements for sales to be carried out by sales partners and multipliers to enable higher market penetration and standardization of the smart service in the following phases.

Although smart services are digital services, personal, direct sales still dominate in the B2B context during standardization. Especially at the beginning of customer relations, when it must be evident what the customer's service requirements are and the integration of the smart service into the existing product and service landscape is necessary, a personal consultation is important. At the same time, digital channels and platforms offer an efficient way to support the customer during use (Demirkan et al. 2015, p. 746). In this way, the benefits realized can be shown to the customer, and further services can be purchased on this basis.

> **E-commerce** sales channels can be highly useful during Standardization. Offering the Smart Service through an Appstore ensures global presence and minimal transaction costs. In addition, costumer data can automatically be gathered and processed. Using an own online platform pursues similar goals, but further automatizes the sales process and allows for a more comprehensive data gathering. This data can then be used in other fields of action such as Segmentation and Value proposition.

To ensure targeted and efficient communication with the customer, both personal and digital sales channels must be developed and used during the scaling phase. It is necessary to define which channel is to be used in which situation, what the transition between the channels should be like for a customer, and how the customer journey is designed for all possible sales, service, and customer management inquiries, to ensure that the customer has a positive and continuous experience throughout.

4.7   Revenue and Price Models

For the piloting phase, pilot contracts with objectives and time frames are to be drawn up as project contracts, so that a transition to market launch can be guaranteed afterward. The focus of these contracts is not on profit maximization, but on cooperation to improve the performance of smart services. One possibility to achieve this is to develop special pilots or test versions of the smart service. High discounts or the offer of freemium models, i.e., free basic versions of the smart service, which can be extended by purchasing additional services, can create incentives for cooperation with the customer during the piloting phase (Frank et al. 2019, p. 8). At the end of the piloting phase, the customer can purchase the smart service as a subscription offer or as a full license product.

> **Licenses** and **Subscription models** are both fitting revenue models for Smart Services but are suitable for different value propositions. The licenses generally only provide access to a Smart Service. They are often used for software and offer advantages through their simplicity. Subscriptions allow continuous data and information exchange between provider and customer leading to a constantly improving and adapting Smart Service. Thus, subscriptions are best suited for services with high complexity, big added value and extensive customization that rely on a back stream of information (i.e. machine data) to the service provider.

The market entry phase requires choosing and elaborating revenue models. For smart services, it is recommended to choose licenses or subscriptions, as these create a benefit over a longer period (Tzuo and Weisert 2018; Wulfsberg et al. 2019).

Since a high level of market penetration is important during the market entry phase, discounts and test phases can also be offered at the beginning as part of the revenue models. In principle, the price of the smart service should be generated using a customer value-based pricing approach. However, because the customer value is not always immediately clear when entering the market, the internal costs of providing the service should not be left out when determining the price.

A subscription as a revenue model gives the customer flexibility to adjust the service, and the continuous provision of services also generates regular revenues. Value-based pricing systems are gaining in importance in the standardization phase through a focus on customer benefit (Bonnet et al. 2014, p. 7). Through the availability of customer data, price metrics can be established for these pricing systems, based on clearly measurable data. Predefined service level agreements can also be offered to the customer to provide services as required (Cordall 2014, p. 1).

During the scaling phase, the availability of detailed customer data, especially during the usage phase, makes it possible to quantify customer benefits more accurately. As a result, the customer benefit and the calculated price for the smart service can be matched well and the ideal value-based pricing model can be selected. When choosing an availability-based pricing model, the customer can count on high system availability. Output-based pricing models focus on remuneration for the increase in productivity, while success-based pricing models allow the provider to receive a share of the customer's cost savings (Cillo and Lachman 2005). Subscription business models offer the opportunity to harmonize customer and provider interests via usage-based pricing models, while regular payments make it possible to adjust the price if the customer value increases. In return, this serves as a reason for the service provider to optimize service performance continuously (Schuh et al. 2019, p. 2).

4.8   External Communication

Due to close cooperation with a few pilot customers, there is no need for extensive external communication during the piloting phase. Because customer feedback is essential for the further development of the smart service, an intensive exchange between provider and pilot customer must be ensured. To increase valuable customer feedback further, customers must be given an easy way to submit suggestions and ideas for improvement. This is achieved, for example, by appointing a central contact person such as a project manager. In this phase, a broad customer base can already be addressed via conferences and trade fairs in preparation for market entry.

The previously carried out pilot projects should be documented as use cases during the market entry phase and published as examples for successful practices. It is useful to work with testimonials as communicators to promote the benefits the customers have received from the smart service during the pilot projects. Additionally, physical and virtual demonstrators can be used to demonstrate the added value of the service (Alexakos et al. 2016, p. 157).

> **Online Customer communities** provide a platform such as a forum for customers, in which they can share experiences, best practices and solutions. This helps saving resources, as the platform provider only has to ensure its availability and potentially appoint a moderator to review the threads created within the forum. Also, customer data can be generated by analyzing the profiles, which the customers created to join the community.

External communication focuses on winning new smart service customers in the phase of standardization: On the one hand, customers who have already purchased other products and services by the same smart service provider in the past can be addressed specifically for upselling. On the other hand, promising contacts can also be contacted and offered a combined portfolio of products, services, and smart services. During this point of selling smart services, external communication can also be used to get in touch with already existing customers and encourage them to leave feedback, for example by offering customer portals and regular feedback meetings.

Due to the scaling of the service offer and the possibility of digital networking, great network effects between providers and customers can be realized in the scaling phase. The customer changes his role from a mere recipient of the service to its co-creator, who is in close exchange with the provider as well as with other customers. Providers can actively promote this behavior in the area of external communication by creating networks and communities for customers such as customer portals.

5   Conclusion

Due to constituent features of smart services such as access to continuously collected data, adaptation to specific customer needs, and high continuous customer interaction, the market launch and selling of smart services differ from existing sales approaches. This chapter provides a holistic approach to introduce smart services successfully to the market. The approach provides design guidelines for the market entry of smart services, structured in four successive sales phases. The goal of the first phase of the market launch, the pilot phase, is to derive as much potential as possible for the improvement of the smart service together with a small number of customers. In the subsequent phases of market entry and standardization, more and more customers are addressed and the organization and processes are professionalized. These phases enable the company to be as efficient as possible in the following last phase of scaling. Once this phase is reached, processes are automated and the expenditure required to acquire new customers is low. The presented approach and the design recommendations provide a framework for companies in the production industry to achieve an efficient and focused design of their smart service market launch.

References

Akkermans, H., Zhu, Q., Fang, F., Lamper, L., & van de Kerkhof, R. (2019). Designing smart services: A system dynamics-based business modeling method for IoT-enabled maintenance services. In *Proceedings of the 52nd Hawaii International Conference on System Sciences*.

Alexakos, C., Anagnostopoulos, C., & Kalogeras, A. P. (2016). Integrating IoT to manufacturing processes utilizing semantics. In *Proceedings, 2016 IEEE 14th International Conference on Industrial Informatics (INDIN)*. Palais des Congrès du Futuroscope, Futuroscope – Poitiers,

France, 19-21 July, 2016. *2016 IEEE 14th International Conference on Industrial Informatics (INDIN)*. Poitiers, France, 7/19/2016–7/21/2016. *IEEE International Conference on Industrial Informatics* (pp. 154–159). Institute of Electrical and Electronics Engineers; INDIN. Piscataway, NJ: IEEE.

Baumbach, E. (2014). Making the intangible tangible: Launch decisions for service innovations. In: AMA winter and summer educators' conference proceedings. *American Marketing Association, 2014*, 21–23.

Bohnsack, R., & Margonlina, A. (2019). Teaching entrepreneurship and business model innovation in a blended-learning curriculum with the Smart Business Modeler. *Journal of Business Models, 7*(3). https://doi.org/10.5278/ojs.jbm.v7i3.2575.

Boldosova, V. (2020). Telling stories that sell: The role of storytelling and big data analytics in smart service sales. *Industrial Marketing Management, 86*, 122–134. https://doi.org/10.1016/j.indmarman.2019.12.004.

Bonnet, D., Buvat, J., & Subrahmanyam, K. V. J. (2014). *Monetizing the internet of things: Extracting value from the connectivity opportunity*. Capgemini Consulting.

Bullinger, H-J., Meiren, T., & Nägele, R. (2015). Smart services in manufacturing companies. In *23rd International Conference on Production Research* (pp. 7–13).

Cillo, P. A., & Lachman, H. (2005). *Pay-as-you-Save™(PAYS®)*.

Cordall, G. (2014). *Service level agreement*. In Keynotes (Ed.). Retrieved November 29, 2019, from https://www.city.ac.uk/__data/assets/pdf_file/0007/133936/Service-Level-Agreements.pdf

Demirkan, H., Bess, C., Spohrer, J., Rayes, A., Allen, D., & Moghaddam, Y. (2015). Innovations with smart service systems: Analytics, big data, cognitive assistance, and the internet of everything. *Communications of the Association for Information Systems, 37*, 733–752.

Doerr, J. (2018). *Measure what Matters. How Google, Bono, and the Gates Foundation rock the world with OKRs*. New York: Portfolio/Penguin.

Frank, M., Rabe, M., Koldewey, C., Dumitrescu, R., Gausemeier, J., von Widdern, H-C., et al. (Eds.) (2019). Classification-based planning of smart service portfolios. In *ISPIM Conference Proceedings: The International Society for Professional Innovation Management (ISPIM)*.

Gallus, J., & Frey, B. S. (2016). Awards: A strategic management perspective. *Strategic Management Journal, 37*(8), 1699–1714.

Geum, Y., Jeon, H., & Lee, H. (2016). Developing new smart services using integrated morphological analysis. Integration of the market-pull and technology-push approach. *Service Business, 10*(3), 531–555.

Hilton, B., Hajihashemi, B., Henderson, C. M., & Palmatier, R. W. (2020). Customer success management: The next evolution in customer management practice? *Industrial Marketing Management, 90*, 360–369. https://doi.org/10.1016/j.indmarman.2020.08.001.

Hou, W-J., Yan, X-Y., & Liu, J-X. (2020). A method for quickly establishing personas. In: *International Conference on Human-Computer Interaction*.

Irlbeck, M. (2017). Digitalisierung und Energie 4.0–Wie schaffen wir die digitale Energiewende? In O. D. Doleski (Ed.), *Herausforderung Utility 4.0. Wie sich die Energiewirtschaft im Zeitalter der Digitalisierung verändert* (pp. 135–148). Wiesbaden: Springer Viewg.

Jussen, P., Kuntz, J., Senderek, R., & Moser, B. (2019). Smart Service Engineering. *Procedia CIRP, 83*, 384–388. https://doi.org/10.1016/j.procir.2019.04.089.

Kagermann, H., Riemensperger, F., Leukert, B., & Wahlster, W. (2018). Smart Service Welt 2018. Wo stehen wir? Wohin gehen wir? In *acatech – Deutsche Akademie der Technikwissenschaften*. München. Retrieved March 30, 2020, from https://www.acatech.de/wp-content/uploads/2018/06/SSW_2018.pdf

Kampker, A., Husmann, M., Jussen, P., & Schwerdt, L. (2018). Market launch process of data-driven services for manufacturers: A qualitative guideline. In *International Conference on Exploring Service Science* (pp. 177–189).

Kauffeld, S., & Lehmann-Willenbrock, N. (2010). Sales training: effects of spaced practice on training transfer. *Journal of European Industrial Training, 34*, 23–37.

Keck, I. R., & Ross, R. J. (2014). Exploring customer specific KPI selection strategies for an adaptive time critical user interface. In *Proceedings of the 19th international conference on Intelligent User Interfaces* (pp. 341–346).

Kim, M.-J., Lim, C.-H., & Lee, C.-H. (2016). Data-driven approach to new service concept design. In T. Borangiu, M. Dragoicea, & H. Nóvoa (Eds.), *Exploring services science* (pp. 485–496). Cham: Springer.

Klein, M. M., Biehl, S. S., & Friedli, T. (2018). Barriers to smart services for manufacturing companies–an exploratory study in the capital goods industry. *Journal of Business & Industrial Marketing, 33*(6), 846–856.

Koponen, J., Julkunen, S., & Asai, A. (2019). Sales communication competence in international B2B solution selling. *Industrial Marketing Management, 82*, 238–252. https://doi.org/10.1016/j.indmarman.2019.01.009.

Lenfle, S., & Midler, C. (2009). The launch of innovative product-related services: Lessons from automotive telematics. *Research Policy, 38*(1), 156–169. https://doi.org/10.1016/j.respol.2008.10.020.

Liddy, C., Drosinis, P., Armstrong, C. D., McKellips, F., Afkham, A., & Keely, E. (2016). What are the cost savings associated with providing access to specialist care through the Champlain BASE eConsult service? A costing evaluation. *BMJ Open, 6*(6), e010920.

Martinez, B., Vilajosana, X., Monton, M., & Vilajosana, I. (2018). Supporting the IoT business value through the platformization of pilots. *IEEE Pervasive Computing, 17*(4), 29–39. https://doi.org/10.1109/MPRV.2018.2873857.

Moogk, D. R. (2012). Minimum viable product and the importance of experimentation in technology startups. *Technology Innovation Management Review, 2*, 23–26. https://doi.org/10.22215/timreview/535.

Moser, B., Leiting, T., Frank, J., Stich, V., & Rödel, L. (2019). Sales of smart services: How industrial companies can successfully sell smart services. In *2nd smart services summit* (p. 66).

Mullen, T. R., Kroustalis, C., & Meade, A. W. (2006). Assessing change in perceived organizational support due to training. In *Proceedings of 21st annual conference of the society for industrial and organizational psychology*.

Newcombe, R. (2003). From client to project stakeholders: A stakeholder mapping approach. *Construction Management and Economics, 21*(8), 841–848.

Poeppelbuss, J., & Durst, C. (2019). Smart service canvas – A tool for analyzing and designing smart product-service systems. *Procedia CIRP, 83*, 324–329. https://doi.org/10.1016/j.procir.2019.04.077.

Salesforce. (2019*). How salesforce success teams use wave and intelligence to take proactive action*. Salesforce. Retrieved November 29, 2019, from https://www.salesforce.com/video/301382/

Schuh, G., Anderl, R., Gausemeier, J., ten Hompel, M., & Wahlster, W. (2017). Industrie 4.0 maturity index. In *Managing the digital transformation of companies*. Munich: Herbert Utz.

Schuh, G., Frank, J., Jussen, P., Rix, C., & Harland, T. (2019). Monetizing industry 4.0: Design principles for subscription business in the manufacturing industry. In IEEE (Ed.), *2019 IEEE international conference on engineering, technology and innovation (ICE/ITMC)* (pp. 1–9).

Teckchandani, A. (2018). Slack: A unified communications platform to improve team collaboration. *Academy of Management Learning & Education, 17*(2).

Töytäri, P., Turunen, T., Klein, M., Eloranta, V., Biehl, S., & Rajala, R. (2018). Aligning the mindset and capabilities within a business network for successful adoption of smart services. *Journal of Product Innovation Management, 35*(5), 763–779.

Tzuo, T., & Weisert, G. (2018). *Subscribed. Why the subscription model will be your company's future - and what to do about it*. New York: Portfolio/Penguin.

Wulfsberg, Jens P.; Hintze, Wolfgang; Behrens, Bernd-Arno (2019): Methodology for the risk and reward evaluation of industrial subscription models. In Jens P. Wulfsberg, Wolfgang Hintze, Bernd-Arno Behrens (Eds.): Production at the leading edge of technology: Springer, Hamburg pp. 613–622.

Part III
Smart Service Architecture

Introduction to Smart Service Architectures

Sebastian R. Bader, Can Azkan, and Ljiljana Stojanovic

Abstract Smart services exist in the intersection of several different fields, reflecting the combined findings from various communities. Understanding the resulting impacts and dependencies requires the understanding of the core influencing factors. This chapter outlines the developments enabling smart services and explains their relations to latest developments and the relevant technology trends driving smart services.

1 Introduction

Architectures of smart services have to reflect their specific purpose. Depending on the targeted environment, different system designs and compositions are plausible and legitimate. Solutions working in a certain environment might be inappropriate for another. No single approach is feasible for all applications. Nevertheless, a generally accepted reference model helps to create a common ground, outlines best practices, and helps to recognize and communicate fundamental principles. Many consortia and organizations have therefore initiated standardization activities, resulting in an overwhelming amount of reference architectures, frameworks, interaction models, interface descriptions, etc. Due to different priorities and backgrounds, the resulting frameworks present stronger focus on cloud architectures, edge computing, cyber-physical systems, IoT interactions, business workflows, or many other aspects.

S. R. Bader (✉)
Fraunhofer IAIS, Schloss Birlinghoven, Sankt Augustin, Germany
e-mail: sebastian.bader@iais.fraunhofer.de

C. Azkan
Fraunhofer ISST, Dortmund, Germany
e-mail: can.azkan@isst.fraunhofer.de

L. Stojanovic
Fraunhofer IOSB, Karlsruhe, Germany
e-mail: ljiljana.stojanovic@iosb.fraunhofer.de

© Springer Nature Switzerland AG 2020
M. Maleshkova et al. (eds.), *Smart Service Management*,
https://doi.org/10.1007/978-3-030-58182-4_9

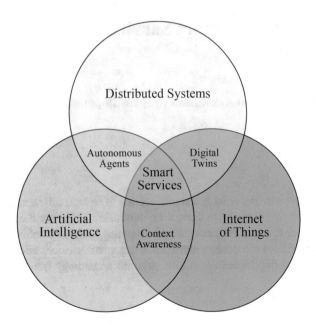

Fig. 1 Smart services use concepts from AI, distributed architectures, and Internet of Things

Smart services, in general, are at the intersection of artificial intelligence, distributed systems and have interactions with the physical world (cf. Fig. 1). A core characteristic is their ability to autonomously decide and influence their environment. This "smartness" can be reached through artificial intelligence techniques based on Machine Learning or other sophisticated patterns allowing a smart service to recognize, evaluate, and finally select between alternative actions. Independent of the implemented internal logic, a smart service requires a certain degree of context-awareness and an internal information model about its environment and the consequences of its actions.

The potential of the smart service concept, however, can only be realized if the automated decision-making is supported with the appropriate degrees of freedom. While, for instance, the question of how an autonomous driving car can reflect moral principles in the case of an accident might be more theoretical than an actually appearing challenge, a certain set of independently selectable options is a prerequisite of any smart service. Defining and assuring the boundaries of this granted decision space is however crucial in order to benefit from their speed and flexibility while at the same time ensuring a safe and secure behavior.

Smart services form data-driven workflows and scalable networks in order to fulfill their task. The ability to collaborate with each other requires standardized interfaces both for incoming and for outgoing information. Smart services are therefore data prosumers, consumer, and producer of information at the same time (Maleshkova et al. 2019). Their APIs need to follow standards and shared conventions, whereas heterogeneity in interaction patterns, protocols, or data formats is the most urgent challenge to tackle.

In the recent times, a consolidation of practices and patterns can be identified. The following sections outline this development and analyze the consequences for all involved stakeholders. The prerequisite to align and organize these developments is a reference structure as introduced in chapter *Reference Architecture Models for Smart Services*. Chapters *Business Aspects of Smart Services* to *Transport and Internet Layer* are outlining the complete architecture stack and explain the relevant features and characteristics of smart services and smart service networks.

2   Value Co-creation of Smart Services

The necessity of smart services only becomes obvious when examining upcoming business models. While data do not contain value in itself, the derivation of insights and activities imposes the game-changing nature of digital services. This leads to business models at the point where different economic actors combine their respective resources and start collaborating. Different to traditional business interactions, the data economy is data-driven and creates its value on the fly. Co-creation evolves from an optional process pattern to a fundamental aspect of conducting business.

By the end of the 20th century, most data were still used to digitalize business processes with the help of, for instance, enterprise resource planning (ERP). At that time, data were seen as a side product of the transformation from analog to digital processes. Today, data are a central component of innovative business models and data-driven products and services. The key drivers for this development are among other things increasing computing capacities, interconnected products, the possibilities of storing large amounts of data at low cost, and the use of procedures such as artificial intelligence (AI). As a result, new complex socio-technical networks—the so-called data ecosystems—are emerging in which actors interact and collaborate with each other in order to find, archive, publish, consume, or reuse data as well as to foster innovation, create value, and support new businesses such as smart services (Oliveira et al. 2019).

In such a data ecosystem, data form the key resource, are understood as independent economic goods, and are exchanged and monetized within the ecosystem (Attard et al. 2016). This data exchange offers new growth opportunities through interconnection with other participants and acts as a driver for innovative services and novel customer experiences. It illustrates a fundamental change in the digital economy: innovations are increasingly taking place in ecosystems consisting of several companies, research organizations, intermediaries in the form of electronic marketplaces, authorities, and customers (Otto et al. 2019).

The merging of partners and the formation of an ecosystem are driven by the co-creation of value from which everyone benefits. A company and even cross-sector data aggregation and subsequent data analyses provide the participants with new insights and ultimately the derivation of efficiency-enhancing activities. This, in turn, is accompanied by requirements for an ecosystem, so it can develop and successfully exist, which have an impact on the architecture of smart services. These are discussed in the following chapters.

3 Prerequisites and Underlying Innovations

The disruptive development arising from internet-based communication and data exchange are the enabling factors for the arising potential of smart services. New solutions become evident, not only enabling the interconnection of heterogeneous devices, services, and networks but also linking components and systems along whole ecosystems. Most underlying technologies have proven their maturity and have been already in use for several decades. The game-changing nature is therefore not depicted by the novelty or an innovative character of the technology stack itself.

Instead, the dissemination of digital concepts, mainly the internet-based exchange of nearly any kind of information, has reached an overwhelming acceptance level and thereby created a common infrastructure, which acts as the core enabler for all further developments. The recent progress made in the context of AI inspired many actors to merge the thereby gained autonomy and self-awareness with data exchange protocols. This change in the mindset of both implementers and deciders is equivalently responsible for the upcoming smart service systems as the progress of the underlying technologies.

The great success of the internet, mainly perceived in the form of the World Wide Web, has proven that the key building blocks for huge decentralized networks exist. The combination of these enabling technologies on the IT side, the progress in related domains, and the demand for data-driven business models drives the disruptive nature of smart service systems. While each single part is on its own neither new nor really disruptive, merging them together leads to a completely new way of organizing processes, economic collaboration, and complete business models.

Acknowledgments This work has been supported by the German Federal Ministry of Education and Research through the research project "Industrial Data Space Plus" (grant no. 01IS17031) and the EU H2020 project "BOOST4.0" (grant no. 780732).

References

Attard, J., Orlandi, F., & Auer, S. (2016). Data value networks: Enabling a new data ecosystem. In *2016 IEEE/WIC/ACM International Conference on Web Intelligence (WI)* (pp. 453–456). IEEE.

Maleshkova, M., Philipp, P., Sure-Vetter, Y., & Studer, R. (2019). Smart Web Services (SmartWS)– The Future of Services on the Web. Preprint. arXiv:1902.00910.

Oliveira, M. I. S., Lima, G. d. F. B., & Lóscio, B. F. (2019). Investigations into data ecosystems: a systematic mapping study. *Knowledge and Information Systems*, 1–42.

Otto, B., Korte, T., Azkan, C., Spiekermann, M., Lis, D., Gelhaar, J., et al. (2019). Data economy. status quo der deutschen wirtschaft & handlungsfelder in der data economy. Whitepaper.

Reference Architecture Models for Smart Services

Sebastian R. Bader, Can Azkan, and Ljiljana Stojanovic

Abstract Speaking about smart services requires a shared understanding of their capabilities and characteristics. Grouping those into views allows their structured analyses by clustering related requirements together. This chapter gives an outline of commonly used categories, represented through stacked layers. Based on international standards and well-accepted conventions, the outlined reference architecture arranges smart services from business considerations down to the physical data transmission and explains the necessary considerations from security and governance perspectives.

1 Introduction

Several works aim to create a framework for software architecture descriptions. ISO/IEC/IEEE 42010 (2011) proposes architecture descriptions derived from a list of so-called *concerns*, being addressed by several *architecture views*. An architecture view is a projection and therefore a simplification of the abstract architecture in order to describe specific topics. For instance, many reference architectures cover both interoperability and security related aspects. Though there are many inter-dependencies, describing both concerns in one view decreases readability and significantly increases complexity.

Despite the variety of models and frameworks, a number of best practices and similarities can be identified. One recurring pattern is the structuring the

S. R. Bader (✉)
Fraunhofer IAIS, Schloss Birlinghoven, Sankt Augustin, Germany
e-mail: sebastian.bader@iais.fraunhofer.de

C. Azkan
Fraunhofer ISST, Dortmund, Germany
e-mail: can.azkan@isst.fraunhofer.de

L. Stojanovic
Fraunhofer IOSB, Karlsruhe, Germany
e-mail: ljiljana.stojanovic@iosb.fraunhofer.de

© Springer Nature Switzerland AG 2020
M. Maleshkova et al. (eds.), *Smart Service Management*,
https://doi.org/10.1007/978-3-030-58182-4_10

115

architecture views in hierarchical layers, organizing components, requirements, and functionalities in separated categories. Usually, the dependencies between different layers are restricted to the direct neighbors—a pattern simplifying the relations and reducing the respective complexity.

Most modern reference architectures start with a **Business Layer**. This layer contains definitions about the independent stakeholder roles of a system or network, which might have economical or otherwise originating interests of the described systems. System administrators, developers, service suppliers, or of course customers are typical entities of a Business Layer. Their intentions, conditions, and workflows need to be specified in order to depict the requirements for the following layers. Diagrams using Business Process Modeling Notation (BPMN) or similar notation patterns may support a generally understandable provisioning of information.

The task of the **Usage Layer** is to illustrate the interactions of the previously mentioned Business Layer. Workflows are separated into interaction sequences and processes. UML-based sequence diagrams are commonly used to indicate information flows. The purpose of this layer is the definition and specifying of the basic interactions and information flow between the system's components, depicting a common set of exchange patterns.

Depending on the selected framework, the **Functional Layer** might even occur before the Usage Layer. It explains the mandatory and optional features of each component, documents inputs and outputs, and states side effects. The Functional Layer should not contain API documentation or specification, as those depend on implementation-specific decisions like used protocols or data formats. Still, it needs to further outline each functionality mentioned in the Usage Layer and define its characteristics as far as the other relevant components are effected.

The **Information Layer**—or sometimes called Data Layer—specifies the meaning of entities and processes. While at the one hand the description of data objects is supported by the provisioning of annotations and attributes through a shared terminology, the thereby defined common understanding also eases the communication between the stakeholders themselves. The resolution of synonyms and homonyms is essential to collectively reach a common goal and to prevent misunderstandings. That means that in addition to the definition of data objects, their syntax, and meaning, the Information Layer also aligns the different terminologies of the various stakeholders through a lingua franca.

Depending on the specifications of the Information Layer, the **Implementation Layer** targets the actually used technology stacks, created software artifacts, and APIs. The abovementioned interactions and functionalities need to be backed up with applicable solutions and reflected in code. The Implementation Layer is the first one containing executable code, and realizes the above outlined characteristics with actual systems.

While the Implementation Layer represents the lowest section of most reference architectures, a smart service system fundamentally relies also on network and communication functionalities. The Internet Protocol Suite (Leiner et al. 1985) depicts a standardization framework for structuring the underlying communication stack. Developers and users of smart services need to understand their relevance. For instance, security-critical services need to ensure that proper encryption mechanisms are applied and that also no unintentional uncovered metadata can compromise their usage. That implies that a requirement for protected communication at the Functional Layer can easily be prevented through insufficient configurations at the Transport Layer. Routing information or interaction frequencies can be observed even if the message content itself is properly encrypted. Observing such meta-information may be valuable already to identify communication partners or guess their intentions.

Different to the other layers, the variety of patterns and used technologies generally decreases toward the Transport and Internet Layers. One can identify an informal agreement that the Internet Protocol (IP) more and more acts as a common denominator not only for smart services but digital communication in general. The Data Link Layer and any lower functionalities are therefore less relevant for this chapter and are only briefly reflected in the following.

As already mentioned, considerations about the **security** of a smart service itself but also how it affects the whole network architecture are an indispensable necessity. Different to the previously mentioned features, security must be regarded across all layers and functions (cf. Fig. 1) and it affects distinct smart services and smart service networks at the same time. Although sometimes treated as a functional characteristic in order to reflect its importance, the implementation of security must

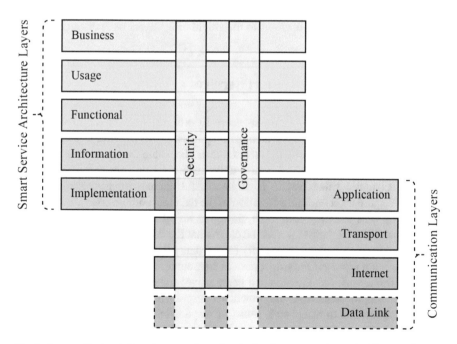

Fig. 1 Layers (horizontal) and perspectives (vertical) of smart services. Architecture Layers describe higher-level concerns and interactions while the Communication Layers contain the message exchange functionalities

not be seen as a present characteristic but as an ascending vector and a dynamically evolving goal. A sufficient security level needs to be defined individually, taking the intended environment, the purpose, and the costs of the smart service into account.

Smart services interact and impact their surrounding in many ways. Business processes and message exchange as regarded in the respective layers only represent a subset of relations and dependencies. The *Governance Perspective* covers the concerns of less obvious stakeholders, for instance, governments, external market players, or socio-political organizations. Closely related is the concept of *Compliance*. Both concepts intend to achieve the main goals in a way that all applicable laws and regulations are met and at the same time adhering to their own standards and values. Such values can contain the desire to create eco-friendly and sustainable solutions but also to prohibit discrimination of certain user groups. The distinct derivation of values is certainly a sophisticated challenge, especially as social norms change over time. The target of the Governance or Compliance Perspective is however to ensure that the legitimate rights of each stakeholder are respected and the long-term success of the service is ensured.

The general reference architecture outlines a structure to organize the requirements and features at each layer and perspective. The specific concerns and regarded topics are presented starting with the Business Layer. The selected sequence reflects the belief that smart services are created to generate a certain value of any kind, not necessarily only reflecting in monetary effects. Independent of this consideration, a discussion on smart services can start at any point of the outlined reference architecture and derive implications to the neighboring layers and perspectives.

2 Business Aspects of Smart Services

To ensure that smart services can be successfully created and offered, various factors must be fulfilled for all data ecosystem participants as well as for the overall system. The driving mechanism behind ecosystems is the value co-creation of services with data as the key resource. Consequently, data must be considered as an asset with an economic value behind it. A successful exchange and trading of data therefore require an economic evaluation of the data sets and concrete monetization approaches, thus enabling data to be viewed as an operational asset. In particular, from a business perspective, it must be clear what the data can be used for and how it supports decision-making, especially for the data provider.

As a starting point for the use of data as a resource, it is necessary to establish a strategic framework (cf. Governance Perspective) for efficient data management. The definition of roles and assignment of responsibilities for data handling is of high importance to establish a sense of responsibility for data and to enforce corresponding guidelines.

Another aspect relates data security and data protection. Data must be protected against falsification, destruction, and unauthorized disclosure. They can also contain sensitive company information. If companies are to be willing to disclose and exchange their valuable data, sovereignty over this data must be guaranteed. This can, for example, be implemented on the technical level via so-called usage policies (Eitel et al. 2019) for data, or contractually with the business partner.

In the development and provision of smart services, as outlined above, a wide variety of participants are often involved, playing different roles. In a smart service system, this includes in particular the data and service provider. For example, while a manufacturing company in its role as data provider supplies process information, the service provider analyzes this data with the help of algorithms and can return important insights to the data provider in order to optimize the production process. To ensure that the service provider can operate the service, the service provider in turn requires companies that host the IT-infrastructure (e.g., cloud-, platform-, or payment solutions), may need to obtain analytical knowledge or obtain data from other sources such as Data Marketplaces. This leads to a complex ecosystem of different cooperating actors to provide a smart service.

The following Fig. 2 shows an example of such an ecosystem. Here, a plant manufacturer provides smart services to a plant operator, who thus achieves higher

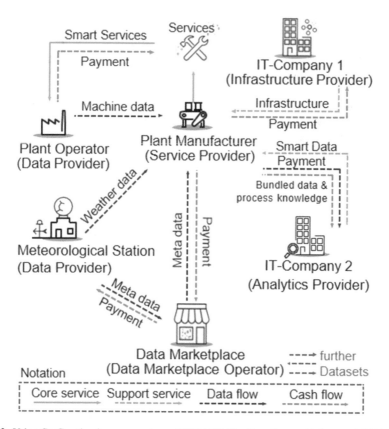

Fig. 2 Value Co-Creation in an ecosystem—DEMAND Use Case Report (Azkan et al. 2020)

machine availability and thus minimizes unplanned downtimes. To achieve this, the plant operator provides machine data and pays for the used services. The plant manufacturer however has the necessary know-how to analyze the data with the help of external data scientists (IT Company 2). The provision of the service takes place via Analytics-Dashboard. To do so, an additional IT company is integrated, which provides the necessary cloud infrastructure. Another important factor in this ecosystem is the data marketplace. The engineers of the plant manufacturer know precisely that they can expand or even improve the offered smart services with additional data sets such as weather data. To this end, a targeted search for such data sets over meta data is carried out on data marketplaces. After finding suitable data, they are sent directly from the meteorologist to the plant manufacturer. The figure clearly shows that everyone in such an ecosystem benefits from cross-company data exchange. This is done either through services received or through payment for the provision of data.

However, there are several **Concerns and Requirements** in such service networks that need to be addressed. In a study conducted by the Institute of German Economy, companies were asked what they consider to be the biggest obstacles for the implementation of data-driven products or services (Azkan et al. 2020). More than every second company stated that they do not implement data-driven offerings due to the unclear benefits. Many companies also have difficulties developing a long-term data strategy (49.5%) and generating new ideas for digital offerings (41.8%). A lack of technical experts is an obstacle for 54% of the companies surveyed.

Challenges are especially to convince customers to pass on their data and to motivate them to exchange it. To do this, it is elementary that the security of the data is guaranteed and that the use of the data does not extend the agreed purposes. The decisive factor here is that the customer (data sovereign) agrees to the appropriate use of his data. Furthermore, the rights of use or ownership of data must be explicitly clarified. For this purpose, individual contractual regulations must be created to eliminate ambiguities. The question of data rights is essential for the sale of data and subsequent data trading, explicitly regulating who may do what with which data objects. If several customers and partners join the data ecosystem, it is also possible to achieve network effects. Data from several sources and ideally across different stages of the value chain lead to more detailed statements about the behavior of machines and plants and with different environmental conditions. Thus, an even more dense knowledge can be created and services can be continuously improved, so that in the end the customers benefit once again from their involvement in the overall system. Further information about the challenges and potential of data-driven networks can be found, for instance, in the BDVA Strategic Research and Innovation Agenda (Big Data Value Association 2017).

3 Usage Aspects of Smart Services

After identifying the stakeholders and necessary capabilities of the business parties, the interactions and roles need to be defined. The Usage Layer serves as a bridge between actors and technical roles. Clients and suppliers are mapped to system operators, users of smart services, or provider of data. While the former are determined by their interests, the latter contain attributes, capabilities, and permissions.

Business interactions driven by the exchange of resources, money, and value are translated into interaction workflows and processes. Relations between organizations and legal entities need to be represented through information flows between systems and networks. Business process models are replaced by sequence diagrams and vice versa.

The Usage Layer is therefore an indispensable bridge between the general idea about how to create value and which components and interactions are required to realize that. Detailed workflows and sequence processes depict the various involved components, both smart services and human actors, and specify the mutual dependencies. Thereby, the Usage Layer clarifies the responsibilities and enables the derivation of technical requirements.

A simple example for analyses performed at this layer is the onboarding of a new organization in a smart service network. The new entity might be registered, provided with a digital identity, and announced to the existing members. Already in this simple example, an identity provider, an exchangeable identity proof, and a notification mechanism can be derived, which then need to be reflected through functional definitions. The information flow needs to be specified and declared to all involved parties. More information about usage-related aspects can be found in the Usage View of Asset Administration Shell (Braune et al. 2019).

4 Functional Aspects of Smart Services

The core capabilities of smart services, in particular their APIs and interfaces, the behavior, delivered quality, and other characteristics affect the perceived value of a smart service. At the core are the technical preconditions required to execute a smart service. These *functional* features include the necessary inputs, input formats, the activation sequence, and other dependencies required to interact with the smart service. Furthermore, the capabilities to discover, compose, orchestrate, and deploy a service instance are depicted.

In addition to the preparation steps, the functional aspects of a smart service also include a documentation of the executed transformation and the service's output in terms of interactions with the environment and the produced data. The capabilities to interact with other parts of the network need to be defined and the life-cycle stages specified.

However, even though the description of the core functional features allows the understanding on how to interact with a smart service but does not explain whether or not the offered service is actually appropriate in the given situation. *Non-functional* requirements are crucial information to enable a well-founded decision in this regard. Most importantly the Quality of Service and the price per interaction determine the suitability of a distinct offer to actually solve a task. Other categories of non-functional requirements include the maintainability or usability of systems but also the reliability or availability of smart services. As those aspects are also framed by the Security and Governance Perspectives, it is obvious that these sections do actively affect each other and cannot be treated independently.

Another category of relevant features is depicted by the *behavioral* characteristics of smart services. This category discusses the operations and states which can be reached. Especially as smart service comprises a certain autonomy and the ability to independently adjust their decision-making, their behavior is not strictly determined anymore. In particular, this implies that definite predictions of their behavior are not possible. Still, in order to ensure safe executions, the boundaries of their operation space need to be described. This information allows other components to prepare for effects in this given limits. For instance, a control unit for an electric power grid might dynamically adjust its voltage output autonomously and self-controlled but needs to respect the safety norms for electronic devices. The IoT-Architecture description (Bassi et al. 2013) offers more information about the Functional Layers.

All these features and capabilities need to be described in ways which both human and other smart services can read and process. The unambiguous and logically consistent provisioning of these descriptions requires extensive data models and vocabularies. While these definitions are crucial for the composition, orchestration, and therefore operation of smart service networks, they are usually treated in the next section, the Information Layer.

5   Data Formats and Semantics of Smart Services

Smart services are the actuators in an environment defined by digital information. The ability to request, transform, analyze, and forward data objects is at their core. The challenges at this point can mainly be grouped into the two categories of *syntactic* and *semantic* heterogeneity. While humans are usually capable to guess the meaning of unknown data based on the delivered context or their personal experience, Smart services require formal methods and explicit world models. Both are hard to accomplish and require elaborate techniques and significant additional efforts.

Syntactic heterogeneity frames the variety of data formats and provisioning methods. Information is stored in closed silos and proprietary formats, exchanged through customized interfaces and implicit and intransparent dependencies. Tackling this issue, an informal movement toward JSON-based data exchange can be recognized which to some degree reduces this hurdle. While other data formats (for instance, XML or relational data sets) certainly have their justification and will not be abolished, the adoption of JSON imposes reduced efforts and requirements for developers, technology stacks, and maintainers.

Recognizing and communicating semantic meaning of data entities is another significant challenge. Smart services provide their full potential in areas where previously unexpected information appears and needs to be processed. Controlled vocabularies are a lightweight approach to accomplish a shared understanding, usually applied in distinct domains or industries. Taxonomies add further hierarchical structures in the form of part-of or subclass relations add further knowledge. Successful examples are eCl@ss[1] and the IEC Common Data Dictionary (IEC 61360 2019) for domain-specific identifiers.

Even more explicit formalizations and machine-interpretable logic are provided by ontologies and logically grounded vocabularies. The Semantic Web Stack, based on the graph-based Resource Description Format (RDF), proposes a formal ecosystem of technologies, standards, and tools to represent information in both human and machine-readable manners. Linked Data extends this further and allows the distributed provisioning of RDF data using the established practices of the web (Bizer et al. 2011). This enables the direct linking to a publicly available, distributed knowledge graph using web standards, called the Linked Open Data Cloud. Another benefit of the formal definitions of RDF and Linked Data is the usage of upper-level ontologies. These well-known and widespread dictionaries serve as logical anchors for references and more fine-grained derivations. Smart services can use the thereby supplied terms and attributes to directly express meaning. For instance, an attribute referring to the Dublin Core property "creator"[2] unambiguously tells the data consumer who the originator of a certain data resource is.

A huge amount of semantic description languages for interfaces and federated systems has been proposed already. The SOAP technology stack and its service description language WSDL, for instance, have been extended with the WSMO and WSMO-Light ontologies (Domingue et al. 2005). OWL-S is a similar OWL-based ontology for semantic descriptions of interfaces and especially for smart services. Furthermore, description languages for REST-APIs have recently gained popularity, most prominently OpenAPI, previously named "Swagger".[3] Similar, API Blueprint[4] and RAML[5] but also the RDF-based Hydra (Lanthaler and Gütl 2013) vocabulary illustrate the great need to unambiguously describe remote interfaces in both human and machine-readable manners. A detailed information

---

[1] https://www.eclass.eu.

[2] See http://purl.org/dc/elements/1.1/creator.

[3] https://swagger.io/docs/specification/about/.

[4] https://apiblueprint.org.

[5] https://raml.org/.

layer is outlined in the Reference Architecture Model of the International Data Space (Otto et al. 2019).

6 Implementation Aspects of Smart Services

The Implementation Layer contains the technology-specific considerations of a smart service. The accessible remote interfaces and APIs are specified and their concrete instantiations designed. This layer serves as the bridge between the upper-level sections used for describing the smart service and smart service networks and the communication-specific characteristics. According to Fig. 1, this layer fairly corresponds to the Application Layer of the Internet Protocol Suite. The interactions with resources, operations, and interactions are translated into executable code, relying on the respective functionalities provided by the network layers below.

The Implementation Layer thereby abstracts the actual implementation logic for the description and presentations at the Information Layer. Relevant interaction patterns in smart service networks include request/response and publish/subscribe. While the former is suitable for point-to-point connections where a distinct client initiates the communication and asks for data, the latter pattern has its strengths in one to many communications. In a publish/subscribe scenario, both the provider and consumer of data interact with an internet server, which receives and then further publishes them based on prior subscriptions.

Both patterns support a loose coupling of components over internet networks. The thereby defined distinct roles and responsibilities ease the integration of new components and actors and allow the network to grow dynamically. Especially for the request/response pattern, the further restrictions imposed by the Representational State Transfer (REST) are currently considered as the de facto standard for resource-oriented systems on the web. The clear interaction model and the deep integration with HTTP reduce complexity both for the client and the server.

In addition, also bidirectional point-to-point interaction is necessary in certain scenarios. WebSockets create a virtual tunnel on top of HTTP, enabling the exchange of data from both ends. Relying on HTTP offers easier integrations with current networks and firewalls as those are typically well-configured for HTTP connections. Still, with the upcoming of more and more resource-restricted devices equipped with internet connections, a significant demand for lightweight and resource conserving protocols appeared. While modern web browsers can cope with the requirements of HTTP-based communication, machine to machine—or smart service to smart service—scenarios do often not rely on the thereby created overhead. Driven also through the Internet of Things (IoT) development, the Constraint Application Protocol (CoAP) presents a downsized alternative for request/response interactions. The MQ Telemetry Transport (MQTT) protocol can similarly serve for publishing and subscribing to messages with only a limited network bandwidth.

In contrast to this relatively simple protocols, OPC UA outlines a complete technology stack highly integrated for industrial manufacturing facilities. The goal of OPC UA is not to replace existing protocols, but rather to support transmission of information for new services in Industrie 4.0. OPC UA is a client/server protocol based on TCP/IP that defines service calls for the interaction with a server-side information model over the network. Recently, the OPC UA specification has been extended for communication based on the publish/subscribe communication paradigm. Two options are supported: (1) broker-based message distribution according to the IEC standards AMQP and MQTT and (2) a custom UDP-based distribution protocol, called UADP, based on the multicast mechanisms of the IP standards. Open62541[6] is the world's first open-source implementation of OPC UA publish/subscribe and demonstrated its real-time capability in combination with Time Sensitive Networking (TSN).

A deep discussion on the Implementation Layer and its effects and requirements is outlined in the Industrial Internet Connectivity Guide (Joshi et al. 2018).

7 Transport and Internet Layer

One reason for the success of the internet as the de facto standard for today's digital communication is certainly the acceptance and adaption of a compact set of transport protocols. TCP and UDP constitute the common denominator for all distributed architectures, in particular for smart services. The remarkable success of these two protocols consolidates the approaches of the previously mentioned protocols and establishes the common infrastructure.

That infrastructure is based on the IP network protocol. Currently, the address restrictions of IPv4 led to the introduction of IPv6. Even though the thereby defined address space is drastically larger than for IPv4, the transition happens significantly slower than expected. Network operators and other infrastructure provider have not updated their routers in the originally predicted speed. In addition, a high number of legacy systems is still in place and can only be replaced gradually. Both developments slow down the conversion to IPv6, requiring a set of intermediate approaches.

Underlying technologies ensuring the physical transportation of signals are usually not in the focus of smart service stakeholders anymore. Ethernet or WiFi are examples of mature and proven technologies providing the foundation for the whole digital communication. Their capabilities are well understood and their implementation straightforward.

That does not imply however that developments at those points do not impact smart services. For instance, the transition from 4G to 5G wireless communication techniques is widely regarded as a breakthrough affecting all layers above. The latency, bandwidth, and transportation speed promises disrupt current application scenarios and thereby create completely new business models. Still, while such

---

[6]www.open62541.org.

developments affect the perceived value for smart service users, the functional interactions are expected to stay nearly the same. The transition costs and efforts for providers and consumers are therefore manageable, due to the integrative nature of the Transport and Network Layers.

8 Security of Smart Services

Security is often treated as a necessary but tedious task, an additional feature with significant effort but limited added value. This results in a set of uncoordinated approaches instead of a comprehensive security strategy. While security by design has drawn significant attention in the recent discussions, the lack of even basic mechanisms in current implementations emphasizes the need for further progress here. State-of-the-art encryption or reliable update functionalities are mandatory for each and every smart service and must be part of the basic toolbox of any smart service creator.

One reason for the unsatisfactory state of current implementations is also the complexity of the topic. In the following, six categories are distinguished to better structure discussions, where each category has its own focus and requirements. *Privacy* frames all topics intended to conceal and protect data and to prohibit its unintended distribution. The *reliability* of smart services explains which measures are in place in order to achieve its general functionality over time. *Resilience* characteristics the ability of smart services to withstand attacks and to prohibit penetrations. *Security* as used in the following is related to IT and communication protection and includes, for instance, encryption techniques.

Lower-level priority or even ignored are often the implications of smart services into the physical world. As the influence of smart services further increases, the boundaries between the digital and physical world decline. *Safety*—or the ability of a service to prevent harming humans, equipment, or any other entity in its environment—becomes a relevant topic. Smart services need to understand the context they are deployed in and which consequences their actions may have. Without that, their ability to autonomously decide and act involves an unacceptable risk for their surrounding. While the legal responsibilities have not yet been sufficiently understood or determined, all involved stakeholders of smart service already need to prepare themselves for the disruptive nature of this development.

While most other functionalities and features can be implemented and verified in objective ways, this is fundamentally different for security and related aspects. A certain message format can be recognized or not, a payment process can be executed or not, or a smart service can deliver its data or not. In contrast to that, a designer of a smart service can never know in advance if the amount of protection is sufficient. The only reliable information flow appears after an intrusion or otherwise corrupted system was identified. In any other situation, the obvious uncertainty whether or not a certain security level is sufficient has to be managed.

Therefore, it is impossible to determine whether a system's security mechanisms are sufficient. Furthermore, security cannot be measured objectively but has to be treated as a moving target. Depending on the expected environment, the trade-off between protection, cost, and required usage convenience has to be solved. A perfectly secured service is easily achieved by blocking any interaction. The most convenient option does not restrict any communication with its users. And the cheapest solution in terms of implementation and interaction costs disregards security at all. Obviously, neither of these alternatives is a reasonable solution.

The provider or operator of a smart service should therefore try to prioritize security aspects by answering the question: "Given that a certain incident appeared, how much will this effect the perceived value of my target group?" If a restart of the smart service restores already to a not corrupted state, the protection against intrusion might be less important. If however personal or customer data can be leaked, the placed protections must be significantly improved.

Independent from the context of a certain smart service, a basic set of guidelines can be formulated:

- State-of-the-art encryption and authentication mechanism
- Constant and promptly updates of all externally accessible components
- Provide recovering strategies for corrupted states or intrusions
- Revocation mechanisms for lost identities
- Notification strategies for affected Data Owners

Using up-to-date communication encryption is certainly without question. In case of long-living systems however, the rapidly changing capabilities and computing powers can significantly impact the appearing protection level. The only reliable strategy to sufficiently secure interconnected services is therefore by regularly supplied updates. Especially functionalities located close to or directly interacting with the open networks must be treated with high priority.

As already stated, security is not absolute but always determined by the trade-off between potential risks, costs, and usage restrictions. Consequently, no system is completely invulnerable, arising the need for adjusted response strategies. In case of a detected intrusion or otherwise misbehaving smart service, a further intrusion must be prohibited and ongoing damage limited. A reset to a non-corrupted backup might be already sufficient for state-less smart services. State-full services require more elaborate strategies as even revocation of most parts might leave malicious code untouched. Appropriate activities highly depend on the service architecture and the used technologies, therefore a generally valid process is not possible.

In any case, the smart service operator must follow a transparent notification strategy toward its stakeholders, especially the ones which data has been affected. The revocation of credentials, tokens, or any kind of digital identity has the highest priority to prevent a further distribution. In addition, the fast provisioning of information to affected parties is the only way to regain trust and to enable them to limit the entailed consequences. The unavoidable loss of reputation can only be countered with quick reactions and a well-organized communication strategy. The details of the reaction strategy are depicted in the Governance Perspective.

Further starting points for security guidance are provided in NIST Special
Publication 800-82 (Stouffer et al. 2011), ISO/IEC 27001 (2013) and ISA/IEC
62443 (2005).

9   Governance and Compliance

Smart services operate and interact with their environment. Their activities therefore
have to be evaluated regarding the surrounding context. While the main considerations at creating smart services usually focus on technical features and the attempt
to provide technical solutions to the occurring requirements, Governance demands
a wider perspective. Indirectly involved stakeholders, for instance, the government
with legislative regulations or society as a whole, do impose relevant factors.

Especially in the data economy, major questions are still unanswered. The most
obvious difference to traditional business interactions is certainly the ownership on
digital information and products. Copyright and licenses do support the enforcement
of financial interests for certain scenarios. Still, the immanent nature of the data
economy is depicted by the fact that copying and sharing of information are cheap
while their creation is expensive. The production cost might be determined by the
invested money but also by the amount of other resources needed to create a piece
of information. The perceived value, and thereby the price, is usually determined
by totally different factors and therefore only indirectly affected by the original
production costs.

This results in a demand for new concepts and principles how digital services
and information need to be treated. For person-related data, the European General
Data Protection Regulation (GDPR) imposes one framework to define and control
the usage and dissemination of data. However, GDPR regulations are in general not
applicable for other types of sensitive data in the context of business-to-business
interactions. One approach targeting this challenge is the introduction of *Data
Sovereignty*, declaring that one party in an ecosystem has a principal interest and
right on a certain data resource. The so-called *Data Sovereign* is the only entity
allowed to formulate usage restrictions and thereby control the dissemination of
its resource. Examples for such restrictions might be the access restriction to
third parties, the implementation of certain data protection mechanisms, or also
reimbursing the Data Sovereign for using the resource.

The collaborating parties in such ecosystems might acknowledge the Data
Sovereign's right, adjust their processes accordingly, and provide trustworthy proofs
to the Data Sovereign. This process affects all architecture layers from top to
bottom. While the general agreement and its details must be formulated as textual—
and only thereby legally binding—contracts and approved in the Business Layer,
the respective negotiations (Usage Layer), capabilities (Functional Layer), and
the shared understanding of the included restrictions (Information Layer) need to
be transferred and imported (Implementation Layer). In case of smart services,
these contracts need to be machine-readable and, in cases autonomous decision-

making is effected, also be enforceable. These requirements add significantly more logical refinements to usage restrictions, as the necessary formalization needs to be evaluated in a setting where information is generally uncertain, incomplete, and not necessarily reliable. While human actors have proven their ability to manage such obstacles all the time, the capabilities of AI systems have not yet reached this level.

In addition to the mentioned challenge of enforcing interest in the usage of a digital resource, the potential of moving decision-making capabilities, and thereby responsibilities, from human participants to smart service contains a huge potential for conflicts. While the vision of self-aware acting robots is certainly still more a topic of science fiction, the liability issue directly affects all involved parties in the context of smart services. The developers, operators, and consumers of smart service systems need to realize and then agree on the effects the smart service might have. It is noteworthy that these questions are still not answered sufficiently and require a significant progress in the current state of legal, ethical and social discussions. Nevertheless, they need to be regarded already for a successful system.

A clear understanding of Governance and its intended implementation however is not primarily relevant when the smart service fulfills its tasks in the intended manner but especially at the occurrence of crises and other unexpected incidents. Organizations need to understand their stakeholder's interest and act accordingly. Studies show that putting whose interests above the own in times of crises—independently whether who was actually responsible for the incident—is beneficial in the mid to long run (Coombs 2007) (cf. Sect. 8). Following this approach, regarding reputation as a collectable good (Fombrun et al. 2004), allows its comprehensive management over all affected aspects. Smart services and smart service operators with higher reputation accounts will therefore recover faster. The reputation shift is however not determined by an absolute scale but by the explicit or implicit expectations of the stakeholders. If an organization manages to surpass the expected level, even in times of preventable crisis, the overall reputation score can even increase. This supports the relevance of a comprehensive understanding of the applied values and emphasizes the potential a well-designed governance strategy has.

Acknowledgments This work has been supported by the German Federal Ministry of Education and Research through the research project "Industrial Data Space Plus" (grant no. 01IS17031) and the EU H2020 project "BOOST4.0" (grant no. 780732).

References

Azkan, C., Iggena, L., Meisel, L., Spiekermann, M., Korte, T., & Otto, B. (2020). Perspektiven der Datenwirtschaft. Wirkmechanismen und Wertschöpfung in Datenökosystemen. Whitepaper.

Bassi, A., Bauer, M., Fiedler, M., Kramp, T., Kranenburg, R. v., Lange, S., et al. (2013). *Enabling things to talk: Designing IoT solutions with the IoT architectural reference model.* SpringerOpen. Heidelberg: Springer.

Big Data Value Association. (2017). European Big Data Value Strategic Research and Innovation Agenda. Available online: http://www.bdva.eu/SRIA (accessed 23.09.2018).

Bizer, C., Heath, T., & Berners-Lee, T. (2011). Linked Data: The Story so far, *in* Semantic Services, Interoperability and Web Applications: Emerging Concepts, pp. 205–227. IGI Global.

Braune, A., Diedrich, C., Grüner, S., Hüttemann, G., Klein, M., Legat, C., et al. (2019). Usage View of the Asset Administration Shell. Discussion Paper, accessible at https://www.plattform-i40.de/PI40/Redaktion/DE/Downloads/Publikation/2019-usage-view-asset-administration-shell.html.

Coombs, W. T. (2007). Protecting organization reputations during a crisis: the development and application of situational crisis communication theory. *Corporate Reputation Review, 10*(3), 163–176.

Domingue, J., Roman, D., & Stollberg, M. (2005). Web Service Modeling Ontology (WSMO)-An Ontology for Semantic Web Services.

Eitel, A., Jung, C., Kühnle, C., Bruckner, F., Brost, G., Birnstill, P. (2019). Usage Control in the IDS. Whitepaper, accessible at https://www.internationaldataspaces.org/wp-content/uploads/2019/11/Usage-Control-in-IDS-V2.0_final.pdf.

Fombrun, C. J., Van Riel, C. B., & Van Riel, C. (2004). *Fame & fortune: How successful companies build winning reputations*. Ft Press.

IEC 61360. (2019). Security for industrial automation and control systems. ISA/IEC Standard, International Electrotechnical Commission, https://webstore.iec.ch/publication/19714.

ISA/IEC 62443. (2005). Standard data element types with associated classification scheme for electric components. IEC Standard, https://webstore.iec.ch/publication/7029.

ISO/IEC 27001. (2013). Information technology – security techniques – information security management systems – requirements. ISO/IEC Standard, http://www.iso.org/iso/home/standards/management-standards/iso27001.htm.

ISO/IEC/IEEE 42010. (2011). Systems and software engineering - architecture description. Standard, International Organization for Standardization (ISO), https://www.iso.org/standard/50508.html.

Joshi, R., Mellor, S., & Didier, P. (2018). The industrial internet of things volume G5: connectivity framework. Industrial Internet Consortium.

Lanthaler, M., & Gütl, C. (2013). Hydra: A vocabulary for hypermedia-driven web APIs. *LDOW, 996*.

Leiner, B., Cole, R., Postel, J., & Mills, D. (1985). The DARPA internet protocol suite. *IEEE Communications Magazine, 23*(3), 29–34.

Otto, B., Lohmann, S., Auer, S., Brost, G., Cirullies, J., Eitel, A. (2019). IDS Reference Architecture Model. *IDSA* . Version 3.0, available at https://www.internationaldataspaces.org/ressource-hub/publications-ids/.

Stouffer, K., Falco, J., & Scarfone, K. (2011). Guide to industrial control systems (ICS) security. *NIST Special Publication, 800*(82), 16–16.

Reference Architecture Models for Smart Service Networks

Sebastian R. Bader and Ljiljana Stojanovic

Abstract The trend towards smart services but also edge, fog, and cloud services and the countless related developments and technologies have created the demand for frameworks ordering and relating the various approaches into consistent ecosystems. Several initiatives from both industry and academia have been formed, resulting in a significant set of different reference frameworks and architecture models. The developer of smart services needs to understand their strengths and underlying intentions to select the most appropriate for each use case. This chapter explains the most relevant ones for smart services, outlines their focus, and puts them into context.

1 Introduction

Various organizations have published IoT reference architectures, focusing on different aspects and environments. However, most share a set of implicit assumptions and overlaps. As mentioned, the Internet Layer can be regarded as the common denominator, relying on IP-based data exchange. The differences on the layers above result—among others—through the influences from different industries, disciplines, challenges, or technologies. Consequently, a comprehensive and unified picture of a system architecture is nearly impossible. This chapter briefly introduces the major reference architectures and outlines common propositions but also identifies the key distinctions respectively.

S. R. Bader (✉)
Fraunhofer IAIS, Schloss Birlinghoven, Sankt Augustin, Germany
e-mail: sebastian.bader@iais.fraunhofer.de

L. Stojanovic
Fraunhofer IOSB, Karlsruhe, Germany
e-mail: ljiljana.stojanovic@iosb.fraunhofer.de

2 Industrial Internet Reference Architecture

The Industrial Internet Reference Architecture (IIRA) published by the Industrial Internet Consortium (IIC) aims for a comprehensive model of the industrial internet, independent of specific domains and industries. The wide scope results in a broad coverage of topics whereas concrete implementation guidelines are only partly provided. The main IIRA categorization is based on ISO/IEC 42010, introducing the four viewpoints Business, Usage, Functional and Implementation. Nevertheless, IIRA lacks an explicit set of addressed concerns. While major concerns can be extracted by analyzing the viewpoint descriptions, a specific allocation of concerns to viewpoints is not given. This results in a certain vagueness of requirements for implementations. Therefore, various architectures also describing smart services can be compliant to IIRA requirements while interoperability or data exchange is still not possible out of the box as a matter of heterogeneous implemented patterns.

IIRA groups its guidelines related to interoperability and data exchange in the Functional Viewpoint, further separated into multiple domains. While the main aspects of IIoT are discussed as parts of the Functional Viewpoint, key aspects like connectivity Joshi et al. (2018) and security Mellor et al. (2016) are discussed in separate documents.

3 International Data Spaces

The International Data Spaces (IDS) focuses on secure and trustworthy data exchange patterns on a data-centric level. The IDS Reference Architecture Model (IDS-RAM) consists of five layers to establish interoperability and three crosscutting perspectives for reaching its main target, namely to ensure end-to-end data sovereignty of the data owner Otto et al. (2019). The syntactic interoperability is accomplished by the IDS Connectors as a core gateway to the IDS, with standardized interfaces and exchange protocols.

The Viewpoints of the IIRA map only to a limited extent to the IDS Layer model. The scope of the IDS leads to a stronger focus on configuration, modeling and integration aspects mainly regarded from a system integration point of view. The IIRA scope includes more stakeholders resulting in several 'Viewpoints'. In general, the aspects of IDS Reference Architecture are mentioned in the IIRA's Functional Viewpoint. The layers and perspectives of the IDS-RAM can—to some extent—be mapped to the IIRA domains of the mentioned Functional Viewpoint.

4 FIWARE

The FIWARE Foundation promotes an open-source software stack to accomplish interoperability also beyond the originally regarded IoT use cases. The Next Generation Service Interface (NGSI) is a standardized Web API for the IoT restricted to RESTful interactions. Any IoT protocol can be connected by suitable agents or wrappers, providing data towards the Orion Context Broker as the intermediary component for data and command transformation and translation. The currently specified NGSI-LD Fonseca et al. (2018) provides a semantically annotated JSON syntax for context modeling and guidelines to interact with the respective resources.

The FIWARE reference architecture provides documentation for developers and system architects on cloud computing and how big data possibly enhances IIoT architectures on the higher network levels instead of regarding physical assets where concepts from for example, RAMI4.0 or IIRA are more detailed. In addition to HTTP serving as the suggested protocol with specified bindings FIWARE defines protocol-agnostic methods and context representations.

5 Web of Things

The internet and in particular the World Wide Web offers already a well understood and widely accepted infrastructure to exchange data. Well-established web technologies like URIs, HTTP and hyperlinks have proven to allow easy and reliable communication mechanisms in a decentralized manner. Cloud services and on demand solutions offer fast and flexible deployment of applications, a strict requirement for a smart factory. The Semantic Web further add meaning to data objects and further reduce the integration effort. However, the so-called Web of Things does neither specify the interaction patterns of the regraded things nor does it model the intended relationship with the physical world.

The Web of Things (WoT) is an initiative of the W3C to model and outline common aspects of physical assets and represent them in the web. An elaborate vocabulary and an interaction model demonstrate how independent entities can be described, operated, and orchestrated using the current practices and conventions of web connections. The regarded requirements are technology-oriented and provide system architects and developers with implementable guidelines based on the currently used technologies.

6 Reference Architecture Model Industry 4.0

The Reference Architecture Model Industrie 4.0 (RAMI4.0) is a three-dimensional model designed primarily for applications in the manufacturing industry DIN SPEC

91345 (2016). One axis represents the life cycle stages of an asset according to IEC 62890. The asset themselves are modeled in the hierarchy levels which extend the automation pyramid with products and connected worlds to fulfill the I4.0 requirements. The technical aspects are modeled using six layers covering the physical assets and their integration in the digital world, communication, information, functions and the business aspects.

RAMI4.0 provides a framework for the interoperability in the manufacturing domain. The focus is on the integration of physical assets from the shop floor with services and applications in the office floor. It serves as a strategic framework highlighting relevant aspects and outlining a common understanding on requirements, dependencies and relations. The model does not propose detailed technical implementation patterns but outlines according standards for the manufacturing domain, which have been extracted and analyzed in detail by Grangel-González et al. (2017). The core specification is published as DIN SPEC 91345 and extended towards Linked Data practices by Bader and Maleshkova (2019).

7 Big Data Value Strategic Research and Innovation Agenda

The Big Data Value Association (BDVA) provides frameworks and tools for data-driven applications in the context of a European Big Data initiative. As part of the Strategic Research and Innovation Agenda Big Data Value Association (2017), a reference architecture for big data applications has been published.

The big data scope of BDVA leads to a focus on data provisioning, processing and hosting related concerns. Interoperability, security or composition are only mentioned to a limited extend. The BDVA reference model provides a clear and comprehensive overview of concerns at the intersection of big data and cloud platforms. IIoT is one use case among others but not the major focus. In contrast to the other concerns, BDVA specifically distinguishes between static and dynamic data. A comparable view is neither part of RAMI4.0 nor IIRA, even though both discuss the impacts of data streams and stream processing. BDVA goes further and analyzes current gaps and challenges for dynamic data and formulates a list of necessary advancements.

Finally, BDVA recognized the importance of the IDS and identified key actions that need to be taken to realize of a pan-European data sharing space Big Data Value Association (2019). In contrast to existing implementations which serve the needs of a few entities or is confined to just one industry, this space could allow different vertical, cross-sectoral, personal and industrial data spaces to interoperate, offering broader services and experimentation opportunities to all stakeholders, while adhering to European values.

8 Internet of Things-Architecture IoT-A

The EU flagship project 'Internet of Things-Architecture' (IoT-A) delivered an unified vision and guidance for transforming existing isolated solutions into an integrated IoT Bassi et al. (2013). The outlined Architecture Reference Model presents an extensive list of requirements on many aspects of IoT architectures, allowing a structured categorization of technologies, protocols and best practices according to the defined layers and perspectives. With its focus on achieving interoperability in means of communication and information exchange, the IoT-A Architecture Reference Model serves as major step towards internet-based technical integration of heterogeneous systems.

The IoT-A project aims to pave the way for a common understanding of IoT architectures. The IoT Reference Architecture Model (IoT ARM) provides generic terms and relations for the IoT but also beyond. Abstract concepts, such as *Physical Entities*, *Service* or *Users* provide the foundation for a consistent description of IoT architectures. An additional significant contribution of IoT-A is their list of reference requirements IoT-A (2016).

Acknowledgments This work has been supported by the German Federal Ministry of Education and Research through the research project "Industrial Data Space Plus" (grant no. 01IS17031) and the EU H2020 project "BOOST4.0" (grant no. 780732).

References

Bader, S. R., & Maleshkova, M. (2019). The semantic asset administration shell. In: *International Conference on Semantic Systems* (pp. 159–174). Berlin: Springer.

Bassi, A., Bauer, M., Fiedler, M., Kramp, T., Kranenburg, R. V., Lange, S. et al. (2013). *Enabling things to talk: Designing IoT solutions with the IoT architectural reference model.* SpringerOpen. Heidelberg: Springer.

Big Data Value Association. (2019). Towards a European Data Sharing Space: Enabling data exchange and unlocking AI potential. BDVA Position Paper.

Big Data Value Association. (2017). European big data value strategic research and innovation agenda. Retrieved September, 2018 from http://www.bdva.eu/SRIA

DIN SPEC 91345. (2016). Reference architecture model industrie 4.0. Deutsches Institut für Normung.

Fonseca, J., Guillemin, P., Bauer, M., Frost, L., Privat, G., et al. (2018). *Context information management (CIM); NGSI-LD API.* https://portal.etsi.org/webapp/WorkProgram/Report_WorkItem.asp?wki_id=54473

Grangel-González, I., Baptista, P., Halilaj, L., Lohmann, S., Vidal, M.-E., Mader, C., et al. (2017). The industry 4.0 standards landscape from a semantic integration perspective. In *2017 22nd IEEE International Conference on Emerging Technologies and Factory Automation (ETFA)* (pp. 1–8). Piscataway, NJ: IEEE.

IoT-A. (2016). IoT-A unified requirements list. Retrieved september 25, 2018 from https://web.archive.org/web/20160322053934/http://www.iot-a.eu/public/requirements

Joshi, R., Mellor, S., & Didier, P. (2018). *The industrial Internet of Things volume G5: Connectivity framework.* Needham, MA: Industrial Internet Consortium.

Mellor, S., Buchheit, M., LeBlanc, J., Schrecker, S., Soroush, H., Molina, J., et al. (2016). *Industrial Internet of Things volume G4: Security framework*, Technical report. Needham, MA: Industrial Internet Consortium.

Otto, B., Lohmann, S., Auer, S., Brost, G., Cirullies, J., Eitel, A., et al. (2019). IDS Reference Architecture Model, IDSA . Version 3.0, from https://www.internationaldataspaces.org/ressource-hub/publications-ids/

Smart Services in the Physical World: Digital Twins

Ljiljana Stojanovic and Sebastian R. Bader

Abstract Comprehensive, independently operating digital representations of physical assets, provisioned and manipulated through standardized interaction patterns, dissolve between the tangible and virtual world. Real-world developments are reflected in digital models and vice versa. The concept of digital twins combines these facets to integrated entities, specifying the description, appearance, and behavior of real-world entities in virtual models. This chapter explains how smart services enact as digital twins but also how they interact in flexible, loosely coupled networks.

1 Introduction

Smart services themselves denote virtual services and therefore focus on digital interactions and functionality. However, the ongoing discussions and progress made in the IoT domain and cyber-physical systems expresses the demand for advanced computing capabilities close to the physical objects. While originally targeting simulations for degradation analysis, the terminology of digital twins has become a common reference to any digital representation of real-world objects. While originally Glaessgen and Stargel (2012) formulated requirements for digital twins regarding NASA and US Air Force vehicles. Their focus was to simulate any perceived incident to the physical vehicle at the virtual one in order to get a higher accuracy predicting the current state of the vehicle.

Tao et al. (2017) focus more on the product life cycle (design, manufacturing, service). They identify a research gap in the field of product life-cycle management in the form of a disconnection between the physical object and the virtual infor-

L. Stojanovic
Fraunhofer IOSB, Karlsruhe, Germany
e-mail: ljiljana.stojanovic@iosb.fraunhofer.de

S. R. Bader (✉)
Fraunhofer IAIS, Schloss Birlinghoven, Sankt Augustin, Germany
e-mail: sebastian.bader@iais.fraunhofer.de

© Springer Nature Switzerland AG 2020
M. Maleshkova et al. (eds.), *Smart Service Management*,
https://doi.org/10.1007/978-3-030-58182-4_12

mation available during the several life-cycle stages. Their Digital Twin concept follows the definition of Glaessgen and Stargel (2012) and focuses on information presentation in the form of a virtual objects but do not consider any manipulations of those. Therefore, their Digital Twin concept mainly serves as a virtual model and information container and rather the thing itself as any (virtual) interaction pattern is missing.

The **Asset Administration Shell (AAS)** is the promoted solution as defined by the Plattform Industrie 4.0 and published in DIN SPEC 91345 in accordance with RAMI4.0. The AAS concept contains a data model, protocol bindings, and life-cycle specifications together with a security concept according to Attribute-based Access Control principles.

IoT data is currently mainly exchanged in either JSON or XML. These commonly used data formats ease the serialization and parsing by providing specifications for the syntactic structure of the data objects. Additional information on the meaning of keys/values is usually specified in customized data models and schemata. The latest specification of the AAS also follows this convention (Barnstedt et al. 2019). The AAS is the declared Digital Twin of the German Plattform Industrie 4.0 and encompasses the interpretation of the digital representation of any production-related asset. As such, materials and products, devices and machines, but also software and digital services have a respective digital version.

While the predefined structure and the usage of specific keys reduce the heterogeneity inherent in the data exchange processes of current industrial scenarios, all real-world scenarios still require a thorough understanding of the specific terms and values. Therefore they are dependent on extensive manual work and understanding of the extended AAS model, followed by a time consuming data mapping. A semantic formalization of entities and data objects has several advantages in this context. The mature Semantic Web technology stack around RDF enables clear references to classes, properties, and instances in the form of URIs, beyond the scope of single AAS objects but also across applications, domains, and organizations. The defined meaning of the used entities further allows its combination with predefined logical axioms, which allow the automatic derivation of new knowledge.

The **IIC Digital Twin** concept is a functional analysis and requirement description specifying the virtual behavior. The IIC defines a Digital Twin as a formal digital representation of some asset, process, or system that captures attributes and behaviors of that entity suitable for communication, storage, interpretation, or processing within a certain context (Malakutiand et al. 2019). It is important to note that a Digital Twin does not only provide access to the life-cycle information of its asset. It also models the asset behavior through different types of asset models (such as physics-based, data-driven, etc.) and it offers value-added services (e.g., anomaly prediction) for industrial applications or other digital twins.

The IIC Digital Twin Interoperability Task Group provides a precise digital twin definition, elaborates on advanced digital twin use cases, and considers a digital twin as the interoperability enabler among vendors. The IIC Plattform Industrie 4.0 Joint Task Group—JCG Digital Twin I4.0 Component CG is currently working on identifying the commonalities and differences of the Digital Twin vs I4.0 Component.

More information of the IIC view on digital twins can be found in the November 2019 edition of the Journal of Innovation which focuses on digital twin.[1] According to the IIC (Malakuti et al. 2020), a digital twin is a formal digital representation of an asset that captures attributes and behaviors of that asset. This definition is very broad in order to cover as many as possible use cases and to be applicable to already existing solutions. However, there is still no standard for representing digital twins, which is one of key barriers of applying digital twins. This results in interoperability problems within a digital twin as well as among the digital twins.

From a technical perspective, a digital twin should include attributes, models as well as services of an asset relevant for a certain context. The attributes can be further split into static data (e.g., a name of the asset or its manufacturer), slow-changing data (e.g., a location of the asset in a plant) and dynamic data (e.g., process parameters that were set during the production of the asset or during its usage). This data is of different modality, as not only the structured data, but more importantly the textual data, time-series data, audio signals, images, and videos could be considered. All this data is needed to generate a total view on the asset. Whereas textual data is usually used e.g. for operating manuals or for describing errors during the production, the time-series data is suitable for capturing real-time process data. The audio signals are increasingly getting attention due to their ability to detect problems based on characteristic sounds with relatively minor investment costs, as such sensors are suitable for asset retrofitting. On the other hand, the features extracted from images and videos define the context and thus help even better understand the asset and its behavior. However, having different modalities significantly increases the complexity of data management during data acquisition, pre-processing, integration, etc. and consequently reduces the data sharing opportunities.

To maximize the utility of digital twin data, much broader expertise on how to interpret this data should be considered, which is not possible without having a deep domain knowledge. This requires using standards for representing data and its semantics not only on the meta-level, but rather to take into account the domain specific vocabulary (e.g., companion specifications) to annotate the data. Only in this way both the human- and machine-processability and understandability can be achieved.

Digital twins are not just the simulation of a physical asset (Kritzinger et al. 2018). They unlock the application of advanced forms of data-driven and knowledge-driven AI in manufacturing operations in order to deal effectively with unforeseen events (Rasheed et al. 2019). However, having different independent models introduces the interoperability problem at the level of digital twin models, which is an even more difficult problem due to many reasons such as model type,

---

[1] https://www.iiconsortium.org/journal-of-innovation.htm.

a life-cycle phase it is created for, a (sub)set of parameters it is built on, etc. Each model explains an aspect of the asset. For example, the 3D models are created during the asset engineering phase by using different 3D modeling tools which model geometry, kinematics, etc. The physics-based models (based on statistical and mathematical modeling) are robust against uncertainty of raw materials and are able to handle a large amount of non-causative correlations. The data-driven models provide deeper insights and make prediction based on streaming data.

To gain additional comprehensive insight about an asset, there is a need to exploit symbiosis among the models. The use of a wide variety of different models will allow combining the strengths of different methods while addressing the weaknesses of some approaches. A very common issue, at least for the manufacturing domain, is that not enough data is available to train machine learning models. For example, quality control is based on the detection of out of control situations (events like some deviations in the process parameters), which are generally very little presented in a standard training dataset, since the production is usually under control. Therefore, methods for robust learning from a few examples or synthetically generated data are required. The physics-based models can be used to initially generate high-quality data to be used for a predictive data-driven model. To resolve the above introduced interoperability problem we propose the level-based approach:

- Level 1: Standardized, I4.0-conform digital twins based on I4.0-based standards for representing data, models, and services;
- Level 2: Hybrid twins for achieving higher predictive capabilities by exploiting the symbiosis among the models;
- Level 3: Cognitive twins for dealing effectively with unforeseen situations by exploiting synergy with expert and problem-solving knowledge.

Realizing all these levels will cover many use cases, starting from the detection of anomalies over the integrative prediction of unusual behavior toward the solution for unknown situations. Whereas the standardized digital twins will reduce digital twin development and integration effort, the hybrid twins will increase model transparency and accuracy. Finally, through the "cognitive augmentation" of digital twin data and models, the cognitive twins will facilitate effective decision-making even for previously unseen, undesired situations.

The summary of our contribution is shown in (Fig. 1).

2   Standardized, I4.0-Conform Digital Twins to Resolve Data Interoperability Problem

To deal with data heterogeneity challenge, there is a need for a standard to represent the data in a way which will allow humans and systems to understand it and to easily build applications. The interoperability problem at the digital twin data level can be partially solved by using the meta model for the asset administration shell

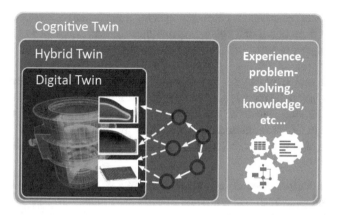

Fig. 1 Evolution of digital twins in the AI era

(Barnstedt et al. 2019), which is also recommended by the joint working group JCG Digital Twin I4.0 Component. By representing the digital twin according to the I4.0 guideline, the digital twin will be asset administration shell compliant, thus will ensure interoperability. In this way a digital twin and its physical counterpart will be integrated into Industrie 4.0 communication and will provide a controlled access to all information (and models) of the asset. This will allow to deal with the syntactic interoperability (i.e., the ability to exchange data e.g. via a REST interface) as well as the semantic interoperability (i.e., the ability to assign a correct understanding to data).[2]

However, as digital twins as active entities that offer different services and collaborate with other entities, the pragmatic interoperability (Asuncion and Van Sinderen 2010) should be achieved. This requires to share the same understanding of the intended and actual use of exchanged messages in a given context. Therefore, it would be mandatory to go beyond the use of digital twin services (such as get/set model or data) and provide the services at the higher abstraction level that make a digital twin an intelligent and self-contained entity (Malakuti et al. 2020) and would guarantee interoperability between the digital twins. To achieve that a digital twin is an active component that has a full control on the usage of models and knowledge facilitating asset understanding, a digital twin should provide analytical and inference functionalities, available through an API. In this way, it will serve e.g. anomaly detection, prediction, (re)scheduling, inferring new facts, causal reasoning, and root-cause analysis in proactive and reactive mode. The following services for management of digital twin models can be foreseen:

- train a model (including automatic generation of "similar" training data);
- using a model to detect and predict anomalies;

---

[2]http://horizon2020-story.eu/in-depth-interoperability-through-embedded-connected-digital-twins.

- reason about the anomalies based on existing models and their dependencies;
- visualize them based on explanation modules for different data modalities (e.g., heatmaps, dashboards, 3D models, etc.) to raise awareness of the cause of the problem;
- explain complex hypotheses by generating credible narratives in order to increase confidence that the models are accurate, controllable, robust, and understandable;
- provide all data, models, and explanations to consumers (humans or other systems) in a secure, transparent, sovereign way, defining not only who, but also how data, and the created knowledge (e.g., through generated explanation) can be used.

The specification of these services will ensure a unified, systematic approach to represent and manage digital twins and to build the applications based on them. For the implementation of these services, all technical aspects of digital twins, which are identified by IIC WG on DTs (cf. Journal of Innovation—edition November 2019), should be taken into account.

3 Hybrid Twins to Resolve Model Interoperability Problems

Having a comprehensive understanding of an asset requires to combine its models. We propose to extend the digital twin concept into the hybrid twins by interplaying different models to achieve higher predictive capabilities and greater potential for industrial applications. The hybrid twin creates a self-improving system that not only manages data and models but also includes services to continuously improve its models.

Indeed, the digital twin models should be employed in such a way that the result is their continuous improvement. There are several possibilities to intelligently combine digital twin models: by generating input for other models, by optimizing parameters of a model based on results of other models, by integrating all models based on winner-takes-all principle, by adding an additional level on the top of all models, etc. For example, the physics-based models can be used to initially generate high-quality data and then construct a predictive data-driven model. The hybrid twin can also apply the resulting data-driven models to enhance the first principle models.

We propose going a step further by introducing industrial knowledge graphs to intertwine all digital models as well as to enable intelligent interlinking of digital twins. As an industrial knowledge graph represents the domain knowledge and mimics how the human brain works, the interaction between different types of digital twin models will be semantically enriched, enabling model interoperability and higher-level inference. Indeed, the industrial knowledge graph will extend the digital twin functionalities by enabling to respond to the questions like "what?," "when?," "how?," "in what context?," "what-if?" along with simpler statistical empirical observations from data. This will be achieved by providing advanced services based on reasoning in knowledge graphs.

Annotating the digital twin models with a knowledge graph allows to understand root causes by inferring explainable hypothesis from complex relationships between individual models that cannot simply be detected by a single model. Since the hybrid twin can deal with less data and can discover the most important parameters, it automatically resolves the problems of missing data or inaccurate models. Additionally, individual model results can be used to generate contextual explanations, which integrate various multi-modal explanation modules to create human-perceivable insights into the asset. The generated explanations can be used to improve the quality of the asset.

4 Cognitive Twins for Resolving Unpredicted Problems

Although digital twins incorporate predictive capabilities, they are still unable to respond appropriately to unforeseen events due to over-simplification of complex situations, low data availability, and poor data quality (Zillner et al. 2018). Currently, a digital twin is still just approximation of a physical asset. Despite the huge amount of data which is ingested, processed, and analyzed and many different models, there are numerous situations where the physical asset cannot be properly understood by the models. In these situations, human involvement and experience play an essential role and can resolve critical situations. Thus, there is a need to engage humans and to benefit from their experience.

The key idea is to combine human tacit knowledge with the power of digital twin models in order to exploit synergies and enable better informed and improved reactions in situations where, when tackling the problem alone, neither human nor digital twin models can perform well without interactions and continuous communication occurring between them. This means that the digital twin should continuously extract, store, share, etc. integrated knowledge both from the experts and from the data in order to assure their sustainability along the asset life cycle. This knowledge should be used for building the transparent models despite the uncertainty existing in the perceptual data, the effects of the generated decisions, and the incomplete information.

A cognitive twin represents the next step in the evolution of the digital twin concept to be well prepared for dealing with unforeseen situations. It incorporates aspects associated with cognition, such as reasoning, planning, and learning. It extends the hybrid twin by incorporating expert, domain, and problem-solving knowledge and thus does not only recognize a problem, but rather has deep understanding of a given situation, supporting the decision if, how and when to react. Indeed, the cognitive twin understands the present and the future situations (including awareness of itself and its environment) and proposes actions to modify the current situation and/or to react to any unpredicted changes in a reasonable way. In this was, it does not only maintain a certain behavioral level, but rather it can improve the behavior in uncertain, time-variant environments (Tomforde et al. 2014).

5   Retrieval and Selection of Reference Frameworks

The necessary effort for both domain experts and newcomers to find suitable guidance is significant. The interested reader can only evaluate the significance of a specific publication after examining the complete text—a substantial challenge regarding the amount of available specifications. In order to target this issue, a publicly available knowledge graph (Bader et al. 2019) containing the latest state of technical specifications with respect to standards, reference frameworks as well as key requirements has been created. The inter-linked nature of the content and its various relations to outside topics led to the design of an RDF-based knowledge graph for technical standards and reference frameworks.

One exemplary usage is constituted by an experienced designer of smart services. She is aware of the technologies and dependencies of her domain. For further iterations of latest guidelines, the expert would like to know about the focus and state of complementary but also competing approaches.

She can use the interactive views provided with the knowledge graph[3] to create the analysis shown in Fig. 2. The significant overlap between the Reference Architecture of the Industrial Internet Consortium on the one hand and the FIWARE platform specification and IoT-A Reference Architecture (cf. Fig. 2 (1) and (2)) are one insight for a targeted investigation.

In another scenario, a system architect looks for relevant information for his next project. Required to ensure the security and protection of his customer's data, he searches for best practices for implementing upcoming technologies and checks the suitability of the latest trends. The co-occurrence matrix of the already mentioned web service depicts which reference frameworks and which respective classifications most probably frame these concerns. Furthermore, he can use the concern hierarchy to aggregate the information of the I40KG (cf. Fig. 3). With this query, the system architect is able to see that the IIC Reference Architecture surpasses the others in terms of its interoperability references (cf. Fig. 3 (1)). However, as data protection is his major target, the IDS Reference Architecture Model seems like a valuable information source (cf. Fig. 3 (2) and (3)).

6   Conclusion

This chapter presents the core principles of smart service architectures. The core building blocks have been presented and put into context. Nevertheless, any selected architecture model must be aligned according to the distinct requirements and context which the targeted smart service experiences. The provided general framework serves as a generic structure to organize the relevant features and aspects and to

---

[3]https://i40-tools.github.io/StandardOntologyVisualization/index.html.

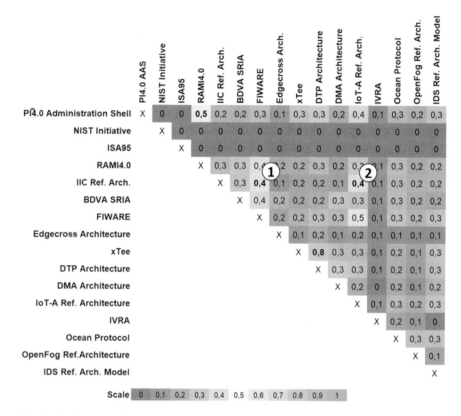

Fig. 2 Overlap of reference frameworks. Symmetric matrix displaying similar frameworks based on the amount of targeted concerns

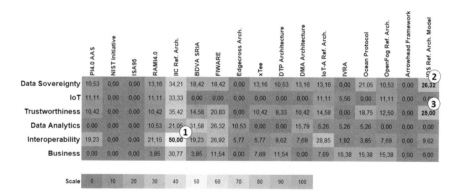

Fig. 3 Focus comparison. Total coverage of requirements by reference frameworks. Higher scores do indicate broader coverage of a topic

support a sound understanding and communication of targeted characteristics. The classification of both the necessary discussions and technical components along distinct layers improves the development processes and establishes transparency.

The currently most relevant conventions, best practices, and technologies are explained organized according to the respective layers and perspectives. A selected set of influential frameworks and reference architectures is supplied to find further inspiration. The similarities between smart services and digital twins might also serve as starting point to ensure the communication and exchange between the different communities and promises mutual benefits. While smart services promote the autonomy and self-regulation of digital entities, the digital twins lift and represent the physical world into digital networks.

Acknowledgments This work has been supported by the German Federal Ministry of Education and Research through the research project "Industrial Data Space Plus" (grant no. 01IS17031), the EU H2020 project "BOOST4.0" (grant no. 780732) and the EU H2020 project "COGNITWIN" (grant no. 870130).

References

Asuncion, C. H., & Van Sinderen, M. J. (2010). Pragmatic interoperability: A systematic review of published definitions. In *IFIP International Conference on Enterprise Architecture, Integration and Interoperability* (pp. 164–175). Springer.

Bader, S. R., Grangel-González, I., Tasnim, M. & Lohmann, S. (2019). Structuring the Industry 4.0 Landscape. In *2019 24th IEEE International Conference on Emerging Technologies and Factory Automation (ETFA)* (pp. 224–231). IEEE.

Barnstedt, E., Bedenbender, H., Billmann, M., Boss, B., Clauer, E., Fritsche, M., et al. (2019). Details of the Asset Administration Shell: Part 1, Technical report, BMWi. Version 2.0.

Glaessgen, E. H., & Stargel, D. (2012). The digital twin paradigm for future NASA and US Air Force vehicles. In *53rd Struct. Dyn. Mater. Conf. Special Session: Digital Twin*, Honolulu, HI, US (pp. 1–14).

Kritzinger, W., Karner, M., Traar, G., Henjes, J., & Sihn, W. (2018). Digital twin in manufacturing: A categorical literature review and classification. *IFAC-PapersOnLine 51*(11), 1016–1022.

Malakuti, S., van Schalkwyk, P., Boss, B., Sastry, C. R., Runkana, V., Lin, S.-W., et al. (2020). Digital twins for industrial applications. In *Industrial Internet Consortium (IIC), White Paper*. https://www.iiconsortium.org/stay-informed/digital-twins-for-industrial-applications.htm, Accessed 14.04.2020.

Malakutiand, S., van Schalkwyk, P., Boss, B., Sastry, C. R., Runkana, V., Lin, S.-W., et al. (2019). Digital twins for industrial applications. In *White Paper, Industrial Internet Consortium*, accessible online: https://www.iiconsortium.org/white-papers.htm.

Rasheed, A., San, O., & Kvamsdal, T. (2019). Digital twin: values, challenges and enablers. Preprint. arXiv:1910.01719.

Tao, F., Cheng, J., Qi, Q., Zhang, M., Zhang, H., & Sui, F. (2017). Digital twin-driven product design, manufacturing and service with big data. *The International Journal of Advanced Manufacturing Technology*, 1–14.

Tomforde, S., Hähner, J., von Mammen, S., Gruhl, C., Sick, B., & Geihs, K. (2014). 'Know thyself'-computational self-reflection in intelligent technical systems. In *2014 IEEE Eighth International Conference on Self-Adaptive and Self-Organizing Systems Workshops* (pp. 150–159). IEEE.

Zillner, S., Gomez, J. A., Robles, A. G., Curry, E., Södergård, C., Boujemaa, N., et al. (2018). In *Data-Driven Artificial Intelligence for European Economic Competitiveness And Societal Progress: BDVA Position St*atement, november 2018'.

Part IV
Smart Service Analytics

Service Analytics: Putting the "Smart" in Smart Services

Niklas Kühl, Hansjörg Fromm, Jakob Schöffer, and Gerhard Satzger

Abstract Artificial intelligence in general and the techniques of machine learning in particular provide many possibilities for data analysis. When applied to services, they allow them to become smart by intelligently analyzing data of typical service transactions, e.g., encounters between customers and providers. We call this service analytics. In this chapter, we define the terminology associated with service analytics, artificial intelligence, and machine learning. We describe the concept of service analytics and illustrate it with typical examples from industry and research.

1 Introduction

As outlined in the previous chapters, modern economies are becoming more and more "servitized"—with over 75% of the gross value added being derived from the tertiary sector (Eichengreen and Gupta 2011) and with an increasing number of industrial companies proceeding to engage in service-type offerings (Neely 2008).

A prominent theory in the field of services—while still being discussed controversially—is the so-called *Service-Dominant Logic* proposed by Vargo and Lusch (2008) that advocates the perspective that value is not "embedded" in products or services but is rather created by the knowledge, skills, and resources employed by both provider(s) and customer(s). The particular challenge then is the so-called *co-creation of value*, i.e., partners aiming at incorporating potential contributions from both sides to come up with a solution that—from an overall system point of view—maximizes the generated value. This goes far beyond the typical customer integration in a traditional service context in that it elevates the viewpoint above the simple provider perspective. Moreover, it opens the view to analyzing and purposefully designing more complex (smart) service systems comprising a larger number of stakeholders (Maglio et al. 2018).

N. Kühl (✉) · H. Fromm · J. Schöffer · G. Satzger
Karlsruhe Institute of Technology (KIT), Karlsruhe, Germany
e-mail: niklas.kuehl@kit.edu; hansjoerg.fromm@kit.edu; jakob.schoeffer@kit.edu; gerhard.satzger@kit.edu

© Springer Nature Switzerland AG 2020
M. Maleshkova et al. (eds.), *Smart Service Management*,
https://doi.org/10.1007/978-3-030-58182-4_13

However, this poses a systemic challenge. Looking at traditional service systems, we realize that one of the key challenges is the availability of the knowledge, skills, and resources available at one integration point to connect the partners. This becomes evident looking at a simple example with data being one of the important resources to be shared: in a supply chain with different providers and their customers, everyone would benefit from understanding and reacting to changes in the production processes within the system. So far, however, individual processes might be measured in real time, but their resulting data are typically not communicated to other stakeholders. Similar situations can be found in other industries. Automotive manufacturers, car dealers, and vendors of value-added services around the car do not know much about the usage of their products and services by the customers. Doctors and other medical service providers do not know about their patients' behaviors and health status once they have left their offices.

As an instrument to overcome this disconnect, modern information and communication technology may assist helping to create a system-wide view and, thus, exploit the inherent potential (Böhmann et al. 2014). For instance, rather than manually reading error logs of machines in a supply chain once a year, smart services could provide regular, more frequent or even real-time updates. At the same time, this data could centrally be made available, and service providers could manage capacity to the advantage of all parties: lower maintenance prices for consumers, faster reaction times, and higher profits for providers. As we can observe, this disconnect is actually overcome more and more with the emergence of new measuring sensor technologies in the field of the Internet of Things (IoT) (Martin et al. in press). An increasing volume of data is already collected by the users/customers themselves (e.g., through smart devices) or by smart services in different fields, like energy services, telematics in automotive and mobility services, RFID in logistics, condition sensors in engineering, data capture solutions in healthcare, etc. The further dissemination of electronic networks, led by the Internet "revolution," will increasingly enable sharing of the captured data across organizational boundaries and support their availability at the point of decision.

Where data are available already today, the potential is clearly visible and is already being leveraged in smart services: by design, these services require connectivity between providers and customers. For instance, customers visit the provider's web pages in order to obtain its service. Thus, the provider is able to analyze the customers' usage characteristics at any level of detail. Typical data of interest are the overall number of page visits, the number of page visits per customer, the time intervals between page visits, the path that an individual customer takes through the website, etc. With these data, the provider can perfectly analyze the behavior and preferences of individual customers, can make personalized recommendations, can assess the general acceptance and attractiveness of the web offering, and can discover possible usability problems related to navigating and finding information on its web pages.

For this process of capturing, processing, and analyzing data taken from a service system—in order to improve, extend, and personalize the service and create new value for both the provider and the customer—we use the term *service analytics* (Fromm et al. 2012).

2 Analytics, Data Mining, Machine Learning, and Artificial Intelligence

But, what is *analytics*? There is no single agreed-upon definition of the term *analytics*. Some authors use the terms *analytics* and *data mining* interchangeably (Kohavi et al. 2002). Others use *analytics* as a synonym for business intelligence (Davenport and Harris 2017). With the rise of artificial intelligence and machine learning, additional concepts are added to this nomenclature, calling for clear definitions of these terms and their interplay (Kühl et al. 2019).

Figure 1 and the terms defined within this section lay the foundation of our understanding of service analytics and the related concepts. However, the overall terminology and the concepts' relationships are discussed controversially (Emmert-Streib and Dehmer 2009).

Traditionally, some dissent is particularly related to the question if analytics should include or exclude data management and reporting technologies. Davenport and Harris (2017) distinguish between "access and reporting" and "analytics," both seen as subsets of business intelligence. Data management and reporting are often considered as basic analytics, which are a prerequisite for advanced analytics, built on methods from statistics and operations research. Recently, however, discussions have been focusing more on techniques labeled as *data mining* and *machine learning*—or *artificial intelligence* as an umbrella term. Not only are the terms *analytics*, *machine learning*, *artificial intelligence*, *data mining*, *deep learning*, and *statistical learning* related, but they also often appear in the same context and are sometimes used interchangeably. While the terms are common in different communities, their particular usage and meaning vary widely.

In the field of statistics, for instance, the focus lies on *statistical learning*, which is defined as a set of methods and algorithms to gain knowledge, predict

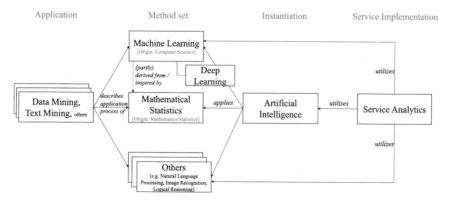

Fig. 1 Overview of terminology

outcomes, and make decisions by constructing models from a data set (Hastie et al. 2005). From a statistics point of view, machine learning can be regarded as an implementation of statistical learning (Bousquet et al. 2011).

Within the field of computer science, *machine learning* is focused on designing efficient algorithms to solve problems with computational resources (Mohri et al. 2012). While machine learning utilizes statistical approaches, it also includes methods not entirely based on statisticians' previous work, resulting in new and well-cited contributions to the field (Huang et al. 2004; Sebastiani 2002). Generally speaking, we can think of machine learning as a set of different tools used to derive meaning from data in an automated fashion. These tools are referred to as machine learning models—specific algorithms that usually take in large amounts of collected data and, through certain mathematical computations (training), accomplish learning general relationships or patterns in said data. There are several, fundamentally different types of machine learning, based on various scenarios that can occur. Three very important types are supervised learning, unsupervised learning, and reinforcement learning.

Supervised learning deals with the so-called labeled data. This means that a supervised model is trained on data that include values for a given target variable (Kühl et al. 2020). Here is an example: Assume we have collected data from a sensor attached to a component of an industrial machine. At a given time, the sensor measures temperature and pressure of the component. We usually call these two variables input features or independent variables. For each collected value pair of temperature and pressure, we also know whether the component was intact or defective; this is our (binary) target variable—or label. The label is also often referred to as the dependent variable. Having collected these data over the course of some time, we are now able to train a machine learning model that can learn a relationship (if any) between temperature, pressure and whether the component is defective or intact. Based on its learning, the model is ultimately able to tell us whether a new, previously unseen combination of pressure and temperature values would rather correspond to a defective or an intact component. An exemplary popular supervised learning algorithm to accomplish this is logistic regression (Nelder and Wedderburn 1972).

Unsupervised learning does not have this target variable, or label, in the data. Instead, imagine a scenario where we have collected consumer data, including age, income, gender, education, etc. with the goal of performing a demographic market segmentation. These insights could ultimately be used to provide personalized online shopping recommendations. In this case, we are not interested in finding a relationship between input features and some target variable, but rather in finding new patterns in the data, i.e., disjoint clusters of customers, such that similar customers belong to the same cluster. In machine learning taxonomy, this approach is called cluster analysis, one of the key unsupervised learning techniques. An exemplary algorithmic implementation of cluster analysis is k-means clustering (Lloyd 1982).

The third of the three main pillars of machine learning is *reinforcement learning* (LeCun et al. 2015). This relatively young discipline started to get a lot of attention after DeepMind's AlphaGo implementation became capable of defeating the world champion in the game of Go (Silver et al. 2017). In brief, reinforcement learning follows a trial and error logic, trying to mimic human learning behavior. Through performing correct actions, i.e., actions that lead to some predefined success (e.g., not losing points in a video game), the algorithm receives a reward and thus learns to distinguish right from wrong. A problem with supervised learning, for example, is that correct relationships between independent and dependent variables are assumed to be known ex ante. However, in the game of Go, e.g., it is intractable to define the full set of correct actions given any specific game scenario. Reinforcement learning is trying to overcome this by learning "on the fly." It is expected that reinforcement learning will have a significant impact on a wide range of real-world applications, such as self-driving cars, robotics, education, etc. (Chollet 2017). A technique often associated with reinforcement learning is called *deep learning* (Goodfellow et al. 2016).

Deep learning has become increasingly popular in machine learning over the past years (LeCun et al. 2015). Generalizing the idea of the so-called *artificial (feed-forward) neural networks* (Basheer and Hajmeer 2000), deep learning models comprise multiple processing layers capable of learning complex data representations with multiple levels of abstraction. Deep learning has drastically improved machine learning's capabilities, for example, with regard to speech (Hinton et al. 2012) and image recognition (He et al. 2016). Despite their superior performance in certain areas, and several breakthroughs in the past, such as Krizhevsky et al. (2012), deep learning models remain challenging to interpret. This is why they are sometimes also referred to as "black box models" (Shwartz-Ziv and Tishby 2017).

Contrary to the above terms, *data mining* describes the process of applying quantitative analytical methods, which help solve real-world problems, for example, in business settings (Schommer 2008). From a machine learning perspective, data mining is the process of generating meaningful machine learning models. The goal is not to develop more knowledge about machine learning algorithms, but to apply them to data in order to gain insights and potentially derive certain actions. Machine learning can therefore be regarded as a basis for data mining (Witten et al. 2011).

In contrast, *artificial intelligence* applies techniques like mathematical statistics, machine learning, natural language processing or image recognition to mimic human intelligence, such as common sense reasoning (Nilsson 2014), in machines. More generally, it can be regarded as an umbrella term for any method with the ultimate goal of achieving machine intelligence.

Service analytics, eventually, applies techniques from all these fields, including machine learning, to improve, extend, and personalize a service, creating added value for both service providers and customers. These enhanced services can themselves be—or at least contain—analytics (e.g., "analytics-as-a-service" Delen and Demirkan 2013).

3 Practical Examples of Service Analytics

In this chapter, we will give some exemplary real-world examples of smart services, which are based on contributions to the minitrack "Service Analytics" from the Hawaii International Conference on System Sciences (HICCS). Other examples can be found in a variety of fields, ranging from industrial manufacturing and mobility to social sciences or health care.

Schoch et al. (2017) propose a paper, in which they propose a way to efficiently collect sensor data in electric vehicles, in order to analyze driving behavior and derive insights around battery degradation. The authors argue that the same sensor data can also be used to improve fleet allocation for car sharing providers or to implement predictive maintenance strategies, among others, both benefiting the end user (increased car availability) and the provider (cost savings through preventive maintenance).

Another example of smart services stems from a paper by Laubis et al. (2017). In this work, the authors describe a machine learning approach for estimating road roughness through smartphone-equipped passenger cars. This allows near real-time road condition monitoring and can benefit road users by warning them of hazardous situations, recommending appropriate driving behavior, or suggesting alternative routes altogether.

A smart service in the field of industrial maintenance is introduced by Wolff et al. (2018). Here, the authors propose the implementation of a technician marketplace that can be accessed by industrial maintenance customers to book technician capacity. They argue that both traditional pricing mechanisms and current dispatching of service workers are inefficient. The newly proposed simulation-based approach allows customers to book technician capacity for fixed time slots, while the price per slot is dynamic, depending on the remaining capacity. That way, the authors claim, customers are incentivized to buy slots in accordance with their objective task urgency, increasing the overall system efficiency.

In the automotive aftermarket domain, Steuer et al. (2018) propose a novel method for inventory planning of spare parts, based on clustering and classification techniques. The authors argue that this approach is particularly well suited for demand forecasting of new parts, where historical demand patterns might not be readily available. More accurate predictions of spare part demands are imperative for stock optimization in a market worth almost €1.0 trillion (Heid et al. 2018).

Steins et al. (2019) propose an approach to forecast the demand of emergency medical services in several Swedish counties. Being able to accurately forecast this demand can "help in providing quick and efficient medical treatment and transportation of out-of-hospital patients," as the authors of this paper phrase it. In addition to historical demands, they incorporate socioeconomic data as well as weather, time, traffic, events, and related information in their model. That way, the proposed method is able to outperform the traditional forecasting practice in place.

Kisore and Reddy (2015) conduct an empirical study to identify and evaluate relationships between demographic and other socioeconomic data on the one hand,

and people's preferences for ATM locations on the other. Based on their findings, the authors then propose a better informed decision-making process regarding ATM location planning for banks in India.

4 Conclusion

In today's connected world, large amounts of data are available and continue to grow every second. While the data can have many origins and purposes, a share is generated from (regular) service operations between providers and customers. Many of these interactions already capture meaningful information that can be utilized to generate useful knowledge as a basis for future decision-making.

The concept of "service analytics" provides researchers and practitioners with different techniques to uncover patterns and insights from data sets from the service space. On the basis of these findings, more sophisticated decisions can be made, and the results can be leveraged to understand multiple perspectives of service operations, which can then lead to further improvements, e.g., by delivering services more efficiently or increasing customer satisfaction.

References

Basheer, I. A., & Hajmeer, M. (2000). Artificial neural networks: fundamentals, computing, design, and application. *Journal of Microbiological Methods, 43*(1), 3–31.

Böhmann, T., Leimeister, J. M. & Möslein, K. (2014). Service-systems-engineering. *Wirtschaftsinf, 56*, 83–90 (2014).

Bousquet, O., von Luxburg, U., & Rätsch, G. (2011). *Advanced Lectures on Machine Learning: ML Summer Schools 2003, Canberra, February 2–14, 2003, Tübingen, Germany, August 4–16, 2003, Revised Lectures* (Vol. 3176). Berlin: Springer.

Chollet, F. (2017). *Deep learning with python* (1st ed.). Greenwich, CT: Manning Publications.

Davenport, T., & Harris, J. (2017). *Competing on analytics: Updated, with a new introduction: The new science of winning*. Brighton, MA: Harvard Business Press.

Delen, D., & Demirkan, H. (2013). Data, information and analytics as services.

Eichengreen, B., & Gupta, P. (2011). The two waves of service-sector growth. *Oxford Economic Papers, 65*(1), 96–123.

Emmert-Streib, F., & Dehmer, M. (2009). *Information theory and statistical learning*. Berlin: Springer.

Fromm, H., Habryn, F., & Satzger, G. (2012). Service analytics: leveraging data across enterprise boundaries for competitive advantage. In: U. Bäumer, P. Kreutter, W. Messner (Eds.), *Globalization of professional services: Innovative strategies, successful processes, inspired talent management, and first-hand experiences* (pp. 139–149). Berlin: Springer.

Goodfellow, I., Bengio, Y., & Courville, A. (2016). *Deep learning*. Cambridge, MA: MIT Press.

Hastie, T., Tibshirani, R., Friedman, J., & Franklin, J. (2005). The elements of statistical learning: Data mining, inference and prediction. *The Mathematical Intelligencer, 27*(2), 83–85.

He, K., Zhang, X., Ren, S., & Sun, J. (2016). Deep residual learning for image recognition. In *2016 IEEE Conference on Computer Vision and Pattern Recognition (CVPR)*.

Heid, B., Huth, C., Kempf, S., & Wu, G. (2018). Ready for inspection: The automotive aftermarket in 2030. Technical report, McKinsey & Company.

Hinton, G., Deng, L., Yu, D., Dahl, G. E., Mohamed, A.-R., Jaitly, N., et al. (2012). Deep neural networks for acoustic modeling in speech recognition. *IEEE Signal Processing Magazine, 29*(6), 82–97.

Huang, G.-B., Zhu, Q.-Y., & Siew, C.-K. (2004). Extreme learning machine: a new learning scheme of feedforward neural networks. In *Proceedings. 2004 IEEE International Joint Conference on Neural Networks, 2004* (Vol. 2, pp. 985–990). Piscataway, NJ: IEEE.

Kisore, N. R., & Reddy, P. G. (2015). Empirical determination and evaluation of factors that impact ATM placement. In *2015 48th Hawaii International Conference on System Sciences* (pp. 1341–1348). Piscataway, NJ: IEEE.

Kohavi, R., Rothleder, N. J., & Simoudis, E. (2002). Emerging trends in business analytics. *Communications of the ACM, 45*(8), 45–48.

Krizhevsky, A., Sutskever, I., & Hinton, G. E. (2012). Imagenet classification with deep convolutional neural networks. In *Advances in neural information processing systems* (pp. 1097–1105).

Kühl, N., Goutier, M., Hirt, R., & Satzger, G. (2019). Machine learning in artificial intelligence: Towards a common understanding. In *Proceedings of the 52nd Hawaii International Conference on System Sciences*.

Kühl, N., Hirt, R., Baier, L., Schmitz, B., Satzger, G. (2020). How to conduct rigorous supervised machine learning in information systems research: The supervised machine learning reportcard, communications of the association for information systems.

Laubis, K., Simko, V., Schuller, A., & Weinhardt, C. (2017). Road condition estimation based on heterogeneous extended floating car data. In *Proceedings of the 50th Hawaii International Conference on System Sciences*.

LeCun, Y. A., Bengio, Y., & Hinton, G. E. (2015). Deep learning. *Nature, 521*(7553), 436–444.

Lloyd, S. P. (1982). Least squares quantization in PCM. *IEEE Trans. Information Theory, 28*, 129–136.

Maglio, P. P., Kieliszewski, C. A., Spohrer, J. C., Lyons, K., Patrício, L., & Sawatani, Y. (2018). *Handbook of service science* (Vol. II). Berlin: Springer.

Martin, D., Kühl, N., von Bischhoffshausen, J. K., & Satzger, G. (in press). System-wide learning in cyber-physical service systems: A research agenda. In *Proceedings of the 15th International Conference on Design Science Research in Information Systems and Technology (DESRIST 2020)*, Kristiansand, Norwegen, November 2020.

Mohri, M., Rostamizadeh, A., & Talwalkar, A. (2012). *Foundations of machine learning*. Cambridge, MA: MIT Press.

Neely, A. (2008). Exploring the financial consequences of the servitization of manufacturing. *Operations Management Research, 1*(2), 103–118.

Nelder, J. A., & Wedderburn, R. W. M. (1972). Generalized linear models. *Journal of the Royal Statistical Society. Series A (General), 135*(3), 370–384.

Nilsson, N. J. (2014). *Principles of artificial intelligence*. Burlington, MA: Morgan Kaufmann.

Schoch, J., Staudt, P., and Setzer, T. (2017). Smart data selection and reduction for electric vehicle service analytics.

Schommer, C. (2008). An unified definition of data mining. Preprint arXiv:0809.2696

Sebastiani, F. (2002). Machine learning in automated text categorization. *ACM Computing Surveys, 34*(1), 1–47.

Shwartz-Ziv, R., & Tishby, N. (2017). Opening the black box of deep neural networks via information. arXiv preprint arXiv:1703.00810.

Silver, D., Schrittwieser, J., Simonyan, K., Antonoglou, I., Huang, A., Guez, A., et al. (2017). Mastering the game of go without human knowledge. *Nature, 550*, 354–359.

Steins, K., Matinrad, N., & Granberg, T. (2019). Forecasting the demand for emergency medical services. In *Proceedings of the 52nd Hawaii International Conference on System Sciences*.

Steuer, D., Hutterer, V., Korevaar, P., & Fromm, H. (2018). A similarity-based approach for the all-time demand prediction of new automotive spare parts. In: *Proceedings of the 51st Hawaii International Conference on System Sciences*

Vargo, S. L., & Lusch, R. F. (2008). Service-dominant logic: Continuing the evolution. *Journal of the Academy of Marketing Science, 36*(1), 1–10.

Witten, I. H., Frank, E., & Hall, M. A. (2011). *Data mining: Practical machine learning tools and techniques* (3rd ed., Vol. 54). Burlington, MA: Morgan Kaufmann

Wolff, C., Vössing, M., Schmitz, B., & Fromm, H. (2018). Towards a technician marketplace using capacity-based pricing. In *Proceedings of the 51st Hawaii International Conference on System Sciences.*

Part V
Smart Service Use Cases

Introduction to Smart Service Use Cases

Maria Maleshkova, Niklas Kühl, and Philipp Jussen

Abstract In the world of smart services, many showcases demonstrate the possibilities of the novel "services". In this chapter, we introduce four different use cases from industry and not only illustrate the specific real-world application but also regard the added value for the individual companies.

1 Introduction

This part showcases how the previously introduced design and development methods for smart services can be put into practice in a number of different domains. In particular, four different use cases are presented in detail. These illustrate not only the specific real-world applicability but also bring forward further added value by discussing lessons learned and met challenges. The use cases include services in the industrial and mobility sectors, which were developed in direct cooperation with industry partners.

The following sections provide a brief overview of each of the smart service use cases.

M. Maleshkova (✉)
University of Bonn, Bonn, Germany
e-mail: maleshkova@cs.uni-bonn.de

N. Kühl
Karlsruhe Institute of Technology (KIT), Karlsruhe, Germany
e-mail: kuehl@kit.edu

P. Jussen
Schaeffler Monitoring Services GmbH, Herzogenrath, Germany
e-mail: philipp.jussen@schaeffler.com

© Springer Nature Switzerland AG 2020
M. Maleshkova et al. (eds.), *Smart Service Management*,
https://doi.org/10.1007/978-3-030-58182-4_14

163

2 Automatic Customer Need Detection with Incident Tickets

The first use case is located in the IT service sector. In many service relationships, customer encounters are not systematically exploited in order to gain valuable insights. However, service analytics methods would provide effective means to systematically screen customer responses and automatically extract relevant business information. We demonstrate how a smart service can be developed for screening incident information in IT services to detect customer needs. We implement and evaluate it with an IT provider covering several thousands of incident tickets per year. As a result, we show that it is feasible to map incoming tickets to a domain-specific selection of needs—and, hence, enable the providers' customer contacts to address unfulfilled needs with tailored service offerings. Thus, we allow service marketing and innovation managers to automatically and scalably monitor their customer base for additional sales opportunities and improvement of customer satisfaction.

3 Digital Sealing Services

The second use case is located in the industrial field, where sensor technology has become increasingly important (e.g., Industry 4.0, IoT). Large numbers of machines and products are equipped with sensors to constantly monitor their condition. Usually, the condition of an entire system is inferred through sensors in parts of the system by means of a multiplicity of methods and techniques. This so-called "condition monitoring" can thus reduce the downtime costs of a machine through improved maintenance scheduling. However, for small components as well as relatively inexpensive or immutable parts of a machine, sometimes it is not possible or uneconomical to embed sensors. We propose a smart service covering a system-oriented concept of how to monitor individual components of a complex technical system without including additional sensor technology. By using already existing sensors from the environment combined with machine learning techniques, we are able to infer the condition of a system component, without actually observing it. As a consequence, condition monitoring or additional services based on the component's behavior can be developed without overcoming the challenges of sensor implementation.

4 Developing Real-Time Smart Industrial Analytics for Industry 4.0 Applications

The third use case focuses on using the power of analytics in order to support the development of innovative services. In particular, it makes use of the abundance of data available through Manufacturing Executing Systems (MESs). The use case shows how to build an integrated view that can make data available in a unified model to support different stakeholders of a factory (e.g., factory planners, managers) in decision making.

Real-data analytics can be enabled by integrating multiple data sources and analyzing these on the fly, thus laying the foundation for building Industry 4.0 smart services. The specific use case is realized in the manufacturing domain and includes key findings and challenges faced while deploying the solution in real industrial settings. The selected use case studies demonstrate the use of smart service management methods for building smart Industry 4.0 applications.

5 How Transformational Management Enabled the Development of a Next Level Condition Monitoring Solution

The fourth use case illustrates the transformational management approach, which industrial component supplier Schaeffler used to develop a disruptive smart service solution for condition monitoring. The management approach emphasizes customer intimacy and scalability as the pillars of a smart service business model. As a result, Schaeffler was able to cut down the development time for the smart service solution by more than 50% compared to conventional approaches, while at the same time uncover a next level of customer value. This use case highlights the management approach on structural, process, and cultural level and highlights from a practical perspective the importance of a management and leadership transformation for smart services.

Designing a Smart Service for Customer Need Identification in B2B Ticketing Systems

Lena Eckstein, Niklas Kühl, and Gerhard Satzger

Abstract In many service relationships, customer encounters are not systematically exploited in order to gain valuable insights. However, service analytics methods would provide effective means to systematically screen customer responses and automatically extract relevant business information. In this chapter, we show how a smart service can be developed for screening incident information in IT services to detect customer needs. We implement and evaluate it with an IT provider covering several thousands of incident tickets per year. We show that it is feasible to map incoming tickets to a domain-specific selection of needs— and, hence, enable the providers' customer contacts to address unfilled needs with tailored service offerings. Thus, we allow service marketing and innovation managers to automatically and scalably monitor their customer base for additional sales opportunities and improvement of customer satisfaction.

1 Introduction and Motivation

Hence, an increasing focus is put on customer needs in order to innovate and offer valuable services. This is especially relevant where a high volume of transactions occur and, thus, huge amounts of data are acquired. A relationship is built by observing customer behavior, remembering past experience, learning from it and acting upon it. Thus, one possibility of gaining information about customer needs is the analysis of service encounters. In services, incidents, problems, or complaints constitute important encounters in the customer relationship. Documentation of these service encounters in the IT sector frequently happens via the so-called *tickets*. Over time, large amounts of these tickets accumulate. Some providers resort to

---

This chapter is based on the paper Eckstein et al. (2016).

L. Eckstein (✉) · N. Kühl · G. Satzger
IBM Deutschland GmbH, Ehningen, Germany
e-mail: lena.eckstein@de.ibm.com; niklas.kuehl@ibm.com; satzger@de.ibm.com

manual ticket analysis in order to identify so far unmet customer needs—relying on knowledge and experience of technical support engineers. However, it becomes obvious that huge and fast growing data volumes as well as the need to externalize engineers' knowledge require more automated, scalable, and data-driven solutions. This chapter demonstrates how to develop a machine learning-based smart service and depicts a feasibility study within an industry setting. Input data are incident tickets of a particular product family of an IT service provider covering several thousands of tickets per year, mainly in B2B settings.

In the remainder of this chapter, we first introduce related work (Sect. 2) and foundational terms (Sect. 3). Subsequently, we portray the smart service for need identification (Sect. 4) and present our findings from the successful feasibility study (Sect. 5). We conclude our chapter with limitations of the current setup and possible extensions of our approach for future improvement (Sect. 6).

2 Related Work

A variety of work exists on the topics *customer need identification* and *incident ticket analytics* with machine learning methods. For *customer need identification*, typical articles focus on needs related to products and feedback in online customer centers is used as input data sources (e.g., Lee 2007; Park and Lee 2011; Jin et al. 2015). There are two related examples of practice-oriented research on using advanced data analytics for customer need identification in services. Bae et al. (2005) extract customer needs from complaints in a life insurance company, while Kühl et al. (2016) determine whether Twitter messages express needs for e-mobility services.

With regard to the topic *incident tickets*, three main groups of research can be distinguished: IT system monitoring (Nair et al. 2015; Zhou et al. 2016), grouping of similar tickets (Di Lucca et al. 2002; Agarwal et al. 2012), and extraction of further useful information from tickets (Godbole and Roy 2008; Chandramouli et al. 2013; Satzger and Hottum 2015; Baier et al. 2020). Among these, the works by Godbole and Roy (2008) and Baier et al. (2020) are most closely related to our approach: They try to judge customer satisfaction from incident tickets and, hence, use a comparable data source. While their setting is similar, we target a different level of insight: We do not intend to analyze whether underlying needs are satisfied but more specifically what these (implicitly) expressed needs actually are.

3 Foundations

In order to provide a common understanding of the terminology used in this chapter, we define some prerequisites.

Needs are "states of felt deprivation" (Armstrong and Kotler 2013, p. 34) created by a "discrepancy between actual and desired state of being" (Homburg et al. 2013, p. 599). In a business context, needs result from the value creation process and are problems for which a solution is desired (Grönroos 2007). Needs influence customer expectations that in turn affect perceived service quality, which is an important competitive factor in services. In other words, high quality service means satisfying customer needs—whether stated explicitly or not—since *quality* is about "the characteristics of a product or service that bear on its ability to satisfy stated or implied needs" (American Society for Quality 2015).

Quality attributes are, hence, an expression of underlying needs. Here, primary needs in services are matched to high-level service quality attributes. Based on an extensive literature review, we identified relevant needs for B2B IT services and validated our findings by interviewing a business expert. This results in the following 14 customer needs (in alphabetical order):

- availability/responsiveness (Parasuraman et al. 1985)
- capacity (Cannon et al. 2011)
- competence (of the provider) (Parasuraman et al. 1985)
- continuity (Cannon et al. 2011)
- convenience (Cunnigham and Roberts 1974)
- customer knowledge (Parasuraman et al. 1985)
- efficiency (Zolkiewski et al. 2007)
- information (Parasuraman et al. 1985)
- performance (Zolkiewski et al. 2007)
- personalization (Bordoloi et al. 2018)
- reliability/dependability (Parasuraman et al. 1985)
- security/safety (Parasuraman et al. 1985)
- simplicity (Cunnigham and Roberts 1974)
- training (of the customer) (Cunnigham and Roberts 1974)

Traditionally, needs of a specific customer are identified via customer interviews or surveys, in one-to-one or group settings, as well as via regular threads of communication like correspondence, phone calls, or meetings. In addition, complaint and incident documentation can be a valuable source for collecting customer needs.

An *incident* in the context of IT services is defined as an "unplanned interruption to an IT service or reduction in the quality of an IT service" (Steinberg et al. 2011, section 4.2). A widespread method for incident documentation is found in the IT Infrastructure Library (ITIL) which lists several best practice elements of a so-called "incident ticket."

4 Designing and Implementing the Smart Service

In this section, we describe how need classification may be implemented in the overall support process. Subsequently, we provide more details about the setup of our need classification system.

4.1 Embedding Need Identification in the Support Process

Knowing customer needs is a prerequisite to offer adequate solutions to customer problems and to provide smart services. However, identifying customer needs in interviews or focus groups can be a cumbersome and time-consuming process. With our approach, needs are retrieved from incident tickets, i.e., a service encounter documentation. By this, we find main needs for a specific customer on the one hand, and, on the other hand, are able to group incidents and, thus, customers with similar needs.

In Fig. 1, we show how our customer need identification approach may fit into the broader context of a support and CRM process. We deliberately introduce a need identification system separately from the ticket management system. First, we assume that a working ticket management system is already in use, and changes

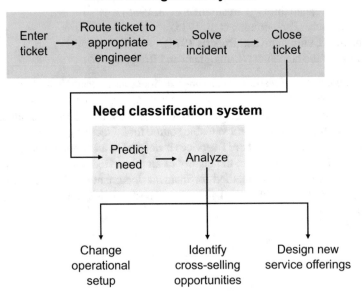

Fig. 1 System design

to it would be complex or even impossible if a standard software is used. Second, ticket management is part of support processes and users are technical staff—while customer need identification and related actions rather belong to CRM processes and are, thus, managed by different job roles.

Figure 1 portrays a simplified ticket management process. When an incident occurs, a ticket is entered into the ticket management system. This is typically done by a phone call, an e-mail, or an online user interface. Then, the ticket is transferred to a qualified engineer who solves the incident and closes the ticket.

Afterward, key data of closed tickets are copied to the need classification system. Here, the corresponding customer need is predicted for each ticket, and further analyses are run. These analyses are, inter alia, accumulations, clustering, or outlier detection and can be performed automatically, semi-automatically, or manually. Finally, the business experts use these insights to derive further actions.

Operationally, gained knowledge may drive more effective behavior in customer interactions: the provider may be able to react faster to customer requests when "availability" is the main customer need or route the incident to the right expert to meet a "competence" need. From a business development point of view, appropriate solutions and offerings can be provided to a customer. For example, for a customer whose main concern is "availability," providing on-site technical engineers might be an attractive offer. Another customer, who is relying on provider competence because of his/her own lack of know-how, might benefit from an education program to improve incident resolution in the future. These constitute cross-selling opportunities. When looking at a customer cluster, i.e. customers with similar needs expressed in their tickets, domain experts may discover trends and previously unaddressed customer needs. Subsequently, new service offerings may be designed to meet those needs. All of these measures aim at improving customer relationship by providing additional value and encouraging long-term business.

4.2 Building the Need Classification System

To extract customer needs from ticket data, we pursue the following approach as depicted in Fig. 2: We generate a list of case-specific needs and then manually label a set of representative tickets as to which, if any, of the customer needs they express. We then prepare the data to be used in a classification model, apply text mining techniques, and evaluate the classification result against a random guess benchmark for performance evaluation.

As stated above, a "long list" of 14 customer needs in B2B IT services has been derived. This is portrayed as input on the left side of the figure. As a next step (1), we reduce the set to a short list of most relevant needs to obtain a more manageable amount of distinct needs for manual labeling. Therefore, the list of 14 customer needs is sent to business experts who select the most important needs. Experts selected for this task need to be familiar with the product group(s) from which the

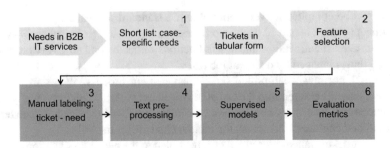

Fig. 2 Approach design

respective tickets arise but also have a thorough understanding of IT services and customer needs.

Next, we have to characterize tickets, our input on the right side, by selecting features (2) that later on can be used to point to particular needs identified above. A good starting point are the incident ticket elements listed in ITIL since ITIL is a known framework providing best practices for IT service management. We assume that a short summarizing free text is available as part of a ticket. This text shall include problem description and solution, i.e. briefly describe problem symptoms and solution steps. Both are important since either problem or solution alone might not be specific enough to determine an underlying need. For example, a "simple" solution like a software update may be an indicator for a lack of competence on the customer side.

Then, tickets are manually labeled by business experts with the one most appropriate, implicitly expressed customer need (3). As a text mining process (4), we choose a bag-of-words approach with stemming and stop word removal. With this method, text is split into chunks of words, and these words are transformed to their root and common words like "and" or "the" are removed.

Then, we train classification models that predict the customer need expressed in a ticket (5). Supervised learning models that are commonly used and suitable for text classification are decision trees, support vector machines (SVM), k-nearest neighbors (kNN), and naïve Bayes models. We split data into 80% training and 20% test data and apply tenfold stratified cross-validation. Overall accuracy and class-specific precision and recall are calculated for each customer need in the final step (6). Precision measures the share of tickets for which the predicted need matches the actual need. Recall regards the share of tickets captured correctly for a given need. Comparing each created model to the outcome of a random guess will be the baseline of evaluation.

5 Feasibility Case Study

In order to validate our need identification design, we apply the presented approach in a feasibility study and discuss the results.

5.1 Application Partner and Case

The feasibility study is set in the context of a large, internationally operating provider of hardware, software, and IT services. The incident tickets arise from software maintenance requests of a specific product group, and customers are mainly B2B private sector companies. For reasons of confidentiality, no further details about the product group of tickets examined can be disclosed here.

The following features are defined as interesting by three business experts for identifying customer needs in this setting: *information on severity during ticket life cycle, product group, total amount of days until closure, solution code and fix number, indicators regarding critical situations with higher management involvement, language preferences*, and *problem and solution summary in textual format*. Table 1 relates these features to the information contained in an incident ticket according to ITIL.

Table 1 Incident ticket features and mapping to ITIL incident ticket

Feature	ITIL
Severity during ticket life cycle	Incident impact, urgency, and priority
Product group	Incident classification
Total amount of days until closure	Date and time of recording and closing
Solution code and fix number	Category; action taken closing the record; known errors
Indicators regarding critical situations with higher management involvement	Incident impact, urgency, and priority
Language preferences	Service catalog
Problem and solution summary	Date and time of recording and any subsequent activities; description of the incident symptoms; details of any actions taken to try to diagnose, resolve, or recreate the incident; details, including time, category, action taken closing the record

5.2 *Results*

First, we send our list of 14 needs to three experts of the feasibility study's environment in order to retrieve essential needs. As a result, the following most important needs are chosen (in alphabetical order):

- availability/responsiveness
- competence (of provider)
- continuity (continuous service)
- customer knowledge (provider knows customer)
- efficiency
- reliability/dependability

Then, 200 randomly sampled tickets are labeled with one of the six corresponding customer needs. As shown in Table 2, 34 tickets are not labeled. These tickets as well as tickets only labeled once or labeled as "other" are discarded from further analyses.

The first results with five need classes are below expectations since classification results are only in parts better than random guess as a benchmark. Hence, we test an additional setup: Instead of distinguishing between all identified need classes, we combine the three classes with few samples, "no need," "continuity," and "reliability/dependability," together to one class "minor needs." Overall, the three-class setup provides models that result in better metrics than a random guess. Table 3 shows classification results on test data, where bold numbers indicate performance better than random guessing. The selection of an applicable model depends on managerial inclination. When the effort for reclassifying, i.e. manually removing tickets that do not belong to their predicted class should be low, precision is weighted more, else higher recall is preferred. Here, SVM shows superior performance compared to the other three algorithms in both metrics.

Table 2 Number of tickets assigned to each customer need

Customer need	Labeled tickets
Availability/responsiveness	57
Competence	62
Continuity	15
Customer knowledge	1
Efficiency	1
Reliability/dependability	6
No need	21
Other	3
(Blank)	34
Total	200

Table 3 Three class classification results, rounded to two decimal places

Algorithm	C4.5	SVM	kNN	naïve Bayes	Random guess
Overall accuracy	0.39	0.45	0.35	0.35	0.33
Average per-class accuracy	0.35	0.42	0.38	0.33	0.33
Micro-averaged recall. precision. f1-score	0.39	0.45	0.35	0.35	0.33
Macro-averaged recall	0.35	0.42	0.38	0.33	0.33
Macro-averaged precision	0.34	0.47	0.40	0.32	0.33
Macro-averaged f1-score	0.34	0.44	0.39	0.33	0.33

6 Conclusion and Outlook

We demonstrated how to develop a smart service based on classification and text mining techniques to identify customer needs from incident tickets. We successfully validated our approach in a feasibility study with a large IT service provider. Results show that the proposed approach is capable of eliciting information from service encounter data in an automated and scalable fashion—after an initial training.

6.1 Lessons Learned

Naturally, the work has certain limitations, and we envision future extensions to further improve results and applicability.

In general, more training data, i.e. more samples of tickets with corresponding need, will improve classification performance, especially for needs that are rarely expressed. Besides, word semantics, like synonyms or abbreviations, could be considered in the future. In addition to that, a broader set of methods and parameter choices for classification algorithms may further drive performance. Finally, also multi-label classifications may be considered, where one or more need(s) are assigned to each ticket.

Despite these limiting factors, this work contributes insights to need identification in services and to methods for customer relationship management and customer insight. Business implications are obvious: Not only can available data be screened for additional (need) information, but also the application of data and text mining approaches will allow to do this in an automated and scalable manner—once the one-time setup effort to calibrate the model has been invested. Tapping incident data from service encounters may yield several advantages: in the short term, providers may benefit from operational improvements dealing with a particular incident ticket, while the mid-term tailored offerings to the customer may enhance business development, and dependency on scarce and futile expert knowledge is reduced. Long-term this will support customer relationship management. In particular, it will back customer intimacy strategies where knowledge about the customer contributes to competitive advantage.

6.2 Additional Implementation Options

One possibility to extend the developed service is need classification during ticket entry. In contrast to our work, where needs are identified from problem and solution, needs would then be extracted from problem description only. Figure 3 displays a possible setup of this smart service. Need classification, in this future scenario, is deployed as a web service. When called during ticket entry, the entry process is automatically adapted depending on the identified need, e.g., simplifying questions for customers with a "competence" need. Likewise, ticket routing considers customer needs, e.g., prioritizing customers with an "availability" need. As described before, the results from need classification are used to gain customer insights. This is achieved by calling the service from the CRM system.

These examples show that need classification as a (web) service may provide a flexible incorporation into existing infrastructures and processes.

The general approach of eliciting information from customer encounters may bear a far richer potential: on the one hand, other sources of available service encounter data, like customer satisfaction surveys, meeting minutes, technician

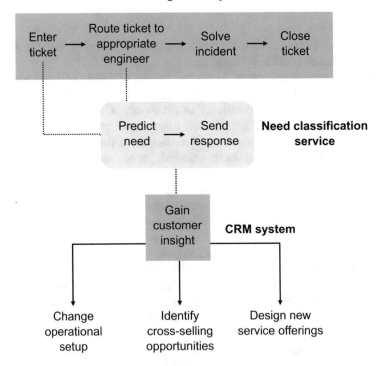

Fig. 3 Future system design

reports, or interaction data itself may be exploitable. On the other hand, service encounter data may be also used to extract other relevant information, like customer experience (Baier et al. 2020) or customer intimacy ratings (Habryn et al. 2012). While our approach focuses on identifying known needs, extracting unknown needs from customer encounter documentation might provide even more value for CRM—though this is a more complex task and research is still in progress (Kühl et al. 2020). Similar to the "need classification service" depicted in Fig. 3, we envision a variety of web services that exploit data which arise in the service process. Examples are a service that maps needs to offerings, a service identifying dissatisfied customer from encounter documentation or a service that builds an overall customer experience rating.

As in all designs for machine learning solutions, certain prerequisites have to be considered: First of all, necessary data have to be available in sufficient quality, and second, regulations like GDPR (General Data Protection Regulation) must be respected. Besides—at least during initial model building—business and technical experts' knowledge is required to understand data and interpretation of results.

We believe that the application of data and text mining techniques will be an effective means to support marketing and innovation managers, specifically, for building individualized offers and lasting service relationships. Thus, this will enhance servitization strategies of enterprises that provide critical differentiation in competitive markets.

References

Agarwal, S., Sindhgatta, R., & Sengupta, B. (2012). SmartDispatch: Enabling efficient ticket dispatch in an IT service environment. In Q. Yang, D. Agarwal & J. Pei (Eds.), *Proceedings of the 18th ACM SIGKDD International Conference on Knowledge Discovery and Data Mining* (pp. 1393–1401). New York, NY: ACM.

American Society for Quality. (2015). *Quality glossary.* http://asq.org/glossary/q.html

Armstrong, G., & Kotler, P. (2013). *Marketing: An introduction* (11th ed.). Boston, MA and Munich: Pearson.

Bae, S. M., Ha, S. H., & Park, S. C. (2005). A web-based system for analyzing the voices of call center customers in the service industry. *Expert Systems with Applications, 28*(1), 29–41.

Baier, L., Kühl, N., Schüritz, R., & Satzger, G. (2020). Will the customers be happy? Identifying unsatisfied customers from service encounter data. *Journal of Service Management.* ISSN: 1757-5818.

Bordoloi, S., Fitzsimmons, J., & Fitzsimmons, M. (2018). *Service management: Operations, strategy, information technology.* New York, NY: McGraw-Hill Education.

Cannon, D., Wheeldon, D., Lacy, S., & Hanna, A. (2011). *ITIL service strategy* (2nd ed.). London: TSO.

Chandramouli, A., Subramanian, G., & Bal, D. (2013). Unsupervised extraction of part names from service logs. In S. I. Ao, C. Douglas, W. S. Grundfest & J. Burgstone (Eds.) *Proceedings of the World Congress on Engineering and Computer Science.* Lecture Notes in Engineering and Computer Science (Vol. 2, pp. 826–828), San Francisco, CA: IAENG.

Cunningham, M. T., & Roberts, D. A. (1974). The role of customer service in industrial marketing. *European Journal of Marketing, 8*(1), 15–28.

Di Lucca, G. A., Di Penta, M., & Gradara, S. (2002). "An approach to classify software maintenance requests. In *Proceedings of the International Conference on Software Maintenance* (pp. 93–102). Piscataway, NJ: IEEE.

Eckstein, L., Kuehl, N., & Satzger, G. (2016). Towards extracting customer needs from incident tickets in IT services. In *2016 IEEE 18th Conference on Business Informatics (CBI)* (Vol. 1, pp. 200–207). Piscataway, NJ: IEEE.

Godbole, S., & Roy, S. (2008). Text classification, business intelligence, and interactivity: automating C-sat analysis for services industry. In Y. Li, B. Liu & S. Sarawagi (Eds.), *Proceedings of the 14th ACM SIGKDD International Conference on Knowledge Discovery and Data Mining* (pp. 911–919). New York, NY: ACM.

Grönroos, C. (2007). *Service management and marketing: customer management in service competition* (3rd ed.). Chichester and Weinheim: Wiley.

Habryn, F., Bischhoffshausen, J., & Satzger, G. (2012). A business intelligence solution for assessing customer interaction, cross-selling, and customization in a customer intimacy context. In *Proceedings of the 20th European Conference on Information Systems, ECIS 2012* (p. 206).

Homburg, C., Kuester, S., & Krohmer, H. (2013). *Marketing management: A contemporary perspective* (2nd ed.). London: McGraw-Hill Higher Education.

Jin, J., Ji, P., Liu, Y., & Johnson Lim, S. C. (2015). Translating online customer opinions into engineering characteristics in QFD: A probabilistic language analysis approach. *Engineering Applications of Artificial Intelligence, 41*, 115–127.

Kühl, N., Mühlthaler, M., & Goutier, M. (2020). Supporting customer-oriented marketing with artificial intelligence: automatically quantifying customer needs from social media. *Electronic Markets, 30*, 351–367.

Kühl, N., Scheurenbrand, J., & Satzger, G. (2016). Needmining: Identifying micro blog data containing customer needs. In *24th European Conference on Information Systems, ECIS 2016*. Bogazici University Istanbul; Istanbul; 12 June 2016 through 15 June 2016. Association for Information Systems.

Lee, T. Y. (2007). Needs-based analysis of online customer reviews. In D. Sarppo, M. Gini, R. J. Kauffman, C. Dellarocas & F. Dignum (Eds.), *Proceedings of the Ninth International Conference on Electronic Commerce* (pp. 311–317). New York, NY: ACM.

Nair, V., Raul, A., Khanduja, S., Bahirwani, V., Sellamanickam, S., Keerthi, S., et al. (2015). Learning a hierarchical monitoring system for detecting and diagnosing service issues. In L. Cao, C. Zhang, T. Joachims, G. Webb, D. D. Margineantu & G. Williams (Eds.), *Proceedings of the 21th ACM SIGKDD International Conference on Knowledge Discovery and Data Mining* (pp. 2029–2038). New York, NY: ACM.

Parasuraman, A., Zeithaml, V. A., & Berry, L. L. (1985). A conceptual model of service quality and its implications for future research. *Journal of Marketing, 49*(4), 41–50.

Park, Y., & Lee, S. (2011). How to design and utilize online customer center to support new product concept generation. *Expert Systems with Applications, 38*(8), 10638–10647.

Satzger, G., & Hottum, P. (2015). Management der Interaktionsqualität in industriellen Dienstleistungsnetzwerken: Ein "Service Analytics"-Ansatz für die Störungsbearbeitung. In L. Grünert, P. Horváth & M. Seiter (Eds.), zfbf Sonderheft 69/2015 Steuerung von Industrial Service Networks (pp. 150–173). Düsseldorf: Handelsblatt Fachmedien.

Steinberg, R. A., Rudd, C., Lacy, S., & Hanna, A. (2011). *ITIL service operation* (2nd ed.). London: TSO.

Zhou, W., Tang, L., Zeng, C., Li, T., Shwartz, L., & Ya. Grabarnik, G. (2016). Resolution recommendation for event tickets in service management. *IEEE Transactions on Network and Service Management, 13*(4), 954–967.

Zolkiewski, J., Lewis, B., Yuan, F., & Yuan, J. (2007). An assessment of customer service in business–to–business relationships. *Journal of Services Marketing, 21*(5), 313–325.

Smart Services: A Condition Monitoring Use Case Utilizing System-Wide Analyses

Dominik Martin, Niklas Kühl, and Johannes Kunze von Bischhoffshausen

Abstract Sensor technology has become increasingly important (e.g., Industry 4.0 and IoT). Large numbers of machines and products are equipped with sensors to constantly monitor their condition. Usually, the condition of an entire system is inferred through sensors in parts of the system by means of a multiplicity of methods and techniques. This so-called condition monitoring can thus reduce the downtime costs of a machine through improved maintenance scheduling. However, for small components as well as relatively inexpensive or immutable parts of a machine, sometimes it is not possible or uneconomical to embed sensors.

This chapter introduces a system-oriented concept of how to monitor individual components of a complex technical system without including additional sensor technology. By using already existing sensors from the environment combined with machine learning techniques, we are able to infer the condition of a system component, without actually observing it. As a consequence, condition monitoring or additional services based on the component's behavior can be developed without overcoming the challenges of sensor implementation. In order to show the feasibility of the presented concept, we also implement an industrial use case.

This chapter is based on the paper (Martin and Kühl 2019).

D. Martin (✉) · N. Kühl
Karlsruhe Institute of Technology (KIT), Karlsruhe, Germany
e-mail: martin@kit.edu; kuehl@kit.edu

J. K. von Bischhoffshausen
Trelleborg Sealing Solutions Germany GmbH, Stuttgart, Germany
e-mail: johannes.kunze@trelleborg.com

© Springer Nature Switzerland AG 2020
M. Maleshkova et al. (eds.), *Smart Service Management*,
https://doi.org/10.1007/978-3-030-58182-4_16

1 Introduction and Motivation

With the rapid development of advanced sensor technology and the decline in hardware costs, an increasing number of machines and products have been equipped with sensors to acquire data on assets behavior (Civerchia et al. 2017; Gubbi et al. 2013; Macskassy and Provost 2017). Condition monitoring uses these data in order to facilitate the detection of machine malfunctions in an early state, thus minimizing consequential damage, enhancing maintenance work scheduling, as well as reducing downtime costs (Jardine et al. 2006).

Industry as well as academia faces the challenge of developing condition monitoring solutions for machines, products, systems, and components. Most research focuses on the development of smart materials equipped with sensors, or equipping machines or components with a large number of sensors designed for this particular purpose (Uluyol et al. 2011; Hodge et al. 2015; Peeters et al. 2001).

However, in many cases, it is either not technically feasible or uneconomic to monitor the components or parts of interest with dedicated sensors (Kassanos et al. 2018a,b; Thompson and Yang 2018). For instance, it is not possible to incorporate sensor technology into a part of interest—such as, i.e., a seal—due to, for instance, technical reasons or unreasonable expenses.

Especially for very complex assets (i.e., aircraft engines, production machines, and wind turbines), the reliability of each individual component is of enormous importance. Such complex assets consist of a number of components that often again are composed of subcomponents produced by various manufacturers. The manufacturing at the entire system level thus requires only little knowledge about the behavior of all parts down to the smallest components. Therefore, the OEMs do not necessarily have the technical know-how to develop high-quality condition monitoring solutions for each individual component.

Nevertheless, it may be interesting to monitor even small and seemingly negligible parts in order to gain insights about the part's behavior within a complex environment, to differentiate from competitors or to be able to offer additional services. Such services could be, for instance, maintenance services, wear prediction, or analysis tools for a specific component or part. Even condition monitoring as a service could be a conceivable business model. Furthermore, condition monitoring allows us to prevent consequential damage to the overall system due to a component malfunction. However, especially for suppliers of very cheap or small components, it is often not possible to offer their own condition monitoring solutions for their products, since an observation of these components in the context of the overall system is too costly. Thus, for instance, embedding special sensors into a part or even customizing the surrounding system of a component that costs a few cents is generally not profitable.

In this chapter, we propose a concept to observe the state of individual parts by a system-wide consideration without actually being able to observe them directly.

By applying machine learning techniques, we show how conclusions about individual components can be drawn by considering the entire system. Thus, our approach allows us to make statements about the behavior or condition of subordinate parts without additional hardware being necessary.

We show that, despite complex interrelations within a system, as described by general systems theory (Bertalanffy 1950; Checkland 1999) and the idea of holism (Oshry 2007; Auyang 1999), condition monitoring of components of a system can be accomplished by means of machine learning.

2 Foundations and Related Work

This chapter considers machines, products, and assets as systems and therefore uses systems theory—an interdisciplinary approach for describing and explaining aspects, properties, and principles of systems—to describe interrelations and the behavior of systems and its components. Subsequently, we introduce the concept of condition monitoring and discuss the related literature regarding the existing condition monitoring approaches.

2.1 Systems Theory

The aim of classical physics was to reduce natural phenomena to an interaction of elementary units—such as atoms—whose properties are independent of the environment, and thus of adjacent units. Similarly, in biology, the assumption was that phenomena of life can be resolved into separate parts that can be considered in isolation. Accordingly, an organism can be thought of as the interplay of various elements—such as cells—that function independently (Bertalanffy 1950).

This traditional scientific theory for exploring single components without regard to the surrounding units is known as reductionism. Reductionism is a bottom-up approach and tries to deduce the understanding of the whole from the understanding of individual parts. However, a whole aggregated of parts is not immediately apparent from the individual parts (Fang and Casadevall 2011).

This problem arises from complex interrelationships between the individual parts, from which a whole emerges. Only the whole gives the parts and their interactions a meaning. For instance, only a living organism gives meaning to the heart or lungs as well as a family to the roles of husband, wife, son, or daughter (Jackson 2007).

According to this assumption, and contrary to the idea of reductionism, modern biology has developed the notion that not only the consideration of isolated parts but also of relations between parts and the resulting dynamic interactions is essential. This results in differences between individual parts considered separately and parts within a whole organism (Bertalanffy 1950; Checkland 1999).

The biologist Ludwig von Bertalanffy proposed systems theory in the 1940s, in which he transferred and generalized this idea to other scientific disciplines

(Boulding 1956). He defines systems as interaction contexts that differ from their environment, which in turn consists of other interaction contexts. Through their interaction with the environment, they can evolve new properties. System theory does not reduce the whole (i.e., the human body) to the behavior or properties of its parts (i.e., organs), but rather describes the relationships and arrangement of the parts which build the whole (Boulding 1956).

Accordingly, holism is the idea that systems (biological, physical, social, economic, etc.) and their properties should be viewed as wholes, not just as a collection of parts (Oshry 2007; Auyang 1999).

Based on this, Ackoff (1981) defines a system as a set of two or more elements that satisfies the following conditions: The behavior of each element has an effect on the behavior of the whole, where both the behavior of the elements and their effects on the whole are interdependent. Additionally, all subgroups of elements have an effect on the behavior of the whole but none has an independent effect on it.

2.2   Condition Monitoring

Observing the behavior of systems and their elements poses a complex challenge in various disciplines, such as biology, physics, medicine, but also in computer science or mechanical engineering. Especially in industry, the continuous observation of machine or product conditions is an important factor for smooth operations.

The concept of condition monitoring describes the regular acquisition and analysis of physical parameters for monitoring the condition of machines. The physical machine parameters are collected by means of sensors and include vibration (Peng and Chu 2004; Carden and Fanning 2004), temperature (Zhou et al. 2007; Bagavathiappan et al. 2013), acoustic emission (Dornfeld and DeVries 1990; Bhuiyan et al. 2016), electricity (Trutt et al. 2002), and many more.

By identifying significant changes in the sensor readings, the occurrence of machine failures is determined by a variety of methods (Nandi et al. 2005). This makes condition monitoring an important basis for predictive maintenance. By being aware of the machine conditions at any time, maintenance work can be better planned and accordingly machine downtimes reduced (Nandi et al. 2005). In addition, further actions can be made to minimize consequential damage as well as the effects of a failure in surrounding components. Condition monitoring allows the earlier detection of machine failures, before their effects can be directly perceived by humans. Thus, condition monitoring is an effective alternative to periodic machine inspections (Alsyouf 2007).

Especially with rotating machines, such as motors, pumps, and compressors, condition monitoring methods can be used effectively (Carden and Fanning 2004). However, interesting research approaches are also available for translatory or even static applications.

For instance, Nandi et al. (2005) describes different components which indicate failures in electric motors. In addition to the typical failure types occurring in different components, common recognition and analysis techniques are summarized. However, the focus relies on the analysis of conditions of the entire electric motor system. A targeted analysis of components such as the bearing or even components of it, without dedicated sensors, is not considered.

Also, Carden and Fanning (2004) summarizes different methods and techniques which appear in literature, which are capable of detecting failures based on the analysis of vibrations. They argue that different methods require a varying number of sensors and the results improve as the number of sensors increases.

This work does neither want to treat the integration of new sensors into a system nor to consider the behavior of the whole system. Our work focuses on monitoring a single component of a system that does not have integrated sensing capabilities by using already available sensors from the component's environment. Thus, we aim to show the feasibility of inferring the condition of such a system component even without dedicated embedded sensors.

3 Approach

The goal of this chapter is to present a concept to gain insights about the behavior of a part of a system based on data gathered from sensors in the part's environment. Thus, we design a concept that allows us to derive the behavior of a part of a system based on system-wide considerations, without being able to observe this directly.

Based on this concept and an industrial use case, we aim to develop a condition monitoring system artifact for hydraulic cylinders, which is capable of detecting seal failures on the basis of sensors within the cylinder, but, however, without being able to observe the seal directly. Thus, we want to evaluate the feasibility of our proposed concept by means of a concrete technical experiment. After demonstrating the feasibility, we also provide a prototype that demonstrates a possible use case.

4 Concept of Holistic System Analytics

As described by Ackoff (1981), systems consist of several elements that are exposed to each other's interactions and thus influence the behavior of the entire system. According to the idea of holism, the total system is more than the sum of its parts. This contradicts the approach of reductionism, which intends to analyze all individual components of a system in order to comprehensively describe the behavior of the entire system. Based on these assumptions, the behavior of a system from a holistic viewpoint cannot be fully explained by the behavior of the individual elements. Thus, no direct inferences from the overall system behavior to its elements are possible, since the behavior of the entire system is influenced by complex interdependent relationships of the system elements.

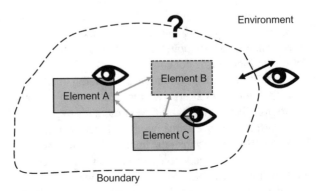

Fig. 1 System-level analysis

However, even if there is no direct relationship between the behavior of the entire system and individual elements of it, each of the effects of an element influences the behavior of the entire system. Thus, by observing these more complex relationships on a system level, patterns can be recognized which are caused by individual elements.

Typically, monitoring of technical systems is achieved by incorporating sensors and observation capabilities into its components. Individual components in complex systems are analyzed separately. Based on this information, conclusions about the behavior of the entire system are derived (Nandi et al. 2005).

Figure 1 visualizes this common approach of a system-level analysis. It shows an open system which consists of a set of elements having interdependent effects on the entire system. The system itself also interacts with the environment. Individual elements of the system can be observed by, i.e., sensors (elements A and C), while other elements are unobservable (element B). Using the observable behavior of elements and the observable interaction of the entire system with the environment, conclusions can be drawn about the behavior of the entire system.

Our proposed concept describes a contradictory approach. This concept describes a method to analyze elements of a complex technical system in which an element of interest on the one hand is not directly observable and on the other hand has no trivial connections between the behavior of itself and the behavior of the entire system. Based on data representing information about the behavior of the entire system, machine learning is used to identify the effects of individual components on the entire system. This approach allows us to observe the behavior and thus the state of system components, which are not observable directly.

This approach is visualized in Fig. 2. Therefore, the behavior of an element within the entire system is of interest. However, this behavior cannot be observed directly. Thus, by observing the interaction of the system with the environment, the impact of the element's behavior (element B) on these interactions is inferred.

This systemic top-down approach, in which the behavior of the entire system serves as basis for the analysis of system elements, requires a technique to identify

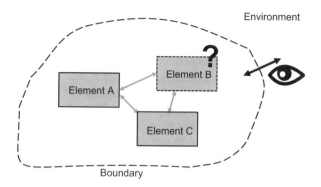

Fig. 2 Component-level analysis

patterns in the interactions of the system with the environment and to isolate the corresponding causers of these patterns.

We use machine learning techniques for tackling this and demonstrate the feasibility of our approach by means of an industrial use case. Thus, our proposed concept of compensating missing sensors in components by applying machine learning techniques to infer component behavior represents a Design Science Research artifact.

5   Evaluation and Discussion

This section evaluates the described artifact (presented concept). Therefore, we use an industrial use case to assess the feasibility of our approach. We define a hydraulic cylinder as a system in which a seal (component) is to be observed without equipping it with sensors.

5.1   Technical Experiment

A hydraulic system is used to transfer power from a hydraulic pump to a piston. By introducing a pressurized hydraulic fluid into a cylinder, the piston within the cylinder is moved. The medium necessary for this is a hydraulic fluid, such as oil, which is usually heavily pressurized. Depending on the application (i.e., an excavator), enormous forces act on the piston that are transmitted from the hydraulic system. The seals which seal the piston rod to the cylinder wall are thus essential for the function of such a hydraulic system.

Seals, even if they seem unimportant and inconspicuous, are an essential component of various applications. The catastrophic incident of the NASA space shuttle Challenger in 1986 caused by a damaged seal reveals that seal failures can lead to dramatic effects (Alsyouf 2007).

As described in Sect. 3, we develop a machine learning model, which is able to infer the behavior, or the state of a seal within a hydraulic cylinder based on sensor time series obtained from the surrounding of the seal itself.

The intention of this model is the real-time detection of failure scenarios. Seals are sensitive components of hydraulic applications. Thus, a malfunction of sealing elements results in inadequate sealing efficiency and thus—in extreme cases—in a failure of the entire application. Due to the high sensitivity, a correct installation of an undamaged seal must be ensured. The model has to be capable to detect, i.e., a possible assembly failure or a damaged seal.

Thus, we define three failure classes: *no failure*, *assembly failure*, and *damage*. Data gained from different tests conducted on hydraulic cylinder test rigs serve as basis for the machine learning model which is able to recognize patterns in the data and derive a class assignment accordingly. In order to obtain a wide range of different failure scenarios, various assembly failures and damages are simulated in several test series.

In order to train the classification model, 400 hours of data with a frequency of 20 Hz captured by 13 sensors are available.

These sensors capture different pressures, temperatures, and rod velocity of the hydraulic cylinder. The data are cleaned and features are extracted. The failure classes are used as labels.

We use a Random Forest Classifier, as it achieves good performance in pre-tests with low training time. For model training and validation by conducting a grid search, we use 10-fold nested cross-validation to avoid overfitting (Cawley and Talbot 2010).

By using the F1-score (Powers 2011) as a performance metric, the classification model achieves an average score of 0.971. In addition, we use neural networks, decision trees, and support vector machines as classification algorithms, all of which, however, yield lower performance (below 0.94).

5.2 Prototype

As described in Sect. 5.1, the condition of seals can be classified by the application of machine learning algorithms. This proves the general feasibility of inferring the condition of seals without directly implemented sensors. This opens up the possibility of making this knowledge accessible and usable for third parties (i.e., customers). Therefore, we deploy the previously developed model as a web service; thus, it can be accessed via Internet.

The architecture of this prototype is shown in Fig. 3. The raw data collected at the hydraulic cylinder are provided unprocessed to an IoT gateway. This gateway allows secure and scalable communication between IoT devices and the cloud and makes the data available to downstream processes, like stream processing.

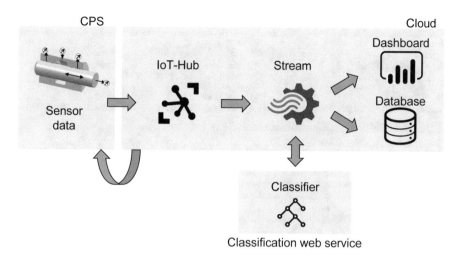

Fig. 3 Architecture of condition monitoring prototype

Streaming allows data to be processed in real time and delivered to the deployed model realized by a RESTful web service. The web service handles the data cleaning and feature extraction and uses the implemented classifier to determine the corresponding failure class of the seal. This information is passed back to the stream module as a response. Subsequently, the raw data, extended to the determined failure information, are passed to the dashboard module. This allows the visualization of real-time data in a browser. In addition, the raw data, extended by the classification results, are stored in a database. Optionally, the determined classification results can be transmitted back to the hydraulic cylinder's control unit in order to initiate appropriate actions there. For practical applications, changing load conditions or switching off the affected cylinder would be conceivable.

Figure 4 shows a screenshot of the dashboard showing the condition of the sealing elements in real time. Thus, visual monitoring of the seal condition is possible with a simple graphical interface. The first tile at the top left shows the current seal condition on a virtual scale from 0 to 1. This is an indicator calculated from the prediction probability and the moving average of historical inferences. The second tile shows the current classified seal condition and the third tile the corresponding probability of a seal failure in the present classification result. The last tile in the first row shows the relative frequency of classified failure classes since system ramp-up. The lower part of the dashboard shows the current sensor raw data in real time.

Fig. 4 Screenshot of condition monitoring dashboard prototype

5.3 Discussion

This work shows how machine learning can be used to obtain insights about the behavior of a system component by data obtained from system-level sensors.

Thus, there are some practical implications. Component manufacturers which previously provided only physical products thus have the opportunity to monetize their domain know-how and offer additional services supporting their core products (Baines et al. 2007). However, collaboration with data owners and manufacturers of the immediate environment of the part or component, including the sensors, is required. Embedding component services to the entire system level, however, also creates additional value concerning the entire system. Furthermore, failure localization within a system is a complex problem, which could be solved hereby. In general, failures are only analyzed at the system level. Thus, an investigation on failure causes needs to be conducted additionally. Knowing the exact location of a failure within a complex system can therefore lead to less time-consuming troubleshooting (Rytter 1993).

The presented artifact is thus able to act as the basis of a new data-driven service. As an example, one could imagine offering a condition monitoring system including maintenance service as a subscription model instead of selling seals in a product-focused manner. The analysis of different failure classes can also help to make application recommendations that lead to longer product lifetimes.

6   Conclusion and Outlook

Due to embedded sensors, machines and products produce large amounts of data which are often only used for a specific purpose. The entire potential of these already existing data is therefore far from being exploited. Furthermore, some manufacturers face the challenge that some components of complex technical systems cannot be monitored because no sensors can be implemented for technical or economic reasons.

Therefore, we propose a concept how this problem can be resolved. By means of a system-wide analysis of the existing sensor data from the immediate environment of the part of interest through machine learning, it is possible to extract patterns that can be used to deduce the behavior of parts of a system.

Based on an industrial use case, we show that the condition of a seal within a hydraulic cylinder, even though no sensors are integrated into it, can be inferred from the sensors in the hydraulic cylinder surrounding the seal. A classification technique analyzes the effects of the different conditions of a seal on the behavior of the entire system and, thus, the system-level sensor values. The results show that patterns caused by the different conditions can be detected within the data captured with surrounding sensors.

In addition to these contributions, this work also has limitations. We assume that the sensors in the environment record patterns that affect a system component. This cannot be proven by the technical experiment presented in this work. In addition, the demarcation of a system in general is not clearly defined. This requires a case-by-case analysis. Furthermore, the application of machine learning also has shortcomings compared to the analysis of physical coherences. The analysis of cause-effect relationships using mathematical models can also be feasible in some cases, however, without the need for collecting training data. However, as with the analysis of physical relationships between components, the sensors used must deliver reliable and stable values over time to ensure the quality of the classification model. A systematic shift in sensor readings over time or a changing sensor configuration can result in decreasing performance.

Nevertheless, we are convinced that this concept provides an exciting research approach. In the next step, it remains to analyze whether the quality of this approach is comparable to sensor-based condition monitoring in use cases where sensors can be equipped. Thus, our proposed concept could potentially replace sensors within components, which could lead to a decrease in overall system costs.

Furthermore, it has to be investigated which effects the behavior of a system component has on the behavior of other system components. Thus, the concept could be extended if the observation of other (observable) components provides additional insights on the (unobservable) target component. This would be a mixture of the traditional approach (observation of individual components to analyze the overall system conditions) and the concept presented in this work.

In addition, it can be analyzed how the quality of this approach, compared with sensing the component itself, changes for other use cases as well as for other system boundaries.

Our presented use case could also be extended by increasing the granularity of the failure classes leading to more detailed insights.

Finally, we are convinced that our concept can be used in many applications and leads to a broader understanding about system components. This holds the potential to make a whole range of applications more transparent and reliable.

References

Ackoff, R. L. (1981). *Creating the corporate future: plan or be planned for*. New York: Wiley.

Alsyouf, I. (2007). The role of maintenance in improving companies' productivity and profitability. *International Journal of Production Economics, 105*(1), 70–78.

Auyang, S. Y. (1999). Foundations of complex-system theories. In *Economics, Evolutionary Biology, and Statistical Physics* (pp. 1–404).

Bagavathiappan, S., Lahiri, B. B., Saravanan, T., Philip, J., & Jayakumar, T. (2013). Infrared thermography for condition monitoring - A review. *Infrared Physics and Technology, 60*, 35–55.

Baines, T. S., Lightfoot, H. W., Evans, S., Neely, A., Greenough, R., Peppard, J., et al. (2007). State-of-the-art in product-service systems. *Proceedings of the Institution of Mechanical Engineers, Part B: Journal of Engineering Manufacture, 221*(10), 1543–1552.

Bertalanffy, L. v. (1950). An outline of general system theory. *The British Journal For Philisophy Of Science, 1*(2), 134–165.

Bhuiyan, M. S. H., Choudhury, I. A., Dahari, M., Nukman, Y., & Dawal, S. Z. (2016). Application of acoustic emission sensor to investigate the frequency of tool wear and plastic deformation in tool condition monitoring. *Measurement: Journal of the International Measurement Confederation, 92*, 208–217.

Boulding, K. E. (1956). General systems theory - the skeleton of sciene. *Management Science, 2*(3), 197–208.

Carden, E. P., & Fanning, P. (2004). Vibration based condition monitoring: a review. *Structural Health Monitoring: An International Journal, 3*(4), 355–377.

Cawley, G. C., & Talbot, N. L. C. (2010). On over-fitting in model selection and subsequent selection bias in performance evaluation. *Journal of Machine Learning Research, 11*, 2079–2107.

Checkland, P. (1999). Systems thinking. In *Rethinking Management Information Systems* (pp. 45–56). Oxford University Press.

Civerchia, F., Bocchino, S., Salvadori, C., Rossi, E., Maggiani, L., & Petracca, M. (2017). Industrial internet of things monitoring solution for advanced predictive maintenance applications. *Journal of Industrial Information Integration, 7*, 4–12.

Dornfeld, D. A., & DeVries, M. (1990). Neural network sensor fusion for tool condition monitoring. *CIRP Annals - Manufacturing Technology, 39*(1), 101–105.

Fang, F. C., & Casadevall, A. (2011). Reductionistic and holistic science. *Infection and Immunity, 79*(4), 1401–1404.

Gubbi, J., Buyya, R., Marusic, S., & Palaniswami, M. (2013). Internet of Things (IoT): A vision, architectural elements, and future directions. *Future Generation Computer Systems, 29*(7), 1645–1660.

Hodge, V. J., Keefe, S. O., Weeks, M., & Moulds, A. (2015). Wireless sensor networks for condition monitoring in the railway industry: a survey. *IEEE Transactions on Intelligent Transportation Systems, 16*(3), 1088–1106.

Jackson, M. C. (2007). *Systems thinking: creative holism for managers.* John Wiley & Sons Ltd.

Jardine, A. K., Lin, D., & Banjevic, D. (2006). A review on machinery diagnostics and prognostics implementing condition-based maintenance. *Mechanical Systems and Signal Processing, 20*(7), 1483–1510.

Kassanos, P., Anastasova, S., & Yang, G.-Z. (2018a). Electrical and physical sensors for biomedical implants. In G.-Z. Yang (Ed.), *Implantable Sensors and Systems: From Theory to Practice* (pp. 99–195). Cham: Springer International Publishing.

Kassanos, P., Ip, H., & Yang, G.-Z. (2018b). Ultra-low power application-specific integrated circuits for sensing. In G.-Z. Yang (Ed.), *Implantable Sensors and Systems: From Theory to Practice* (pp. 281–437). Cham: Springer International Publishing.

Macskassy, S. A., & Provost, F. (2017). A brief survey of machine learning methods and their sensor and IoT applications. In *International Conference on Information, Intelligence, Systems & Applications (IISA)* (pp. 172–175).

Martin, D. and Kühl, N. (2019). Holistic system-analytics as an alternative to isolated sensor technology: a condition monitoring use case. In *Proceedings of the 52nd Hawaii International Conference on System Sciences* (pp. 1005–1012).

Nandi, S., Toliyat, H. A., & Li, X. (2005). Condition monitoring and fault diagnosis of electrical motors - A review. *IEEE Transactions on Energy Conversion, 20*(4), 719–729.

Oshry, B. (2007). *Seeing systems: unlocking the mysteries of organizational life.* Berrett-Koehler Publishers, Inc.

Peeters, B., Maeck, J., & Roeck, G. D. (2001). Vibration-based damage detection in civil engineering: Excitation sources and temperature effects. *Smart Materials and Structures,* June(October 2014).

Peng, Z. K., & Chu, F. L. (2004). Application of the wavelet transform in machine condition monitoring and fault diagnostics: A review with bibliography. *Mechanical Systems and Signal Processing, 18*(2), 199–221.

Powers, D. (2011). Evaluation: from precision, recall and F-measure to Roc, informedness, markedness & correlation. *Journal of Machine Learning Technologies, 2*(1), 37–63.

Rytter, A. (1993). *Vibrational based inspection of civil engineering structures.* Ph.D. thesis, Aalborg University, Denmark.

Thompson, A. J., & Yang, G.-Z. (2018). Tethered and implantable optical sensors. In G.-Z. Yang (Ed.), *Implantable Sensors and Systems: From Theory to Practice* (pp. 439–505). Cham: Springer International Publishing.

Trutt, F. C., Sottile, J., & Kohler, J. L. (2002). Online condition monitoring of induction motors. *IEEE Transactions on Industry Applications, 38*(6), 1627–1632.

Uluyol, O., Parthasarathy, G., Foslien, W., & Kim, K. (2011). Power curve analytic for wind turbine performance monitoring and prognostics. In *Annual Conference of the Prognostics and Health Management Society* (August, pp. 1–8).

Zhou, W., Habetler, T. G., & Harley, R. G. (2007). Bearing condition monitoring methods for electric machines: a general review. In *2007 IEEE International Symposium on Diagnostics for Electric Machines, Power Electronics and Drives* (pp. 3–6).

Developing Real-Time Smart Industrial Analytics for Industry 4.0 Applications

Pankesh Patel and Muhammad Intizar Ali

Abstract Industry 4.0 refers to the 4th Industrial Revolution—the recent trend of automation and data exchange in manufacturing technologies. Traditionally, Manufacturing Executing System (MES) collects data, and it is only used for periodic reports giving insight about past events. It does not incorporate real-time data for up-to-date reports. Production targets are mostly predefined, before the actual production starts. The different production anomalies are known to happen in the real world, affecting the predefined production targets. Moreover, a key challenge faced by industry is to integrate multiple autonomous processes, machines, and businesses.

A broad objective of our work is to build an integrated view that can make data available in a unified model to support different stakeholders of a factory (e.g., factory planners, managers) in decision-making. In this chapter, we focus on designing an approach for building Industry 4.0 smart services and addressing real-time data analytics, which can integrate multiple sources of information and analyze them on the fly. Moreover, we share our experience of applying IoT and data analytics approach to a traditional manufacturing domain, thus enabling smart services for Industry 4.0. We also present our key findings and challenges faced while deploying our solution in real industrial settings. The selected use case studies demonstrate the use of our approach for building smart Industry 4.0 applications.

P. Patel (✉)
Data Science Institute, NUI Galway, Galway, Ireland
e-mail: pankesh.patel@insight-centre.org

M. I. Ali
Data Science Institute, NUI Galway, Galway, Ireland

Dublin City University, Dublin, Ireland
e-mail: ali.intizar@insight-centre.org; ali.intizar@dcu.ie

© Springer Nature Switzerland AG 2020
M. Maleshkova et al. (eds.), *Smart Service Management*,
https://doi.org/10.1007/978-3-030-58182-4_17

1 Introduction

Industry 4.0 or smart manufacturing brings the 4th Industrial Revolution by integrating all digitized services and facilitating automation in manufacturing. The aim of Industry 4.0 is to provide end-to-end connected smart solutions. Cyber Physical Systems are a key pillar of Industry 4.0 as they provide interconnected services between physical assets and their computational spaces (Lee et al. 2015). Industrial data analytics is another important pillar of the Industry 4.0, as it supports intelligent, automated decision-making. With the recent scientific achievements in machine learning and deep learning technologies, it is now possible to analyze a large amount of data and provide actionable insights.

The key goal of this chapter is to demonstrate on how to build smart services for Industry 4.0 domain that can use data analytics to make intelligent decisions (Lee et al. 2014). Among the key challenges to build the smart services for Industry 4.0, the fundamental challenge is *lack of real-time analysis*. The traditional approach in Industry 4.0 is to compile historical data and generate reports for decision-making (Berson and Smith 1997). A common pattern found is that data are stored in the databases. Then, the stored data are retrieved later to generate periodic reports, analyzing the insights about past events. This pattern is not able to incorporate real-time data (e.g., device real-time alarms). An analysis in real time can be a key to accurately predict at more granular time intervals. Therefore, it is necessary to set up an Industry 4.0 data collection infrastructure that can provide end-to-end transparency in real time (e.g., the status of the production in the manufacturing process), allowing for optimization not only across the factory sites but also in the entire supply chain. Moreover, the blend of historical data and contextual data generated by IoT devices can improve the outcomes of decision-making algorithms (Watson and Wixom 2007). A few middleware solutions have been proposed (Gao et al. 2017; Intizar et al. 2017) for real-time analytics. However, the applications of the proposed approaches are missing in the manufacturing domain (Zhong et al. 2017). Another challenge is *lack of interoperability*. The data collection largely is not interconnected. This results into silos of data, making the interoperability of data very difficult. The complex and heterogeneous nature of the equipment used in the manufacturing industry sometimes makes it difficult to get an overall perspective. As the technology advances, the new machines are often delivered with powerful technologies. For SMEs (small-to-medium-sized enterprises) with older machines installed at its factory, it can be challenging to catch up with the complex IT standards that come along. The equipment used in factories is often based on proprietary software that uses proprietary protocols, and it is often difficult to update to more modern protocols. This environment makes it challenging to create solutions that monitor equipment across entire factory floors and across different factories.

By achieving interoperability, it is possible to build Industry 4.0 smart services, in which multiple autonomous systems can be capable of exchanging information on the fly and make automated intelligent decision after analyzing the collected

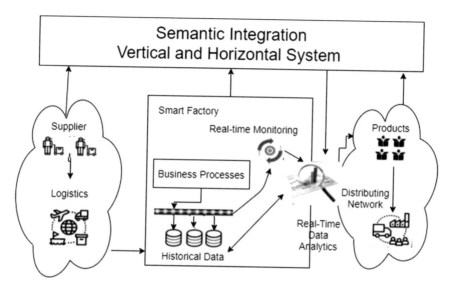

Fig. 1 A semantic-enabled platform for Industry 4.0 systems

information. Currently, the business intelligence is mostly limited to a department level or to a site level at the most. We envision an ecosystem of Industry 4.0 applications, where multiple autonomous systems can share information in real time and collectively make decisions for the common good (see Fig. 1). Imagine a scenario of supply chain management, where multiple stakeholders are involved. An integrated middleware should enable the integration of the systems supported by multiple stakeholders and optimize manufacturing tasks accordingly. In such scenarios, a delay in the supply chain must already alert the manager of the shop floor to optimize manufacturing processes accordingly or a weather calamity event must automatically trigger actions expecting abruption in manufacturing processes and consequently a reduction in daily production goals.

An integrated and holistic view of a factory can be established to improve the decision-making and to reduce the overall complexity. The interlinking includes the interlinking of diverse data sources such as anomalies in real time (e.g., machine breakage), the manufacturing execution system (e.g., production data), business processes, and so on. Although much of these data are already captured by IT system, it largely remains inaccessible in an integrated way without investigating manual effort. Thus, *the broad objective of our research is to build an integrated view that can make data available in a unified model to support different stakeholders of a factory (e.g., factory planners, managers) in decision-making.* Section 3 presents AI- and semantic-based conceptual framework (named SWeTI Patel et al. 2018) to achieve this broad objective.

In this chapter, we focus on designing an approach for building Industry 4.0 smart services and addressing real-time data analytics, which can integrate multiple sources of information and analyze them on the fly. Moreover, we share our experience of applying IoT and data analytics approach to a traditional manufacturing domain, thus enabling smart services for Industry 4.0. Using our open-source and standards-based approach, autonomous systems could be seamlessly integrated using semantic technologies. The proposed approach can analyze large amount of historical manufacturing data by applying machine learning algorithms and collecting and analyzing sensor data on the fly. It facilitates an integrated view of information from historical as well as real-time data perspective and facilitates intelligent decision-making.

We also discuss a real-world production manufacturing use case, provided by a large manufacturer of bio-medical devices (more details in Sect. 2). We elaborate our approach to design a real-time data analytic solution based on production forecasting. The proposed approach uses historical data of production processes to train ML algorithms for future production goals, which help the manufactures to set optimal and realistic goals for production. Contrary to traditional machine learning approach that only considers historical data pattern, the proposed approach supports a real-time monitoring to detect abnormal events (such as machine breakages, head count shortages, and unavailability of raw materials). The impact of these abnormal events is calculated and used to adjust the hourly, daily, and weekly production targets accordingly. Our proposed approach integrates real-time monitoring techniques to trigger notifications for taking the remedial actions in real time.

Outline The remainder of this chapter is structured as follows: In Sect. 2, we take one real-world Industry 4.0 case study. Section 3 presents our AI- and semantic-based conceptual framework (named SWeTI Patel et al. 2018) for building smart services for Industry 4.0. Background and existing approaches to build smart services for Industry 4.0 are discussed in Sect. 4. We discussed our approach to address the objective of the case study in Sect. 5, before concluding in Sect. 6.

2 Motivating Use Case: Smart Industrial Analytics

This section presents a production forecasting use case in the Industry 4.0 domain. We consider a production forecasting of a large medical device manufacturer, which is one of our industrial partners at the CONFIRM SFI Research Centre for Smart Manufacturing (https://confirm.ie/). Our industry partner manufactures orthopedic devices such as knee, hip, and shoulder joint replacements. The organization has multiple manufacturing units at various geographical locations, across Ireland and worldwide.

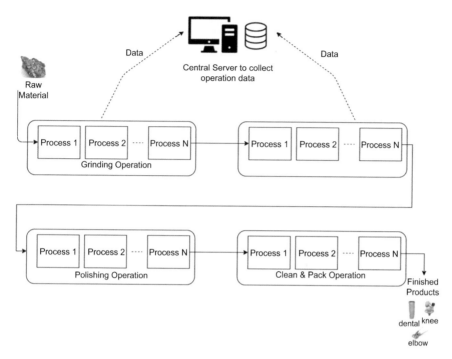

Fig. 2 Production process layout, from raw material to a finished product

Figure 2 presents a production process layout. At a manufacturing unit, a typical line of production at the shop floor is sequential. For simplicity reasons, we present broad steps of the manufacturing process, however, the actual lines of production are usually very complex. Figure 2 presents the production process layout steps from raw material to grinding, from grinding to polishing, and from polishing to cleaning and packing. A machine is responsible for executing one or more steps of an operation (e.g., grinding). Each machine has specific characteristics that restrict a set of products, which can be allocated to it. The manufacturing process is carried out in a batch processing manner. Each machine can only run one batch at a time.

Due to the sequential production process at the manufacturing unit, any kind of anomaly at any stage leads to domino effect on subsequence manufacturing processes. The organization uses an internal Manufacturing Execution System (MES) to keep track of its daily processes and stores relevant information about each processing step of each manufacturing process. The collected data are used to generate periodic reports, summarizing the actual production between requested time frames. The generated reports are used by factory planners to set future production targets.

The current system at the company is facing some challenges, which needs to be addressed to achieve overall goals of the manufacturing company. These goals are to reach production goal on time to meet the product demand, to reduce manufacturing cost, and to maximize utilization of resources. In the following, we present the challenges that need to be addressed to achieve these objectives:

Real-Time Visibility The existing system collects data, and it is only used for the generation of periodic reports giving insights about past events. It does not incorporate real-time data, events for up-to-date reports, and feedback from the supervisor(s) of shop floor. To address these limitations, the company needs a system that allows them to capture data in real time from each process and shows the production targets in real time. If the threshold condition is not met, then deviations are recorded and supervisors are notified. So, the supervisors can take appropriate actions to minimize the effect. Moreover, the deviation reasons can be recorded for future analysis for improvements and production planning. Sections 4.1 and 4.2 present the state-of-the-art tools to address this challenge.

Anomalies at Runtime The production targets are set, before the actual production starts. More specifically, the planners largely define production goals based on the plant's current capacity of producing the number of units, supply and demand consideration, and consideration of past events or situations. The different anomalies are known to happen in the real world. For instance, the anomalies such as machine breakage, raw material low supply due to some external events (e.g., logistics delay, supplier or distributor issues), manpower shortage, quality issues such as scrap and rework. These are not considered during the goal settings, thus affecting the overall production targets. To address this limitation, a company would need a set of tools (state of the art presented in Sect. 4.2) to monitor, detect, and report events. To detect an event, different thresholds based on historical data analysis and domain knowledge from staff members of the organizations are implemented.

Interoperability Data collected at each process (e.g., grinding, polishing, cleaning, and packaging) are not interconnected and interoperable, resulting into silos of information for each process. This largely occurs because the company is using different systems, supplied by different vendors, each has its own data collection software, different communication protocols as well as different data format and files. To ensure accurate prediction, the company would need to integrate data from all relevant processes. Semantic Web approaches discussed in Sect. 4.3 can play a role to achieve this objective.

Self-Configuration Due to the advancement in technologies, the manufacturers may be interested in self-adaptive approaches, which can automatically adjust goals and targets based on current processes. An ideal scenario is to develop a system that can automatically reduce daily production targets according to unexpected events such as machine failure (Wang et al. 2016). This approach would ensure a maximum utilization of available resources.

To address the objectives, such as mentioned above, the next section presents our AI- and semantic-based conceptual framework (named SWeTI Patel et al. 2018) for building smart services for Industry 4.0.

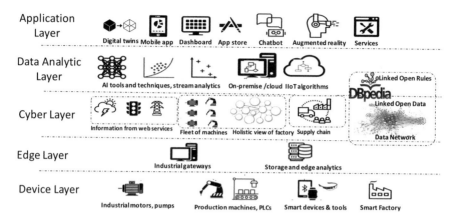

Fig. 3 A layered view of SWeTI platform

3 SWeTI: A Semantic Web of Things Platform for Building Industry 4.0 Smart Services

This section presents a layered architecture of SWeTI platform briefly (Patel et al. 2018). Figure 3 presents an architecture. It begins with the data processing pipeline at the machine level and moves toward intelligent autonomous applications.

Device Layer The shop floor at a factory hosts various industrial devices (e.g., pumps, motors, PLCs, industrial robots) and smart devices (e.g., mobile phones, smartwatches) that enhance human–machine interactions. From a connectivity viewpoint, they could be devices with legacy communication protocols or IoT standard protocols (e.g., OPC-UA, BLE, MQTT).

Edge Layer It transforms raw data generated at the device layer into information. Typically, powerful gateway devices are deployed at this layer. The gateway devices implement various edge analytics techniques such as data aggregation, data filteration, and data cleansing to further refine acquired data (some of the edge analytics tools are presented in Sect. 4).

Cyber Layer It acts as a distributed information hub, preparing a ground for specific data analytics. Diverse information could be collected from different players of a supply chain (e.g., logistics, distributors, suppliers), industrial machines on factory floors from edge devices. The information is pushed to form a linked network of information (Linked Data[1]). Linked data are a natural fit for the connected data as they provide abstraction on top of a distributed set of information.

---

[1] https://bit.ly/29YZz5b.

Data Analytic Layer The massive amount of data collected at the cyber layer creates an opportunity to apply industrial analytics, leveraging AI techniques. The aim is to identify an invisible relationship among data and enhance Industry 4.0 applications for better decision-making. The industrial analytics algorithms can be on premise (state of the art presented in Sect. 4.2) or cloud based (state of the art presented in Sect. 4.1).

Application Layer This layer builds meaningful and customized application on top of data and services exposed by the data analytic layer. In recent years, a wide variety of Industry 4.0 applications are demonstrated. For instance, developers can create digital twin by combining data from the data analytic layer and functionality exposed by an industrial machine. GE digital has demonstrated an advanced digital twin.[2] The customer can ask questions related to the machine's performance and potential issues through a natural language interface and receive the answers. Moreover, a manufacturer can interact with the digital twin through Microsoft HoloLense,[3] an augmented reality (AR) device, and the manufacturer can have a 3D view of an industrial asset to analyze its internal parts.

4 Related Work

This section presents existing approaches to implement the use case, presented in Sect. 2. The existing approaches are largely divided into three categories: (1) cloud-based approaches (Sect. 4.1), (2) open-source tools to develop an infrastructure that enables real-time analytics (Sect. 4.2), and (3) Semantic Web technologies to achieve the interoperability among industrial devices (Sect. 4.3).

4.1 Cloud Manufacturing

To realize the use case mentioned in Sect. 2, different cloud vendors (such as Microsoft Azure, AWS, Google, IBM) provide cloud-based services. A common approach, adopted by cloud, is to ingest data from an IoT device to cloud infrastructure. Then, all processing takes place on top of the ingested data, and appropriate decisions are made. The cloud-based approaches provide a set of services to implement industrial analytics solutions. The following present some of the cloud vendors and describe the services offered by them to implement smart industrial analytics:

---

[2]https://youtu.be/2dCz3oL2rTw.

[3]https://www.microsoft.com/en-us/hololens.

- **Microsoft Azure.**[4] It provides storage services (e.g., data lake) to store structured and unstructured data. Moreover, its streaming service allows the users to ingest data into the cloud from industrial devices. This service is supported by an analytic service to analyze the streaming data and to derive insight out of the streaming data. The analytic service component interfaces data visualization services to implement analytic dashboard, machine learning service to make predictions, and data lake services to store big data in various data formats.
- **Siemens Offers MindSphere.**[5] It is an Industrial Internet of Things/Industry 4.0 solution, hosted on AWS. Using this service, the users can connect various industrial devices. MindSphere provides marketplace of preconfigured industrial analytics solutions, using which the users can quickly prototype a solution.
- **GE Offers Predix.**[6] It is a cloud-based Industry 4.0 solution with a preconfig-ured industrial analytics solution (in form of preconfigured apps and machine learning solutions such as predictive maintenance). Moreover, Predix offers an operating system for Industry 4.0 devices that let manufacturers deploy intelligent algorithms at the edge.

Shortcomings of Cloud Manufacturing The cloud-based approaches keep indus-trial analytics solutions largely at a center (Patel et al. 2017, 2018). Thus, it is easy for maintenance. Moreover, it provides tools and technologies that reduce the application development efforts. However, it is not suitable for some of these Industrial Internet of Things applications. In the following, we present the shortcoming of cloud approaches:

- The cloud approaches rely on the constant Internet connectivity among Industry 4.0 devices and Cloud services. The Internet connectivity may not remain consistent, due to several reasons such as the manufacturing unit setup at remote places or at the area where enough infrastructure for the Internet is not available. Imagine a scenario, where an oil and gas unit is located at the seashore. Even if we accept the fact that the technologies advancements can address the Internet connectivity issues, there will always be concerns related to security and sharing data to the third-party cloud vendors.
- A "development environment" of a cloud vendor can be very specific to a plat-form, because each cloud platform brings its own platform-specific environment. This could be a problem when a developer wants to migrate a solution from one cloud provider to the other cloud provider. For instance, the developer may want to migrate his/her solution from Microsoft Azure IoT hub solution to AWS IoT solution. He/she may have to make changes in the cloud-based configuration and perhaps changes in the application's front-end code as well.

---

[4]https://azure.microsoft.com/en-us/industries/discrete-manufacturing/.

[5]https://siemens.mindsphere.io/.

[6]https://www.predix.io/catalog/services/.

- The innovation path may depend on "cloud vendor specific" offering. For instance, a manufacturer may not be able to customize certain cloud-specific features in a certain way if a cloud vendor is not offering that feature.

A common practice of cloud manufacturing is that developer uses the on-premise tools and technologies (mentioned in Sect. 4.2) for initial prototyping of the solution. Then, the solutions are deployed in the cloud for better scalability, when there is an increase of customer base.

4.2 On-premise and Open-Source Approaches

A common pattern found in this approach is that sensor data are collected using Industry 4.0 standards such as OPC-UA, Modbus, MQTT, BLE. The collected data are sent to the more powerful devices such as gateway, which are responsible to aggregate data or to send control signals back to the devices. Moreover, the processed data are pushed to powerful servers, where the data are analyzed. Various machine learning algorithms are used to make predictions. A set of open-source technologies from the Eclipse foundations have been released to build such on-premise systems for Industry 4.0. In the following, we present some of the open-source tools to build on-premise solutions. Table 1 summarizes all these tools and technologies.

Table 1 Summary: open-source tools to build on-premise Industry 4.0 applications

Tools	Description	Layer
Ditto	It is a platform for building a digital twin. A digital twin is a virtual representation of its physical industrial asset (e.g., electric motor). The Ditto provides HTTP APIs to access industrial asset. Using Ditto platform, the developers do not need to know how or where the Industrial assets are connected, thus it simplifies the development of digital twins	Cloud, edge
Kura	It is a platform for building Industry 4.0 gateway devices. It implements the remote management of gateway devices, deployed in the factory. It provides various APIs that allow the developers to build and deploy customized logic at the gateway devices	Gateway
HONO	It provides service interfaces for connecting Industry 4.0 devices to a back end. It provides interfaces to interact with the devices in a uniform way regardless of the device communication protocol	Gateway, edge
Kapua	It is an open-source cloud platform to manage and integrate devices and their data.	Cloud, analytics
Unide	Unide stands for "Understand Industry Devices." It is a Production Performance Management Protocol (PPMP), which is a lightweight server–client implementation using REST APIs and JSON	Edge

Ditto[7]   It is an IoT technology to build "digital twin," which is a virtual representation of its real-world counterpart. For instance, a digital twin of an electric motor in a smart factory can collect data from a physical motor. The user can interact with the digital twin to know the current status of the motor. Eclipse Ditto provides high-level APIs, connecting devices to the back end and implementing business application on top of the high-level APIs.

Kura[8]   It is a software platform (runs on the edge devices) for building IoT gateways. Eclipse Kura provides several services. These services include (1) I/O services to connect and access sensors and resource constrained devices such as microcontrollers, (2) Data services to store and forward the telemetry data collected by the sensors, (3) Cloud services to push data to cloud servers such as AWS and Azure, and (4) Kura wire services to customize logic on gateway devices. All these services are exposed by Web service interface.

HONO[9]   HONO is an open-source remote service interface for connecting IoT devices to back-end services. It is a quite active project in the community with a lot of documentations and examples. The goal of HONO is to provide a platform to interact with devices regardless of communication protocols. The community has developed solutions for HTTP, MQTT, AMQP, and Kura. Moreover, it allows developers to plug custom device protocols, thus it does not limit the Industry 4.0 developers to only supported protocols. On top of Eclipse HONO, it provides a uniform interface to interact with underlying IoT devices regardless of the communication protocols they implement. HONO supports scalable and secure ingestion of sensor data, and its command control API allows to send and receive command message.

Unide[10]   Unide stands for "Understand Industry Devices." It is a Production Performance Management Protocol (PPMP),[11] , which is a lightweight server–client implementation using REST APIs and JSON. Unide provides tools for the validation of PPMP messages and for visualization and persisting of PPMP data. It provides the public REST API with the purpose of receiving measurement and message data from machine. To validate PPMP messages, Unide offers a validator that compares the payload you send to the given JSON-schema. By sending HTTP-POST requests to the validator endpoint, you receive a message confirming whether the PPMP message is correctly written according to the specification.

Kapua[12]   The goal of the Kapua project is to provide an open-source cloud-based IoT integration platform. The Kapua is a platform to integrate data from various IoT

---

[7]https://www.eclipse.org/ditto/.

[8]https://www.eclipse.org/kura/.

[9]https://www.eclipse.org/hono/.

[10]https://www.eclipse.org/unide/.

[11]https://www.eclipse.org/unide/specification/.

[12]https://www.eclipse.org/kapua/.

devices. The Kapua provides a comprehensive management of IoT devices. The management services include the connectivity to IoT devices supporting different ingestion mechanisms, device configuration remotely, application development on top of the Kapua APIs, controlling the device remotely using appropriate access mechanisms, and sending device updates. The Kapua tools can be combined with the Kura project to develop an end-to-end Industry 4.0 solution. This would accelerate community-driven open-source implementation and avoid proprietary vendor lock-in.

We continue leveraging our IoT tools to implement the discussed application: IoTSuite (Chauhan et al. 2016), a tool suite to develop IoT application rapidly; SWoTSuite, a tool suite to implement Semantic Web of Things applications; and a middleware (Alie et al. 2017) for real-time analytics to implement essential Industry 4.0 components. In the following, we present them briefly:

IoTSuite[13] The objective of this programming framework is to make the application development easy by hiding IoT development-related complexity. It provides high-level and platform independent programming abstractions and specification. The developer specifies high-level specification, which is parsed by IoTSuite to generate the platform-specific code. The high-level specification includes the specification about sensing, actuating, and computational components as well as the device properties. The developers do not need to concern about the platform and runtime-specific aspect of development. More specifically, the following key characteristics of this tool suite make it suitable for building real-time industrial analytics.

- The current version of IoTSuite generates code in C, Python, Java, Android, and Node.js. The code generator is flexible to generate IoT framework in a new programming language. The developers just need to write a small plug-in to generate IoT framework code in new programming language. IoTSuite has been tested on devices such as Raspberry PI, ABB's RIO 600, Arduino, and Android smartphones.
- The current version of IoTSuite plugs MQTT, WebSocket runtime. However, the integration of a new runtime is easy. The IoTSuite simply exposes well-defined interfaces (Soukaras et al. 2015) to integrate a new runtime. The developers simply implement runtime-specific interfaces to plug a target runtime system.

SWoTSuite[14] It is a framework intended to build cross-domain IoT applications by leveraging semantic technologies to achieve interoperability among heterogeneous IoT systems. The SWoTSuite reasoning mechanism over semantically annotated IoT data generates user suggestions. The framework applies Linked Open Data (LOD), Linked Open Vocabularies (LOV), and Linked Open Service

---

[13]https://github.com/pankeshpatel/IoTSuite/wiki.

[14]https://github.com/pankeshpatel/SWoTSuite.

(LOS) to achieve interoperability and derive meaningful knowledge from annotated data (Gyrard et al. 2016).

ACEIS[15]   It contains a set of tools, designed for IoT data analytics. It leverages Semantic Web technologies to build various components including one each for integration on the fly, event detection, and streaming data discovery (Gao et al. 2017).

4.3   Semantic Web Technologies for Industry 4.0

This section presents Semantic Web tools and technologies to achieve interoperability among Industry 4.0 devices. In the following, we present Semantic Web components that can be used to implement the use case, mentioned in Sect. 2.

Data Ingestion   Data ingestion is a process of getting data into an analytic platform. It ingests sensor data for further processing and device description for discovery. The data collection could be in various semantic formats such as JSON, EXI, XML.

Data Representation   A common data representation format such as RDF could be used for data exchange among industrial devices. The work (Grangel-González et al. 2016) notes several benefits of employing RDF as data representation format for Industry 4.0.: first, various data serialization formats are generated easily and transmitted. Second, the data representation can be generated on the fly from the data stored in relational database or other data representation formats. This is very important aspect, because this flexibility enables data sharing among legacy systems and new systems. Third, SPARQL (a W3C standard for an RDF query) can be used on top of RDF data. This would make data available through a standard interface. However, Industry 4.0 devices such as PLCs may not have enough processing power to process RDF data.

The work (Su et al. 2015) emphasizes adding semantic technologies on devices and evaluates several different formats for representing sensor measurements and device properties in terms of energy efficiency for data communication and processing. The evaluation conducted by (Su et al. 2012) finds that JSON for Linked Data (JSON-LD[16]) and Entity Notation (EN) are compact as well as lightweight data representations. Many non-RDF lightweight emerging standards are available for representing industrial devices and sensor measurements in the domain of Industry 4.0. In the following, we present some of the Industry 4.0 standards for representing data from industrial devices.

---

[15]https://github.com/CityPulse/Stream-Discovery-and-Integration-Middleware.
[16]http://json-ld.org/.

- **OPC Unified Architecture (OPC-UA).**[17] It is a machine-to-machine Industry 4.0 protocol. It integrates an information model for information integration. Using OPC-UA information model, the complex data can be modeled.
- **Production Performance Management Protocol (PPMP).**[18] It can be challenging for SMEs to catch up with the complex IT standards such as OPC-UA that come along. To address these challenges and requirements in Industry 4.0, PPMP is designed. It specifies a format that allows capturing data for performance analysis of production facilities. It is structured into three payload formats: measurement payload, message payload, and process payload. The measurement payload contains measurements from machines (e.g., temperature, vibrations of a machine). The message payload contains alerts sent by a machine. A process message consists of information (e.g., tightening process with all their characterizing data), which is needed to describe and analyze it. The Eclipse Unide aims to provide sample implementations and further development of PPMP in and with the Eclipse Open Source community.

Data Transformation This component is responsible for transforming various formats to standardized format. It enables reasoning of sensor data in a uniform way. For instance, the work by Su et al. (2014) transforms Sensor Markup Language (SenML)[19] to RDF. SenML is an industry-driven lightweight solution for representing sensor measurements, accepted by many industrial vendors. Eclipse Unide presents an open-source implementation that transforms PRC7000 format to PPMP format using Apache Camel, Which is a versatile open-source integration framework.

Data Storage and Processing This component is responsible for storing and processing data. Broadly, there are two approaches: first, the use of cloud for processing. Second, edge computing that stores process data locally. The RDF storage on resource-constrained devices may not possible due to the textual representation of RDF. To address this problem, formats such as Binary XML and EXI are promising compact representation, proposed by W3C. The work (Le-Phuoc et al. 2010) proposes "RDF on the Go" that offers a full-fledged RDF storage for Android devices. Similarly, MicroJena and MobileRDF[20] present an approach to store and query RDF data locally.

Reasoning at Edge To derive new knowledge, it is necessary to push reasoning on the edge. However, existing reasoning tools such as RacerPro, Jena, Fact++, Pellet cannot be used for edge devices, due to their high computation cost. The work (d'Aquin et al. 2010) demonstrates reasoning engines require several hundred KBs of memory to process one RDF triple. Thus, technically it is possible to port

---

[17]https://opcfoundation.org/about/opc-technologies/opc-ua/.

[18]https://www.eclipse.org/unide/.

[19]https://tools.ietf.org/html/draft-jennings-senml-10.

[20]http://www.hedenus.de/rdf/.

a reasoner on device with some code-level modification, a reasoning engine can consume a huge amount of resources (Tai et al. 2015).

5 Our Approach and Implementation

This section presents our approach to achieve the objectives of the case study, described in Sect. 2. In the following, we present various data analytics steps, performed on industrial data.

5.1 Data Ingestion

This is an entry point of getting data into the platform. This module has two major roles to play: first, scale to meet the demand of diverse data sources including relational/non-relational database as well as real-time data. Second, move data as fast as possible to the next module for further processing. This module collects data in various formats (e.g., JSON, RDF, XML), discussed in Sect. 4.3. We use Apache Kafka[21] for data ingestion service. Kafka provides a set of standard connectors[22] to query the relevant databases directly, following traditional ETL (Extract–Transform–Load) pattern as well as connectors to ingest real-time data that exhibit a number of interaction patterns such as request–response (Berners-Lee et al. 2001), publish–subscribe (Eugster et al. 2003), and streaming (Aggarwal et al. 2006). Depending on the nature of the underlying information source and the data policy, this module performs either a full ETL on the whole dataset or partial data are acquired using an on-demand ETL policy.

5.2 Data Pre-processing

As a first step, we identified the relevant variables that are important for production forecasting and selected a set of dependent and independent variables. The extracted data spanned over the last three years. Table 2 describes the selected variables, which are collected at each manufacturing step. For the purposes of our analysis, we considered three independent variables, namely (1) Scrap: the number of units scrapped during production, (2) Rework: the number of units sent back for reworking, and (3) Lead time: the overall time it takes for a container to be processed between the first and last operations. We use query-based approach to extract data,

---

[21] https://kafka.apache.org/.
[22] https://www.confluent.io/connectors/.

Table 2 Selected variables for production forecasting

Variables	Description
Scrap	It is a number of units scrapped during the manufacturing process
Rework	It is a number of units (in a given container) that are sent back for reprocessing through a manufacturing operation step
Lead time	It is a total time of a manufacturing process, from process start to finish, including any queue times
Operation process time	It is an actual processing time of a container, including container on-hold time
Operation queue time	It is an actual queued time of a container, before entering the next operation step
Machine uptime	It indicates a time during the manufacturing process a machine is in a productive state
NCR occurrences	It is an event, when a container is non-conforming
Containers on hold	It is a state of the manufacturing process when a container is placed "on-hold," requiring further investigation
Sample tests failed	It indicates a number of samples, pulled for test purposes for the quality control, that have failed an inspection step

in such a way that any future versions of the database can be easily linked to our tool.

We analyzed the extracted data manually and ensured that the prepared data are properly cleaned and free of any missing values or any discrepancies. Figure 4 presents a snapshot of collected data. This process was the most time-consuming part. We leverage a variety of tools for data cleansing including anomaly detection, handling incomplete and noisy data, identifying any missing values, contradictory and out of range values, and an automated features extraction tool to identify relevant features before applying to the next step, discussed in Sect. 5.3.

5.3   Machine Learning Algorithms for Prediction

We applied regression-based ML algorithms over collected data to identify the best performing algorithms. We used models such as Multiple Linear Regression, Support Vector Regression, Decision Tree Regression, and Random Forest Regression. The models were trained using 80% training dataset, and 20% validation dataset was used for testing.

```
theday,scrap,rework,leadTime,stdmvoutput
2014-12-08,46,,,
2014-12-09,50,,83,629
2014-12-10,88,11,83,1461
2014-12-11,92,4,83,1669
2014-12-12,76,204,83,1801
2014-12-13,22,,83,117
2014-12-14,0,,83,133
2014-12-15,74,86,83,1873
2014-12-16,111,335,83,1921
2014-12-17,111,13,83,1964
2014-12-18,73,113,83,1750
2014-12-19,92,36,83,1374
2014-12-20,27,,,64
2014-12-21,3,,,118
2014-12-22,93,163,83,2062
2014-12-23,34,39,83,1658
```

Fig. 4 Data collection from MES before data pre-processing step

Figure 5a–d presents the results of our evaluation of the four, respectively. The results demonstrate a comparison between the actual value (as a blue line) and predicted value (as an orange line) for the number of units manufactured during 6 months. We employed Root Mean Square Error (RMSE) mechanism to evaluate the accuracy of an algorithm. This mechanism helped us to select a most appropriate algorithm for our use case. RMSE shows how close a trained model is to a set of actual points. This is calculated by taking the distances from the points to the regression lines and squaring them before taking the root for the final value. The smaller RMSE indicates a best fit. Table 3 presents the results of RMSE value of each regression ML algorithm. As we can see that, Random Forest model shows the smallest RMSE value.

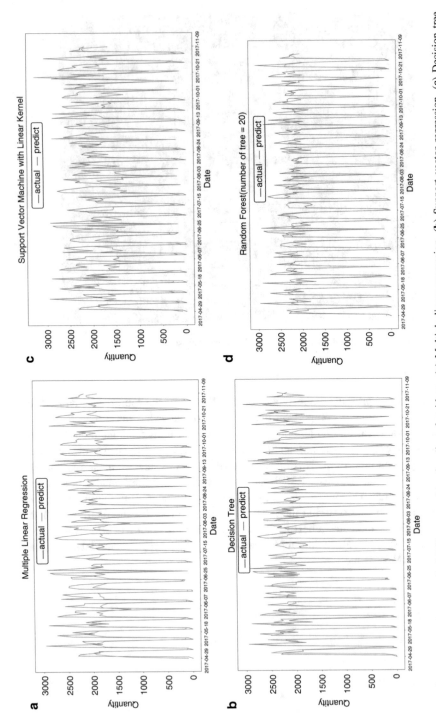

Fig. 5 Results of predictions using different machine learning algorithms. (**a**) Multiple linear regression. (**b**) Support vector regression. (**c**) Decision tree regression. (**d**) Random forest regression

Table 3 RMSE scores for different regression models

Regression types	RMSE
Multiple linear	467.89
Support vector	587.84
Decision tree	434.54
Random forest ($n = 20$)*	312.37

*The most accurate algorithm with lowest RMSE score

5.4 Real-Time Event Monitoring and Notification

The limitation of the existing system at the factory is that there was lack of tools to visual data in real time, to set production targets for the supervisors, and to record events that could affect the overall production and their causation. To address the limitation, we have developed a set of tools. To detect events, we set different thresholds based on historical data analysis and domain knowledge from staff members of the organization.

The major benefit of real-time analytics is to support a detection of events. An event can be defined in various ways, such as continuously looking for the occurrence of any predefined pattern or continuously monitoring the streaming data values and trigger an event whenever a pre-specified threshold for the values is breached. This module implements a real-time event detection mechanism for streaming data. A set of predefined thresholds are used for production data for granular time interval. We use the live production data to monitor real-time events and then continuously analyzed and matched values of the production data by comparing the values against the predefined thresholds. We reported an event whenever the values observed from the live data streams go beyond the defined threshold values. We also introduce a buffering mechanism, which ensures that events are generated only when the live production data deviate beyond the threshold by a certain margin, e.g., ±5% of daily average production.

We developed a set of tools to monitor, detect, and report events. In the following, we present each module in detail:

Real-Time Analytic Module The first goal of a real-time analytics module is to capture data in real time and visualize them on a dashboard. The second goal is to set realistic production target and use these thresholds for deviation detection. The third goal is to alert supervisors at a factory when a processing step deviates from a predefined target. If the threshold condition is not met, then deviated containers are recorded and notifications are sent to supervisors.

Target Definition and Threshold Setting The objective of this module is to alert users when a processing step deviates from a predefined target. To achieve this objective, we defined a realistic target and use it as threshold for deviation detection. We used parts per minute (PPM) to define as a target for each type of product. However, we leveraged the outcomes of historical analysis and used the predicated values automatically to define targets. We also provided a web interface to allow shift supervisor to set goals of each shift manually and to log the reasons if a target is increased or decreased from suggested target.

Event Detection and Event Logging In order to provide a mechanism for event detection, we build a tool to log all detected events. The UI in the tool, lets supervisors to input why deviations happened are provided by the supervisors. These reasons can provide later on an additional information for the historical analysis model. This additional column perhaps helps the prediction model more precise. We used the following notations for event detection:

- P: It is a process that is defined as a set of work-flow steps. Each P is assigned with a target T.
- $R = \{r_1, r_2, \ldots, r_n\}$ is a set of reasons that are either defined by users or detected automatically by the system. Each reason r_i can have a positive or negative effect on target T. Let $f(r_i, T)$ be the effect value that r_i produces on T, where $f(r_i, T) > 0$ ($f(r_i, T) < 0$) represents a positive (negative) effect.

Given a target T and a set of reasons R. Assume that each reason in R holds a different level of effect on the overall target, i.e., some reasons can adversely affect the overall target more or less compared to another. Hence, different weights are added to each reason. Any R can have either a positive or a negative effect on T, which can be calculated based on the following formula:

$$f(R, T) = \frac{\sum_{i=1}^{n} w_i f(r_i, T)}{\sum_{i=1}^{n} W_i} > 0 \text{ (or } < 0),$$

where $w_1, \ldots, w_n$ are the weights of the contributions of reasons $r_1, \ldots, r_n$, respectively.

Alerting and Notification This module is responsible for the generation of notification whenever an event is detected. Upon the detection of an event, this module triggers an action for the detected event. The action can be either a notification, an alarm, an alert or even an email to the relevant person who can take appropriate action. We implemented two types of notification delivery methods: first, an alert system was integrated within the dashboard. The factory supervisor was able to monitor the real-time progress of the production by following a visual interface installed at the shop floor. Second, a system-generated email is sent to the selected managers whenever there are any unexpected events.

5.5 Capacity Planning Tool for Production Forecasting

We developed a capacity planning tool facilitating the factory managers to set long-term production targets. Figure 6 shows the production forecasting results, where the blue line is an actual production and red line indicates the predicted values. Moreover, this tool lets the managers to adjust the values of different dependent variables to perform what-if analysis. Historical data analysis provides an estimated value for each of the days as auto-filled value that can be changed by the manager to see an impact of the change.

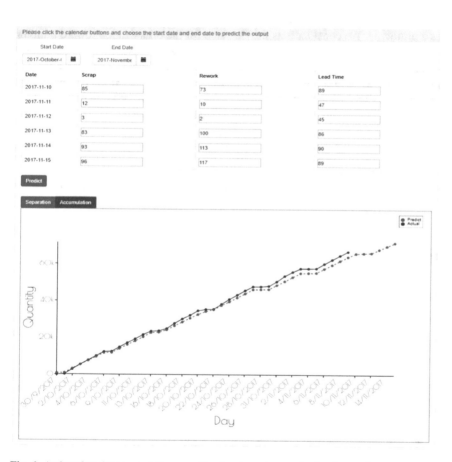

Fig. 6 An interface for accumulative capacity planning using production forecasting

6 Conclusion and Future Work

In this chapter, we presented an approach for event detection for smart manufacturing in real time. We presented a use case for the application of data analytics in the context of smart manufacturing. We reviewed the existing practices and solutions supported by the industry and discussed the key challenges faced while designing Industry 4.0 applications. We presented detailed components of our proposed approach, which can collect, integrate, and analyze historical as well as real-time data. We showcase the practical use of our approach by showing how an industry's use case was implemented using our proposed solution.

The proposed approach has been successfully deployed at a manufacturing unit as a prototype. We consider it as the first step for the organization toward building a larger vision of Industry 4.0. We plan to extend this deployment for all processes within the factory and design more business intelligence tools. Particularly, we will focus on the integration of multiple autonomous systems and show the integration and analytics of data collected from disperse autonomous systems for the supply chain management and manufacturing processes optimization.

Acknowledgments This publication has emanated from research supported in part by a research grant from Science Foundation Ireland under Grant Numbers 16/RC/3918 (CONFIRM SFI Research Centre for Smart Manufacturing) and 12/RC/2289_2 (Insight SFI Research Centre for Data Analytics), co-funded by the European Regional Development Fund. We thank Chan Le Van for his valuable contribution to acquire and process data provided by the industry partner.

References

Aggarwal, C. C. (2006). *Data streams: Models and algorithms (advances in database systems)*. New York, NY: Springer.

Ali, M. I., Ono, N., Kaysar, M., Shamszaman, Z. U., Pham, T. L., Gao, F., et al. (2017). Real-time data analytics and event detection for IoT-enabled communication systems. *Web Semantics: Science, Services and Agents on the World Wide Web, 42*, 19–37.

Berson, A., & Smith, S. J. (1997). *Data warehousing, data mining, and OLAP*. New York, NY: McGraw-Hill.

Berners-Lee, T., Hendler, J., Lassila, O., et al. (2001). The semantic web. *Scientific American, 284*(5), 28–37.

Chauhan, S., Patel, P., Sureka, A., Delicato, F. C., & Chaudhary, S. (2016). IoTSuite: A framework to design, implement, and deploy IoT applications: Demonstration abstract. In *Proceedings of the 15th International Conference on Information Processing in Sensor Networks, IPSN '16* (pp. 37:1–37:2). Piscataway, NJ: IEEE Press.

d'Aquin, M., Nikolov, A., & Motta, E. (2010). *How much semantic data on small devices?* (pp. 565–575). Berlin: Springer.

Eugster, P. T., Felber, P. A., Guerraoui, R., & Kermarrec, A. M. (2003). The many faces of publish/subscribe. *ACM Computing Surveys, 35*(2), 114–131.

Gao, F., Ali, M. I., Curry, E., & Mileo, A. (2017). Automated discovery and integration of semantic urban data streams: The ACEIS middleware. *Future Generation Computer Systems, 76*, 561–581.

Grangel-González, I., Halilaj, L., Coskun, G., Auer, S., Collarana, D., & Hoffmeister, M. (2016). Towards a semantic administrative shell for Industry 4.0 components. arXiv preprint arXiv:1601.01556.

Gyrard, A., Patel, P., Sheth, A. P., & Serrano, M. (2016). Building the web of knowledge with smart IoT applications. *IEEE Intelligent Systems, 31*(5), 83–88.

Intizar, M., Patel, P., Datta, S. K., & Gyrard, A. (2017). Multi-layer cross domain reasoning over distributed autonomous IoT applications. *Open Journal of Internet of Things, 3.*

Lee, J., Bagheri, B., & Kao, H. A. (2015). A cyber-physical systems architecture for industry 4.0-based manufacturing systems. *Manufacturing Letters, 3*, 18–23.

Lee, J., Kao, H. A., & Yang, S. (2014). Service innovation and smart analytics for industry 4.0 and big data environment. *Procedia Cirp, 16*, 3–8.

Le-Phuoc, D., Parreira, J. X., Reynolds, V., & Hauswirth, M. (2010). RDF on the go: An RDF storage and query processor for mobile devices. In *Proceedings of the 2010 International Conference on Posters & Demonstrations Track—Volume 658*, ISWC-PD'10 (pp. 149–152). Aachen: CEUR-WS.org

Patel, P., Ali, M. I., & Sheth, A. (2018). From raw data to smart manufacturing: AI and Semantic Web of Things for Industry 4.0. *IEEE Intelligent Systems, 33*(4), 79–86.

Patel, P., Ali, M. I., & Sheth, A. (2017). On using the intelligent edge for IoT analytics. *IEEE Intelligent Systems, 32*(5), 64–69.

Soukaras, D., Patel, P., Song, H., & Chaudhary, S. (2015). IoTSuite: A toolsuite for prototyping internet of things applications. In *The 4th International Workshop on Computing and Networking for Internet of Things (ComNet-IoT), Co-Located with 16th International Conference on Distributed Computing and Networking (ICDCN)* (p. 6).

Su, X., Riekki, J., Nurminen, J. K., Nieminen, J., & Koskimies, M. (2015). Adding semantics to internet of things. *Concurrency and Computation: Practice and Experience, 27*(8), 1844–1860 (2015)

Su, X., Riekki, J., & Haverinen, J. (2012). Entity notation: Enabling knowledge representations for resource-constrained sensors. *Personal and Ubiquitous Computing, 16*(7), 819–834.

Su, X., Zhang, H., Riekki, J., Keränen, A., Nurminen, J. K., & Du, L. (2014). Connecting IoT sensors to knowledge-based systems by transforming SenML to RDF. *Procedia Computer Science, 32*, 215–222.

Tai, W., Keeney, J., & O'Sullivan, D. (2015). Resource-constrained reasoning using a reasoner composition approach. *Semantic Web, 6*(1), 35–59.

Wang, S., Wan, J., Zhang, D., Li, D., & Zhang, C. (2016). Towards smart factory for industry 4.0: a self-organized multi-agent system with big data based feedback and coordination. *Computer Networks, 101*, 158–168.

Watson, H. J., & Wixom, B. H. (2007). The current state of business intelligence. *Computer, 40*(9), 96–99

Zhong, R. Y., Xu, C., Chen, C., & Huang, G. Q. (2017). Big data analytics for physical internet-based intelligent manufacturing shop floors. *International Journal of Production Research, 55*(9), 2610–2621.

How Transformational Management Enabled the Development of a Next Level Condition Monitoring Solution

Philipp Jussen and Jarno Suomela

Abstract This chapter illustrates the transformational management that global automotive and industrial components and systems supplier Schaeffler used to develop a smart service solution for condition monitoring. The management approach emphasizes customer intimacy and scalability as the pillars of a smart service business model. As a result, Schaeffler was able to cut the development time for this smart service solution by more than 50 percent compared to conventional approaches. At the same time, Schaeffler was able to uncover a next level of customer value. This chapter highlights the management approach on structural, process, and cultural level.

1 Situation and Challenges in the CM Market

Condition monitoring (CM) is a summarizing term for the acquisition and analysis of physical measured variables with the aim of evaluating the condition of machines and plants. Depending on the type of machine, there are different approaches and technologies for this purpose. Since the 1990s, a broad market has developed for different technology and service providers. Driven by constantly increasing demands on machine availability, optimization of maintenance and lifecycle costs, or safety requirements, the CM market is enjoying steady growth.

The market can be roughly divided into the following business models:

- Technology providers mainly provide hardware-driven measurement and analysis systems. Generally, they have a product-driven business model. Their target customers are OEMs of machines, system providers, service providers, or asset

P. Jussen (✉)
Schaeffler Monitoring Services GmbH, Herzogenrath, Germany
e-mail: philipp.jussen@schaeffler.com

J. Suomela
Schaeffler Finland Oy, Jyväskylä, Finland
e-mail: jarno.suomela@schaeffler.com

© Springer Nature Switzerland AG 2020
M. Maleshkova et al. (eds.), *Smart Service Management*,
https://doi.org/10.1007/978-3-030-58182-4_18

217

owners who install the measurement and analysis technology in machines and assets or offer services with the help of these. CM technology can be divided into permanently installed sensors and evaluation units, portable measuring devices (handhelds), or analysis tools (software).

- Service providers sell services for condition assessment of machines and plants. They rely on various business models, ranging from hour-based services or pay-per-measurement models to performance or output-based contracts. In each case, the service provider has extensive CM know-how coupled with an understanding of the application. It is not uncommon for service providers to simultaneously take over the role of a distributor for spare parts or provider of maintenance services.
- Full portfolio providers have a wide range of technology and services at their disposal and combine them in modular service bundles according to customer requirements. It is not unusual for these companies to also be manufacturers of individual components or units (from bearings to pumps or motors). In addition to measurement technology and CM services, the remote analysis of data by experts in a Remote Service Center is one of the classic service offerings of these providers.

The CM market is subject to various trends. On the one hand, the conception and engineering, installation, and configuration as well as operation of CM systems including analysis often requires extensive CM and application know-how. On the other hand, CM experts are rare and expensive to train. Many companies have only one or two people per production site who have the necessary know-how and are confronted with the challenge that the experts are often close to retirement.

From a technology perspective, traditional wired CM systems provide accurate data but often require deep expertise to analyze it. The aim of these systems is to provide precise and high-quality insights and analysis of the condition of complex machines. Since technology providers mostly focus only on hardware and sensors, analytics, or services but generally do not offer end-to-end solutions, the integration of different IoT layers to create an end-to-end solution has to be performed by the asset owner or a service provider. Typically, CM systems are fine-tuned to specific machine component types which additionally limit scaling up their use in other environments. As a result, CM systems are often expensive to deploy due to the wiring and infrastructure costs and required expertise.

At the same time, new players push onto the CM market. Driven by the promise of emerging data analytics and prediction technology like machine learning and artificial intelligence (AI), these new players promise a new level of insights from existing data. These services are usually offered under the term predictive maintenance promising that not only the current condition of a machine or asset will be detected, but on top a prediction about the future condition and especially the prognosis of faults is possible. However, the providers of these services require mass data as a foundation for machine learning and AI technology and seldom offer a solution to acquire this mass data.

As a summary CM is an integral part of modern production facilities. However due to the substantial cost and required expertise, current CM systems lack the necessary scalability and affordability to be deployed on a massive scale. Only the most important machines for the production process are usually monitored, rarely adding up to more than 5 to 10 of the machines in a production site. Occasionally added manual handheld measurements for another 20 to 40 percent of the machines are used. Overall, it can be concluded that the condition of most machines and assets in a production site is unknown to maintenance and production managers for a large amount of time. This results in frequent unplanned downtimes and production losses in the millions in asset-intensive industries.

2 The Challenge to Develop a Next Level Condition Monitoring Solution

In the existing CM market, the Germany-based company Schaeffler can be qualified as a full portfolio provider. Schaeffler offers a global portfolio of CM measurement devices as well as different CM services like remote monitoring or on-site assessment (e.g., handheld measurements or endoscopies). At the same time, Schaeffler is a key innovator and manufacturer in the field of high precision and high-performance bearings. Schaeffler has deep knowledge on rotating machines and assets. As an established player in the CM market, Schaeffler was looking for ways to further develop its portfolio.

Based on the assessment of the current CM market, Schaeffler identified a strategic opportunity to take CM to the next level and offer a superior business model based on digital technology. The key challenge was to create a CM solution which can provide a new level of customer value by drastically increasing the number of monitored assets in a production site. At the same time, the solution should be highly scalable across multiple industries. To achieve this, a couple of key requirements were defined to outline the scope of the new CM solution. The key requirements are directed to solve the current key problems preventing massive scale of CM: cost and effort.

The first key requirement was a target price range. It was necessary to substantially lower the cost to monitor a machine in order to make it economically feasible for a maintenance or production manager to deploy this solution across hundreds or thousands of machines per production site including non-production critical machines. Technologically, it was clear that the new CM solution needed to consider the entire IoT range, from the data acquisition in the measuring device to connectivity to questions of analytics to visualization and user experience. At the same time, the overall effort and expertise to implement and deploy the solution needed to be kept to a minimum. Therefore, as a second key requirement it was concluded that the solution should be extremely easy to install. Not only the solution cost in total but also the installation cost needed to be lowered by rapidly decreasing the amount of effort needed for installation also in terms of training or configuration.

Derived from these key requirements that were put in place to ensure the customer value, it was possible to outline a technology strategy for the new CM solution. A wireless sensor was to be developed based on newly available precise but inexpensive MEMS components for vibration measurement. A central challenge with wireless sensors is the energy supply or energy efficiency. For the transmission of data, a particularly energy-saving low power wireless MESH network protocol proven in scale was therefore chosen. For the overall connectivity, it was imperative to lower the amount of complexity and integration effort. So, in addition to wireless sensors, a gateway with direct cellular connection was a second key piece of the solution. Using this setup potential, customers do not have to integrate into their own networks and can make use of the self-configuring MESH technology. The gateway transfers the measured vibration and temperature data to a cloud-based IoT platform—also selected to enable digital services scalability for quickly growing customer base. As a third key element, automated analytics of the vibration data in the cloud was determined as a third key piece of the solution. Vibration and temperature data need to be analyzed and interpreted to become useful for maintenance and production in decision-making processes. Usually this analysis results in alarms or even recommendations including analysis of possible failure types of machines or suggestions for maintenance actions. In conventional CM, automated analyses based on thresholds generate alarms and provide a baseline for transparency for asset operators. However, this way of analyzing data is prone to errors and in practical use often either generates a lot of faulty alarms or detects a deteriorating machine status very late. For this reason, CM experts perform additional analysis of the data manually and conclude based on their expertise. In order to meet the requirements of creating a cost-efficient and easy-to-use CM solution that could still provide sufficient quality of alarms and recommendations for practical use in maintenance and production, Schaeffler decided to use machine learning technology and combines it with its core know-how on bearings and vibration-based CM. Thus, a highly automated but powerful analytics engine was to be created which could deliver precise alarms and recommendations while minimizing the amounts of configuration needed. Bringing Schaeffler's deep knowledge into the core of the product was also a necessary step to keep its competitive edge as solely technology-based differentiation factors would vanish over time.

As a summary, to meet the key requirements of creating a highly scalable, affordable, and easy-to-use CM solution Schaeffler made various key technological decisions. On different levels, the new CM solution had to combine Schaeffler's know-how in machine condition analysis and diverse technologies (wireless MEMS sensor, MESH network, IoT connectivity, cloud, machine learning). The approach was viewed to potentially be revolutionary for the established CM market since it would result in a CM solution which could achieve a never seen before scale and transparency in production environments. It became clear that the development of this new CM solution would be a challenging task on different levels. At the same time, a complex set of new digital technology and a visionary market approach had to be combined while not losing focus on customer value and achieving a short time to market.

3 Focal Points of Industrial Management and Innovation

Conventional industrial management faces several challenges when trying to achieve drastic changes in business models as well as utilizing digital technology. It is not uncommon that in established market new technology providers not only threaten the position of existing players based on technological but also organizational advantages.

In classical industrial management, customer value is mainly associated with using expertise to deliver complex engineering concepts. Precision, reliability, and safety are typical technical requirements that industrial organizations aim to achieve. This is especially true for industrial component suppliers since these components get built into machines and assets and first and foremost must fulfill the defined technical specifications. This is equally true for CM systems which in the past typically are designed to deliver high precision measurement and analysis and recommendations as precisely as possible. The management of these organizations reflects this. Typical industrial organizations are in their structure and processes designed to achieve efficiency, continuity, and controllability. This is strongly reflected also in the culture of a typical industrial organization where a chain-of-command hierarchy, budgets, reports and documentation, role descriptions, and clearly defined levels or responsibility play an important role. Employees are supposed to follow defined rules and structures to make large industrial organizations manageable.

The typical innovation processes of industrial organization are there also designed to guarantee high reliability, precision, and safety of the development result. Usually, the innovation process follows a classical stage-gate approach. Technical requirements must be documented and frozen early in the development process to estimate a budget for the development. Afterward multi-year development projects are undertaken to deliver the defined products.

Even in sales and marketing, the technology focus of industrial organizations becomes visible. Classical industrial sales processes aim at convincing the technical decision maker on the customer side first. After that economical and business value discussion follows. Marketing evenly focuses on communicating the technological advantages of a company often highlighting certain technical specifications and unique selling points.

Because of these characteristics of conventional industrial management, Schaeffler decided to deploy a different management approach. In the newly built Industry 4.0 business unit of Schaeffler, it was agreed that the challenge to create a next level CM solution using a lot of new digital technology and an aggressive market approach would also require a different management approach.

4 Schaeffler Transformation Management Approach

The goal of the strategic business unit Industry 4.0 at Schaeffler is to make use of digital technology to create new business models and customer value. Because of this strategy, a new transformational management approach was outlined and first deployed for the development program of the new CM solution (Fig. 1).

The new management approach was designed to emphasize customer value and innovation speed. Strategy, structure, and processes as well as culture should reflect this emphasis. The main aspects of this approach are outlined in the following part of this chapter. It is described how the management approach unfolds from the strategic and business model perspective, through the setup of the development program, to the marketing of the new CM solution. It is also illustrated how the culture and overall innovation approach supported the development of a highly complex but disruptive solution to an established market within only 12 months from idea to market launch.

4.1 Strategic Level

The strategy for the developed solution was based on the strategic big picture around the business unit's targets.—the unit is looking for aggressive growth utilizing latest technologies. Two reasons led to the setting of a super-aggressive go-to-market timeline:

- Business growth needed portfolio expansions by new products quickly.

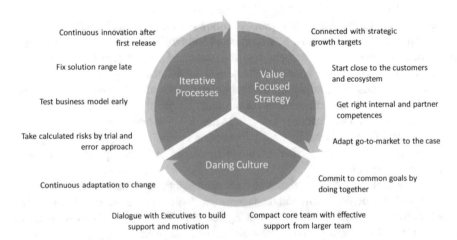

Fig. 1 Schaeffler transformational management approach

- Few technological developments provided window for market disruption—especially good quality MEMS sensors combined with low power MESH communication. The players who can maximize the potential during this disruption win the most.

An essential part of the solution development was the selected strategy to set up the development project's core into a new location with a very strong ecosystem nearby where both pilot customers and technology providers are present. In this case, it meant Finland where industrial customers have traditionally searched for competitive edge by cooperating with technology vendors and piloting solutions. For the technology needed, Finland also provided existing technology ecosystems around the MESH technology, including several players to choose from for the smart devices, MESH communication devices, and IoT platform. Schaeffler's leadership also quickly utilized an opportunity to set up a competitive team that had the required competence mix for such development.

The core team started by evaluating all aspects of the project based on the key requirements for the CM solution. Instead of focusing on the technical details, the created project plan's structure was heavily focused on the customer value:

- What is the customer problem we try to solve?
- Business opportunity for a specific industry—customer voice
- Value proportion analysis
- Current solutions' weaknesses
- New Schaeffler solution for disruptive market entry—creating blue ocean
- Competitive landscape and Schaeffler positioning
- Draft business plan
- Project setup and initial time schedule
- Summary

After the first 5 weeks, the preselected partners were evaluated along with studying internal competences and processes. Soon the partnering network was founded, an internal project team grew which included product management, condition monitoring, legal, and procurement experts, and a teaming kick-off was held with the partners.

A key element was to confirm the business case very early by direct customer feedback. Even at an early stage, quantitative aspects of the business model were discussed and validated with trusted pilot customers. On the technological side, the strong partner network delivered a working prototype within 1.5 month which led to growing support from the top management. This early proof of value became a foundation for the successful solution and created the necessary trust to conduct the rest of the development program in a short amount of time as in such a short program several quick decisions were required, e.g., project approvals, partner contracts, and hiring of the project team.

The new CM solution was to set up a potentially disruptive product with multiple unique selling points. Therefore, it required a highly differentiating marketing approach. Despite utilization of state-of-the-art technology, the most appealing story turned out to be the one that earned 100% hit rate with pilot customer acquisition. The approach focused heavily on the key customer pain points not only from a business value level but also from a personal level addressing roles and personas within a production environment. This approach was evaluated and improved each time after presenting to the customers, eventually turning into the core marketing message.

The product was estimated to have very high market need—too high to handle only by one or two sales channels. Therefore, a several channels approach including direct sales, e-commerce, service partners, and distributors was chosen early on which was also important as this had an impact on business model definition and to some core SW back-end features.

4.2   Cultural Level

As the target was to create a high value providing solution to the customer in only a year's time, innovation only on technology was not enough. The whole operating environment and culture had to support the target.

The first and foremost cultural aspect was very deep focus on the customer value. Everything, even the most interesting technological gadgets in the solution, had to support the customer value proposition or to be considered outside the scope. The very basic targets were repeated and the fit of the solution to the key requirements was checked constantly to ensure that sufficient evolution was achieved and the team internalized them. Continuous iteration around the material kept the team honest to themselves and supported boldness to challenge the deeply lying assumptions without proper explanation of *why* a certain feature is required.

Secondly, it was necessary to ensure that the team can focus on providing their best performance without feeling negative pressure about the challenges and potential failure. In any high-performing team, the feeling of working together for a common goal is the most important force. Quality time was invested to ensure the team building had enough time and user story creation workshops in small cross-functional teams were used to form the team. This ensured a common understanding, but also a buy-in into the customer value as everyone invested substantial time to understand the customer problems. The motivation and fast pace of the project was maintained by motivating the whole team, including the customers and partners by executive discussions by Schaeffler.

Another leading aspect was to keep things simple. A compact core team was used to reduce internal communication overhead and consider which processes support the aggressive go-to-market goals and which of the processes need to get adjusted to reach the goal. One of the most difficult challenges in the program was the inevitable transition from a compact core team into growing team over months. Since the new CM solution was supposed to scale and be sold and delivered globally, the team had to grow and effective ways had to be built to utilize the supporting competences in the organization without stressing them about the new ways of operating the development. A key success factor in this transition is the identification of the required knowledge and qualification within the global organization of Schaeffler to expand the team. In the case of Schaeffler, the core team to develop the new CM solution included several new hires which had to first uncover the location of the needed knowledge and qualification to expand the team.

Finally, the fast and disruptive development program required the ability for continuous adaptation. There were times when the rapid pace of the program brought up potential showstoppers that could potentially threaten the entire success of the program on a weekly basis. At times like this, it became essential that the team had invested in trust building and a deep understanding of the customer value. That enabled to keep the focus on the overall development goals and to use an objective basis to decide whether escalations were necessary.

4.3 Process Level

Not only in strategy, overall structure, and culture but also on a process level, customer centricity was implemented. In most industrial organizations, processes are designed to guarantee stability and reliability. They are designed to shield the organization from external influences and avoid potential risks as much as possible. However, in an aggressive disruptive development program an openness to external influences is required. After all, it is the strategy to let external impulses like the voice of the customer or guidance from experienced technology partners guide you through the steps of your development. The strategy to deal with risks is not to avoid them entirely but rather to tackle some of the risks in a calculated manner by a trial and error process. The goal is to find out if a potential risk turns into an actual risk by testing your assumptions on key hypothesis for the development program. One of the examples in the case of Schaeffler was the decision to discuss the business model with potential customers in the very first stages of the development program. On the one hand, this exposes the risk that certain expectations are raised which cannot be met later on or this would put Schaeffler in a bad negotiation spot with the customer at later stages or information about prices would leak to potential competitors very early. On the other hand, validating the business model early was a huge upside for the focus and direction of the overall program as it helped to understand the customer problem in better detail and gave a clear guidance for cost parameters.

Therefore, a key element in the management of the development program was to establish an iterative process that allowed for several quick steps to validate the approach and secure the planning assumption. Key user stories were defined in the beginning and the customer value proven early. The steps included:

- Proof of value
- Proof of concept
- Early release to first pilot

- Scale to several pilots ensuring solution fit to generic market needs
- Pre-launch sales approach

In each of the steps, the underlying assumptions on the business model, business value, technological setup, sales approach, etc. were tested with feedback from customers. This way, not only the development of the technological solution but also the development of the entire go-to-market followed an iterative approach. Sales pitches were first tested in the acquisition of the pilot customers, improved based on the feedback and learnings from these meetings, and again tested with more information with additional customers that were approached months before the actual launch. Therefore, once it came to the actual market launch, the sales pitch already was very mature and tested multiple times in actual sales situations with customers.

One of the challenges of this approach is that the complete solution range is fixed relatively late in the iterative design and testing phases. Whereas conventional stage-gate-based development approaches tend to fix most details early in the concept phase, the iterative approach allows for late changes in the design of the solution of customer feedback that makes this essential. The reason for this is that only after several learning iterations together with the customer, the necessary knowledge about the real customer needs is acquired to make those decisions based on as much information as possible. However, this approach forces all other processes surrounding the development process to also take an iterative approach to maintain a fast go-to-market speed. Since setting up the necessary organization and processes for logistics, delivery, marketing, sales, operations, documentation, etc. takes time, those processes have to do with the technical solution being much less defined compared to classical development approaches. On the other hand, by using an integrated view of business model and technological solution, it is possible to use feedback.

The last element of the process level setup of the Schaeffler management approach is to allow for continuous innovation. To increase time to market, the first release of the new CM solution focused on the most important requirements and functions from a customer perspective. At the same time, this inevitably means that there is constant room for additional value and improvements after the first release. On a technological level, the solution needed to be built to allow for easy additional releases in the future. But the organization and processes also needed to account for that. A vital element of this continuous innovation process is to establish a constant feedback loop between customer, product management, and development. The future direction of the solution has to be constantly evaluated to choose the most effective items for future releases which always need to be seen from the customer value perspective. This approach ensures that teams can focus on getting the first release done and the solution out on the market even though not all the possible functions are yet included. The team is aware that good ideas are not lost or dropped but rather put into a second (mental) bucket which will be delivered later.

5   Conclusion

Smart service innovation requires not only technological changes but first and foremost management and cultural transformation. Schaeffler was able to introduce a disruptive condition monitoring solution to the market within 12 months from idea to market launch. Schaeffler relied on transformational management for the development program. This transformational management approach ensures focus on customer value and speed and dedication of development on strategic, cultural, and process level.